They Also Serve

An Armorer's Life in the ETO

by

John B. Henkels

DORRANCE PUBLISHING CO., INC.
PITTSBURGH, PENNSYLVANIA 15222

ISBN # 0-8059-3998-9
Printed in the United States of America

First Printing

For information or to order additional books, please write:
Dorrance Publishing Co., Inc.
643 Smithfield Street
Pittsburgh, Pennsylvania 15222
U.S.A.

Dedication

I dedicate this book to my comrades in arms, the two hundred and fifty-two enlisted men of the 511th Fighter Squadron, 405th Fighter Group. Every enlisted man in the squadron was a citizen soldier who had either enlisted or been drafted for the duration of the war. The enlisted section of the squadron was split into two entities. One was made up of the ground crews who worked on the line and maintained the planes. The safety of the pilots was their only concern. No hours were too long and no task too difficult for them to perform to insure that our fliers had safe planes to fly. Pilots were keenly aware that every time they took off, their lives were on the line. They never had to worry about flying a substandard aircraft. Every ground crew member made certain that each plane was in tip-top condition before it was certified as airworthy.

The P-47 was a fine new type of aircraft and was very reliable, but like any man-made mechanism, it could and did have its failures. Combat flying put such a tremendous stress on the engines, very few lasted more than two or three hundred hours at the most. Changing engines was a major operation but our mechanics quickly developed short cuts that radically reduced the downtime of our planes.

Unfortunately, engine failures were not the only problems we faced. It required constant vigilance on the part of every member of the ground crews to make certain that all failures were caught before they put a pilot's life in jeopardy. All maintenance had to be done in the field under wartime conditions and frequently in adverse weather. The fact that few planes were forced to return before completing their mission was a tribute to the dedication and zeal of the ground crews.

It would have been impossible for either the pilots or the ground crews to perform their jobs without the support of the administrative staff. These individuals took care of such essentials as cooking meals, looking after the health of all of us, keeping us supplied with food and ammunition, handling all types of communications and performing other necessary functions. They were as important to the successful operation of the squadron as any other group. Poor administration resulted in low morale, poor performance in the field, and in the air. Our administration was first-rate.

We had an outstanding group of enlisted personnel in the 511th Fighter Squadron and I am proud to be numbered among them. In the annals of the war, the ground crews of the air forces remain unsung. I hope that this narrative will serve as a small tribute to a fine group of men who worked so well together in a common cause.

Contents

Preface

I hope that this book will give every reader an insight into the important part played by the ground crews of the Ninth Air Force in World War II. Our job was to facilitate operations for the pilots who risked their lives every time they hopped into the cockpit. They, in turn, saved thousands of lives of the embattled infantry and tank corps who faced the Wehrmacht head on.

When I first decided to write this book, I did not realize how difficult it would be. I thought that my letters and my memory would be sufficient, but I soon found there were too many gaps in both. I wrote to Washington to obtain the official records of our squadron which had just been declassified. When they arrived, I found to my dismay that most of the entries were so dark that they were illegible. They were not much help, so the gaps remained.

Many thanks go to pilot Homer Smith for his discovery of a log of our many missions.

My comrade-in-arms and best friend, Len Hitchman, filled me in on some important technical details and also sent me a copy of an armorer's manual. This enabled me to bone up on the details of our job on P-47s.

My wife, Jean, has supported and continually encouraged me while I was writing. She also performed an invaluable job in proofreading the manuscript as I went along. She also did yeoman service in correcting my English and sentence structure.

When I started writing, I forgot to divide the manuscript into chapters. Charlotte Fishburn, my computer mentor, bailed me out of this crisis and some others as well. This greatly facilitated my ability to make corrections and additions.

I sent a copy of the completed text to my good friends, Bob Skotheim and his wife, Nadine, for their perusal. Bob is a first-class historian and an excellent writer. He is also president of the Huntington Library in California. Both of them took time from their very busy schedules to read through the manuscript and to suggest some pertinent changes which I quickly incorporated into the finished text.

However, it was my mother, who had the foresight to save all my correspondence, who really made this book possible. She saved every note I wrote to the family and even procured some I had sent to mutual friends. These letters are the backbone of my book.

Writing these memoirs has been a very rewarding experience. It has enabled me to relive many of the exciting events of my army career, both here in the U. S. and throughout Europe. My greatest pleasure, however, has been in remembering the many fine friends I made in the service. Even though I cannot recall all the names of those I met at New Cumberland, in basic training at Miami Beach, or in armament school in Denver, Colorado, I still remember many of them and the fun we had together as we faced the vicissitudes of life as greenhorns in the army. While I would not want to go through any of it again, I certainly would not want a single moment of this part of my life deleted.

In my narrative, I sometimes use the word "army" and at other times "the air forces." I apologize for any confusion this may cause the reader. However, it is not as inconsistent as it may seem. During the war, the air forces were an integral part of the army. Army regulations applied to us as much as to the infantry, tank corps, the signal corps, or any other part of the Army. Our basic training was virtually identical with any of the above. After basic, our training was specialized as was theirs.

I have tried to avoid the use of bad language in this narrative. However, non-coms are not noted for the breadth of their vocabularies, so bad language was endemic in all the armed forces. It would be inconsistent on my part to speak in an early chapter about the universal use of bad language and then quote a sergeant as saying something innocuous like "golly gee", so I have put in such language as I felt was necessary to make the story credible.

Chapter One
How it All Began

Let It Begin Here
—John Parker

Thanksgiving Day is *the* major feast for my wife and me here in Salt Lake City. Most of our scattered brood visits us for the long weekend and traditional dinner. It was at our Thanksgiving dinner in the mid-1980s that our youngest daughter brought up the subject of World War II in connection with a high school project she was working on.

It had been over forty years since my army discharge and I thought of the war as many people think of the American Civil War. For some reason, I could hardly picture myself as a participant, though I had spent the better part of three years in the air forces here and abroad. The books I read about the war were always written by participating generals or by military experts. All of them dealt with tactics, individual battles, and various campaigns, and in all these learned tomes, the individual soldier was regarded as a statistic and not as a human being. None of them touched on the realities of war, bodily disfigurement, death, going hungry, or the constant exposure to miserable weather. It was through reading these books, however, that I learned the true scope of what occurred in the areas of Europe where I served my time during the war.

Although I served in some of the epic campaigns of the European theater, I was aware of only a minuscule part of what was taking place. The newspapers knew far more than the fighting man of what was really happening. For example, though I realized that the Germans had met with disaster at St. Lo and in the Falaise Gap, I was not cognizant that this fiasco was the direct result of one of Hitler's brainstorms. He committed a colossal tactical error by using virtually all his reserves in an ill-advised counterattack east of Normandy. Nor was I aware that this blunder was the answer to General Omar Bradley's prayer. I had supposed that the vast forces we surrounded and destroyed were the German armies guarding the French coast and Brittany whom we cut off before they could be withdrawn safely.

As we talked during our Thanksgiving feast, it suddenly struck me that none of my family was aware I had spent almost three years in the air forces during this conflagration, including some nineteen months overseas in the European theater of operations. Like every GI, I kept some souvenirs of this important part of my life. I left the table, went to my room, dug through my closet and returned with a small dusty ammo box which contained my wartime trophies. I hadn't opened this box for at least thirty years and had almost forgotten it existed. My mementos consisted of some dog-eared photos, coins of every country I visited, old campaign ribbons, and post cards of London, Paris, Rheims, and some of the other historic places I had the good fortune to visit while abroad.

Everyone chuckled a bit when I came across my moldy Good Conduct Ribbon. All present were aware that obedience is not high on my totem pole of virtues, in or out of the army. All present wondered aloud how I had managed to contain myself long enough to qualify for it. I didn't tell them that it was far easier for the brass to award it than to explain why they had not. I did not mention that everyone else in the outfit was also awarded this coveted (?) medal. After all, a bum medal is better than no medal.

Retrieving these dog-eared relics from the box brought back a host of memories. I repeated a few of the more interesting episodes of my army career—as much for myself as for them. I realized they were fascinated by my recitations so I felt it would be fun to commit them to paper. Thus, my kids would know not only that I had served but also what I had done and where I had done it.

Unfortunately, I had not kept a diary. This neglect on my part was partially offset by the fact that I had been a faithful correspondent to my family and my mother had carefully preserved all my letters for posterity. She gave them to me just prior to our move to Salt Lake City in 1970. My job here kept me so busy for the next eighteen years that I forgot all about these epistles and scarcely remembered where they were.

When I finally found them, at the bottom of a bureau drawer in our bedroom, I pulled them out and read a few. As I read on, my memory was refreshed and my interest in my army career was rekindled. I contacted Washington and learned that microfilm of our group history had been declassified, so I ordered a set which took some five weeks to arrive. As luck would have it, many of the sheets were so dark that they were indecipherable, but those of our sister squadron, the 510th, were much more legible. This was not a total loss, since both squadrons had flown together on many missions and this, together with a good memory, enabled me to recall a lot of the events of our most important missions with reasonable accuracy.

At this juncture, I received an invitation from Homer Smith to a group reunion that was to be held in Clearwater, Florida. While I was unable to go to this particular reunion, Homer mentioned his discovery of our squadron history that he found in Wisconsin. This history covered every mission in detail: the location of the targets, the names of the pilots who flew, the quantity and types of armament used, and the losses we sustained. I ordered a copy from him posthaste and it has proved to be invaluable.

Reading over these logs made me realize how fortunate I was to be present and serve in some of the greatest events of that historic war—the Invasion of Festung Europa, the Battle of the Bulge, the capture of the bridge over the Rhine River at Remagen, the ultimate defeat of Germany, and the surrender to us of Stuka pilot, Hans Rudel. I also realized how close to oblivion the history of our outfit had come. A dog-eared log found in a small flea market in a small village in Wisconsin was all that stood between the knowledge of our squadron history and a complete loss to the world of all that we had accomplished!

After some thirty-eight years in the contracting business, twenty of which I spent in Philadelphia and the rest in Utah, I decided to retire and fulfill a longtime ambition to earn a Master's Degree in History. After some consultation, with various members of the History Department at the University of Utah, I decided on a Master of Science degree which required neither a foreign language nor a thesis. It did have the disadvantage of being a dead end street; I forfeited any possibility of going on to a PhD. This was no great loss since I had neither the time nor the ambition to go on any further anyhow.

As time went on, I started to feel unfulfilled when people questioned me on the subject of my thesis and I was forced to reply that I had not written one. It suddenly occurred to me that perhaps an objective history of my place in the war might suffice to fulfill this omission. I discussed this possibility with the History Department at the University of Utah where I had earned my degree. Without giving me a definite "yes" or "no", they expressed some interest, provided certain criteria were observed. By now, I had already decided to write the following for my own satisfaction and perhaps to aid in preserving the memory of our squadron and our accomplishments in the war.

Much has been written about the Eighth Air Force, whose heavy bombers devastated Germany, but I am unaware of any written history of the unglamorous duties and adventures of the ground crews of the Ninth Air Force whose planes had the dangerous and unrewarding task of supporting the various Allied ground forces in their struggle against the German Wehrmacht. This account is just a microcosm of the story of the Ninth Air Force, but no history is complete without the inclusion of every facet, the sum of which makes up the whole.

Millions of GIs had served in Europe during this great conflict; each one had unique adventures. For the first few years after we were discharged, those stories were virtually the only topic of conversation when two or more veterans got together. Each felt in his heart of hearts that he had played an essential role in the successful completion of the war. We all maximized our part and minimized the part of the guy we were talking to. This is the nature of the beast. It's a form of what is commonly known as "one upmanship" and is really quite harmless.

In conversations concerning personal adventures such as wartime service, fishing, golf, etc., it is important to remember that he who speaks first loses the game. The reason for this is obvious and it was certainly true with the tellers of WW II adventures. More enemy tanks were destroyed, planes shot down, ships sunk than either the Germans or the Japanese could possibly have built in a hundred years. Bigger and better battles were fought in every bar than had ever taken place in Europe or Asia, or even at sea if an ex-gob was present.

However, this kind of talk put me at a disadvantage since the only enemy planes I had ever seen in the air was a flight of Me 109s and Stukas which flew into our base at Kitzingen in Germany to surrender. My dull tales quickly paled to insignificance when I conversed with those who claimed to have seen more action. There was nothing glamorous about loading planes with caliber-fifty machine gun ammunition or loading and fusing various types of types of bombs, even though you might be close enough to the front at times to be able to differentiate between friendly and hostile fire.

The very human habit of exaggeration is one of the more harmless traits of our sinful nature, and all of us are addicted to this vice to various degrees. War was a unique experience for civilian-minded Americans and we made the best of it in the telling. This was particularly true on the few occasions when one encountered a virgin wide-eyed audience. It was almost as much fun to listen as to talk. I had a ball trying to sift the wheat from the chaff from others' conversation, and I guess they did the same with mine. This relating of combat stories lasted for about a year and a half before both tellers and audiences got bored stiff.

By early 1947, the war was put on the back burner and gradually faded from our daily thoughts. When I got married in 1950, my wife knew that I had served in the war and had been overseas, but she had no idea of the specific places I had been nor what I had done, since the topic never came up. I was aware that her brother had been in the Navy, but what he had done or where he had been were both unknown since it had never occurred to him to tell me or for me to ask.

The first time the subject of my place in the war came up was just after I returned to school in 1987, as I began my quest for a degree at the University of Utah. Someone in our Middle Ages course mentioned Normandy, and I inadvertently mentioned that I had been there during the war, had disembarked at Omaha Beach shortly after D-Day, climbed the hill, and was based at a nearby airstrip. This created a bit of a stir, and I held an informal class on the invasion and my part in the war for twenty minutes after our class was dismissed. Since I was forty years senior to any of my classmates, WW II was comparable to the Revolutionary War to them. They would have been no more surprised had I said that I had served at Yorktown or had shot a long bow at Agincourt. Two major wars had been fought by the U.S. since WW II so it had become ancient history to all who had not served.

All this buttressed my determination to write something of the war before it was too late. I began rereading over the letters my mother had so painstakingly preserved. At first glance, they appeared as dull as dishwater. Gradually, they refreshed my memory and I was able to extract interesting material from them which I supplemented with some of my personal recollections and the priceless log. The letters I had written before going abroad were gold mines of information. Those I wrote shortly after landing in England were censored to a fare-thee-well, but they did jog my memory a bit so were not completely useless. The subsequent ones were more informative after we had a short but unpleasant scrimmage with our censors. They relaxed and we became more adept at skirting their scrutiny. My memory and that of some of my companions of our stay in England was clear because everything there was so new to us. None of us had ever been across the Atlantic before, so it was all one big, exciting adventure and hence easy to recollect. The indispensable log was a priceless source for filling in the details of our combat missions.

It has been a pleasant *deja vu* going over this material, since it brought back fond memories of people who were very close to me during the war and whom I had not seen or heard from, for almost fifty years, many of whom I will probably never see again. I met some of the finest people in my life in the army and reliving my experiences with them is a joy. Even better is the fact that time has softened my views on the few "heavies" in our outfit whom I had the pleasure of taking on in the course of my career.

I hope that the material that follows will enable those who read it to understand what it was all about to serve in the ground crew of a fighter squadron flying ground support and what life was like for those of us who did.

Chapter Two
The Background

There is properly no history, only biography.
-Ralph Waldo Emerson

Environment plays a crucial part in our actions, and life prior to my induction into the army certainly affected my reactions to the many new and strange situations I encountered there. I hope the digression below will give readers some idea of why I embarked on my bizarre adventures in the service.

The Great Depression still hung over the country like a dark, venomous cloud when I first was old enough to take an interest in events outside my home. Conversations around our dinner table were running commentaries on current events. They focused particularly on the doings of President Franklin Roosevelt, the hero, and Herbert Hoover, the heavy. Nine Old Men of the Supreme Court callously struck down the NRA and the AAA as being unconstitutional, ending the country's hopes for quick end to the Depression. My parents made many references in their daily conversation about how difficult it was to make ends meet. These discussions have affected my life to this day.

Gambling was the number one sport in the army, but not for me. Any temptations I ever had to gamble quickly evaporated because of my fear of losing big money. The thought of winning always meant far less to me than the agonizing thought of losing. This restricted me to peripheral penny-ante poker games which were a challenge but still inexpensive. To me, Las Vegas is a glitzy dive, not a place to strike it rich. Despite this, I have never been a tightwad; spending money was fun, but wasting it was criminal. Thus, high-stake gambling or betting was a no-no. My upbringing also gave me a strong dislike for loaning money. I didn't need Polonius to teach me that. It was ingrained in me from the first.

The first historical event I remember was the flap between Edward the Eighth, who had just succeeded to the throne of England, and Prime Minister Stanley Baldwin. They battled over Edward's desire to marry Wally Simpson, an American divorcee. My father always taught us that it was a major crime to quit on a commitment once made, so he despised Edward. His feelings in this affair spilled over to me. I was thirteen at the time so I could not understand why any sane person would give up a throne for a woman and particularly for one as plain as Wally Simpson. The pros and cons of this row were big news for several months until Edward finally abdicated in December of 1936 and slipped into obscurity. He was succeeded by his brother, George, who became a hero in the forthcoming war.

In 1937, when I was in eighth grade, the Spanish Civil War broke out and split the U.S. into two camps. As a Roman Catholic, I favored the Nationalists because they were anti-Communists and the Church was opposed to Communism. While I just followed the party line of the Catholic Church at this time and was too young to have any input of my own, nothing I have heard since has caused me to change my mind. This savage war was also my introduction to Hitler and Mussolini, both of whom gave essential aid to Franco and the Nationalists. I have seen replicas of Picasso's moving painting, "Guernica," which depicts a brutal air raid on that small Basque village. However, in the Cathedral at Cordoba, I have also seen a long list of Catholic priests and other religious officials executed by the Republicans. Neither side had a monopoly on brutality, which is par for the course in a civil war.

The U.S., Britain, and France remained neutral, while Germany and Italy actively assisted the Nationalists. Communist Russia did what she could for the Republicans, thus putting the Catholic Church solidly behind Franco.

The egg heads and most of the media favored the Republicans. In his book, *Witness to A Century*, George Seldes went so far as to state, "Every intelligent person who knew what was going on...favored the Republicans." This is not the way I recall it. Both camps had their adherents who overlooked the excesses of one side and exaggerated those of the other side. I learned an important lesson—this is *modus operandi* for politicians and the media. It became evident to me that neither of these two august groups gave the average person credit for having the intelligence to figure things out for themselves. This, unfortunately, is still the case.

At that time, no one knew that this was just a prelude to the horrors of World War II. Watching newsreels, I was struck by the realization that it was always the innocent civilians who suffered in these conflicts. The media was full of pictures of refugees from the war slowly carrying their meager possessions to the rear or crossing the border into southern France. They also featured many scenes of devastated and deserted cities.

The more I saw of this war, the more firmly I believed that we should steer clear of any armed involvement in Europe. These conflicts were just another chapter in feuds that had existed for centuries and we had no business in getting mixed up in them. This feeling was buttressed by what I read about our involvement in the First World War. None of the countries involved in that conflict made any attempt to repay their war debts to us except Finland, and I heard rumors that the British used our money to finance the war and hoarded their own resources to build up their commerce for the future.

I guess Hitler's success in assisting Franco conquer Spain inflated his ego and increased his belief that Britain and France would not impede his ambitions of territorial gains for Germany. Shortly thereafter, German troops marched into the Rhineland in violation of the Versailles Treaty.

When both countries did nothing, he occupied Austria and Czechoslovakia in quick succession. England and France accepted these conquests with the hope that such concessions would satiate his ambitions. Unfortunately for the world, the opposite was true. He turned his greedy gaze eastward toward Poland, the free city of Danzig, and the Polish Corridor—a narrow strip of land taken from Germany and awarded to Poland after World War One so she would have access to the Baltic Sea.

When he was unable to regain Danzig and the corridor by peaceful means, Hitler attacked, thereby precipitating the greatest war the world has ever known. By this time, both England and France had lost patience with Hitler's double-dealings and declared war on Germany.

Germany attacked Poland in September of 1939, just two weeks before I started my junior year in high school. One of my courses was English History, which served as a good introduction into the workings of British foreign policy and the nature of the English people. England had always been heavily involved in European affairs, so my history course gave me an insight into many of the timeless feuds and petty nationalisms of Europe. I realized that the causes of this great conflict were not as simplistic as the media would have had us believe.

While our course only took us to the end of World War One and the Versailles Treaty, we had many discussions on current affairs in Europe and the background of all the principals involved. Since we started at 2 P.M., ours was the last class of the day. We could hang around after class and discuss with our instructor and with each other such issues as the rise of Hitler, the Munich Pact, the partition of Czechoslovakia, and Germany's alleged territorial "grievances" against Poland.

Virtually every geopolitician knew from the word go that the Polish Corridor would be a bone of contention since it separated Germany proper from its East Prussian Province. We had discussed this in my sixth grade history course back in 1935. Vindictiveness often raises its ugly head in peace negotiations, and the Versailles Treaty was a classic example of this. At that time, Germany was thoroughly beaten and forced to accept harsh terms. She lost all her African colonies and enough European territory to form much of Poland and Czechoslovakia. The seeds of World War Two were sown at Versailles. It was only a question of time before

Germany, like the Phoenix, came to life and demanded the return of the corridor. This aspect of the treaty enabled Hitler to galvanize the German people into action. Why the Allies were unable to foresee the problems that this particular clause would create was something I could not fathom.

Most Americans felt that Hitler had to be stopped somewhere and that this was as good a time as any. When Germany attacked Poland on September, 1, 1939, many military experts felt that Hitler had finally overreached himself. The French Army was rated the best in the world, and that of England was, although very small, very tough.

My Uncle Harry Johnson, who had served in World War One and was a major in the National Guard at the time, could not understand why the British and the French did not attack the German West Wall while the Nazis were occupied in Poland. He was an avid follower of all things military and was as close to an expert as I knew. He thought that the German attack on Poland was a bluff and that the Nazis were not prepared for an all-out war because they hadn't had sufficient time to build a complete war machine. He thought that any type of attack would bring Hitler scurrying to the peace table. The non-aggression pact that Germany and Russia had signed only two weeks prior to this invasion didn't change his thinking. This pact gave Germany assurance that their eastern front was secure from attack, thus giving them a green light in Poland. I have since discovered that British military writer, Basil Liddell-Hart, in his landmark book, *History of the Second World War*, with the advantage of hindsight, took the same position.

Polish tactics were strictly orthodox—on several occasions they even employed cavalry charges which surprised the Germans so much that they almost succeeded. However, the German blitzkrieg quickly prevailed. Then the opportunistic Russians poured in from the east and in a short time, Poland ceased to exist. Germany and Russia divided up the spoils according to a prearranged and secret agreement.

In the meantime, Britain and France were paralyzed. According to Liddell-Hart, there were two reasons for this inertia. First, they did not expect Germany to conquer Poland as rapidly as they did and second, neither had taken the trouble to do any advanced planning or mobilization. Liddell-Hart claims that the lack of a determined attack by the Allies at this time was tragic. He states that resolute action at any time prior to the complete conquest of Poland would have resulted in a hasty retreat by Hitler, since neither he not his generals desired or were prepared for a major war.

Two interesting characters were *vis-à-vis* with each other: Hitler with his gross arrogance and bluff and Neville Chamberlain with his consuming desire for peace at all costs. Did Chamberlain enter negotiations with

Hitler with the feeling that the latter would be satisfied once Germany had regained its pre-World-War-One size or was he striving, as he always maintained, to obtain peace at any price? He must have realized at some point that long-term peace was impossible without correcting the inequities of the Versailles Treaty. There is no question that this pact deprived Germany of territory that was essentially German in character and that ultimate peace was impossible until these inequities were corrected.

Winston Churchill disagreed with Chamberlain on this issue and wanted the Allies to take strong measures to stop the war in its infancy. However, the only permanent solution lay in addressing the root cause of the trouble, the inequities created by the Versailles Treaty.

We had many discussions on the pros and cons of the treaty and whether the Allies should attempt to rectify alleged German grievances. Many of my acquaintances were hard-liners who felt that Germany had gotten her just deserts, while others felt that concessions to relieve Germany of the onus of the treaty were the only way to avoid a cataclysmic war.

After swallowing Poland, Hitler made peace overtures to Britain and France which were rejected out of hand. Neither country had any confidence in his word. A period known as "The Phony War" followed. For the next five months, an eerie calm existed—there was no overt action by either side.

Behind the scenes, however, both sides were busily preparing for offensive action. The Allies toyed with the idea of invading Norway while Germany dusted off its old Shlieffen Plan for invading France via Belgium and Holland. The conquest of Norway by Allied forces would put a severe crimp in Germany's already successful submarine campaign against Allied shipping, since it would make it difficult for submarines to leave the Baltic Sea without detection by the Royal Navy. Germany did not wish to widen the war, but she made provisions to forestall any British attack on Norway by making plans to do so herself. None of this information came to light until well after the war was over.

At this point in time, a significant event occurred which changed the course of the war dramatically. In early 1940, the British Navy chased the German pocket battle ship, the *Graf Spee*, which had been harassing Allied shipping in the South Pacific and Atlantic Oceans into Montevideo harbor where it was bottled up and then scuttled by its own crew. While on the high seas, this ship had sunk some seven or eight Allied merchant vessels and had placed the captured crews on its supply ship, the *Altmark*.

While the Royal Navy was distracted in destroying the *Graf Spee*, the *Altmark* slipped away. It was finally chased into a Norwegian port with the expectations of being interned there. However, Norwegian neutrality didn't phase the Royal Navy. They promptly entered the harbor, seized the German ship and released the prisoners. The Norwegians made only token resistance which galled the Germans no end. The international reaction to this bold act by Britain was split. Anglophiles, who were in the majority, were delighted, while the Anglophobes who constituted a noisy minority were indignant. One thing was certain—the lack of any effort by the Norwegians to interfere boded them no good.

This incident and the fear that an Allied invasion of Norway was forthcoming galvanized Germany into action. While the Allies assembled troops to invade and then vacillated, Germany struck. Denmark was rapidly overrun and despite the preponderant strength of the British Navy, Germany quickly seized most of Norway by air and sea. Only Narvic, an important port in the far north, failed to fall immediately and was the scene of desperate fighting. The British maintained a foothold there until the invasion of France when all Allied troops were evacuated and German control of Norway was complete. The occupation of Norway by the Allies would have severely impeded German access to the North Sea and thus crippled her submarine campaign, so the German reaction to the Allies' threat to Norway could be understood if not condoned.

The results of this invasion were threefold: five years of misery for the Danes and Norwegians, the access of Germany to Norwegian ports as submarine bases from which they were able to harass Allied shipping, and the ability of the Germans to use airbases in both countries to bomb northern England. Later in the war, these airbases were very convenient for the bombing of Allied convoys on their way to supply Russia. All of the above seemed to be a high price to pay for the rescue of several hundred merchant seamen. Literally hundreds of British merchantmen and much loss of life resulted from the easy access that German U Boats had to the sea from Norwegian ports.

The German attack and success against the supposedly invincible French Army was a shock to the entire world. They surprised the Allies by striking from the Ardennes, which was only slightly defended. I can remember following the German advances of some thirty to forty miles per day on newspaper maps. Dunkirk seemed to be a small consolation for the string of German victories, since the evacuees were forced to abandon all their equipment. It later became apparent that the escape of the British troops from mainland Europe at this time was a major factor in the final Allied victory.

To most of us, the onset of the war soon became another unpleasant incident in world affairs. Many people in the U.S. were still smarting from its disillusioning experience in World War One, when Clemenceau and Lloyd George punished the German people for the "sins" of the Kaiser. There was a strong feeling that we should never allow ourselves to be coerced into another involvement in the internal affairs of Europe.

Both my parents firmly believed that our involvement in the First

World War had been an unmitigated disaster. Pacifists by nature, they feared that intervention in the present conflict would result in permanent U.S. involvement in European feuds which didn't concern us. This view, though not held by the majority, was, nonetheless a popular one. My folks thought that Clemenceau and Lloyd George had hoodwinked Woodrow Wilson at Versailles. They became members of a group known as "America First" which stood for strict neutrality. Charles Lindbergh was a prime mover in this movement. He had just returned from a visit to Germany where he had received a medal and had been courted by both Hitler and Goring. During his visit, he had the opportunity to observe the German Luftwaffe and had been very impressed.

While I never doubted his patriotism as President Roosevelt did, I did not share his pessimism, so I remained neutral. I did, however, share my parents' feeling about our role in World War One and the necessity of our avoiding European entanglements.

President Roosevelt was a staunch supporter of the Allies from the word go. He made every effort to circumvent the Neutrality Act which Congress passed to prevent our involvement. He tried to sway public opinion from its neutral position for one favoring the British.

My folks were staunch supporters of Roosevelt until he attempted to pack the Supreme Court when they declared that much of his legislation designed to cure the Depression was unconstitutional. Roosevelt had a vindictive streak in his makeup. It was dangerous to cross him, since he never forgave those who did. At any rate, both of my parents thought that this move on the part of the president was a blatant move to seize power and to circumvent the division of powers so important to good government. They were outraged. This feeling was buttressed when FDR ran for a third term. My father believed that George Washington was not only the greatest American who had ever lived but also that he was one of the five greatest men of all times. Washington had refused a third term because he felt that no president should be in office for more than eight years. Our entire family felt that this was true and thought that Roosevelt's attempt was an unwarranted grasp for power. Unfortunately, the Republicans ran Wendell Wilkie who was not much competition. I admit that I had serious doubts about Wilkie's ability to run the country in those critical times. However, I just could not accept the concept of a three-term president. I regretted that I was too young to vote.

After his election in 1940 on the same platform which Woodrow Wilson had used so successfully to gain his second term, i.e. "He kept us out of war", Roosevelt dropped any pretense of keeping the country neutral and opted for active open assistance to the Allies. With the example of Wilson staring me in the face, I was disappointed but not surprised. For some reason, I had expected him to live by his campaign promises. The

Neutrality Act was quickly gutted and finally repealed. Next we traded fifty overaged destroyers to Britain for military bases throughout the world.

This was not difficult for a man of President Roosevelt's stature, since he was a convincing speaker. The massive air raids by the German Luftwaffe on London and the plucky resistance by the RAF swung popular opinion toward some type of intervention to assist the hard-pressed British. All of the above made me feel that it would only be a matter of time before one of the Axis hotheads, Tojo or Hitler, under the provocation of our government, would lose patience and Roosevelt would have his excuse to involve us.

I was not a pacifist, but I favored strict neutrality. I opposed lend-lease and the trade of the old destroyers for bases in such places as Bermuda and the Bahamas. I feared that these were the first steps to outright intervention. I thought that most Americans opposed going to war. Despite Roosevelt's warning to the contrary, I was certain that forty million Germans could not conquer the world.

For the first time, I felt some concern that we might be involved but the Battle of Britain relieved me of my fears. England was safe for the foreseeable future. Surrounded by the Anglophobes of my family as I was, I thought that our government's concern was for the fate of Britain alone, not Democracy as was trumpeted by government spokesmen and the media. It appeared to me that as a country, we had little concern for France or other nationalities such as the Polish, Yugoslavs, etc., whose countries Germany had overrun, since they did not share our culture. I felt that our main concern was the preservation of the British Empire.

In the Spring of 1941, everybody followed the campaigns of Rommel in North Africa as we might the pennant races. He captured the imagination of many Americans and built up quite a following here in the U.S. He did much to alleviate the dislike of Germany for almost a year. The changing fortunes of the Afrika Corps and the British Eighth Army had the effect of a tennis match. As the fortunes of both teetered back and forth, it was difficult for us to realize that men were killed and the assets of both countries were being destroyed.

My entire senior year in high school was unmarred by military concerns. Basketball, baseball, and problems with math and physics swept all else from my mind. Several weeks after graduation, in June, 1941, Germany attacked Russia, an act I still cannot understand. This finally brought home to me just how vicious Hitler was. It had taken awhile, but at last I got the message. Though I didn't approve of many of his previous moves, I could understand them from a strategic point of view. The invasion of Russia was aggression, pure and simple, and there was absolutely no justification for it. I was certain that German preoccupation with Russia would make our entry into the war unnecessary. At any rate, I went back to my war maps.

In September, I entered the University of Pennsylvania to study chemical engineering. Getting accustomed to college life consumed virtually all my waking hours. College was very different from high school. No one gave a damn whether I flunked a course or passed as long as I paid my tuition on time. I was overwhelmed by an independence I was not prepared to handle. I fell behind in my studies and didn't know how to catch up. I also became enmeshed in the fraternity rat race, visiting one house after another to see which I liked and which liked me. I still followed the actions of the German Army as it drove relentlessly toward Moscow, but I had enough troubles in college to worry about anything else.

At the beginning of December, both combatants were engaged in a titanic struggle for the city of Moscow. For almost six weeks, the Germans fought in the outskirts of the city and it appeared that they would succeed. Finally, the Russian winter and the dogged defense by the Russkies prevailed and the Germans had to retreat. This was really the turning point of the war. Moscow was the heart and soul of Russia and the German failure to capture it enabled the Russians to recover and go on to ultimate victory.

In the meantime, the U.S. was rearming and giving active aid to both England and Russia. Military experts had written Russia off and were wondering what the Nazis would do after their victory. I could not understand this. I thought that Hitler had taken on the impossible. Russia was just too large for any country to conquer. It didn't take a military expert to figure this out.

Roosevelt and Churchill voiced fears that England would soon be facing a victorious Germany alone. I thought that the attack on Russia was a godsend, two immoral empires in conflict with each other. I looked at the map and saw how minute the German advances were in comparison with the entire Soviet Empire. In my mind, it was only a question of time before the Nazis ran out of men and equipment and it would be 1812 all over again. I hoped that Roosevelt would let nature take its course and not get us involved before this took place.

Only the adventurous and bored students enlisted at this time. All the others continued their studies. Since I had an aversion to being shot at and no desire to shoot at anyone else, I hung on. If Uncle Sam called, I would answer, but no volunteering for me. This was my situation on the morning of December 7, 1941.

Chapter Three
Drafted!

There is a time for War
-Ecclesiastes

Sunday, December 7th, 1941, was a typical early winter day in Philadelphia. It was cloudy and raw. The familiar walk down Woodland Avenue was as rugged as ever. For some reason, this road always acted as a wind tunnel. A stiff breeze perpetually blew along it and, as on a golf course, it always blew in one's face. That Sunday was no exception. As Mort Shilbret and I walked along, we lowered our heads to lessen the effect of the blast. Dried sycamore leaves scurried along the road and blew in our faces while whirlpools of dust sent irritating particles of grit into our eyes and mouths.

As freshmen at the University of Pennsylvania, we were on our way to visit a bunch of fraternity houses which were conducting Rush Week, the period when they solicit new members from the Freshman class. Mort was a business major and I was an aspiring chemical engineer. We were more acquaintances than friends, but since in unity there is strength, we went together for mutual protection from overzealous brothers. For several weeks prior to this particular Sunday, we had visited many of the fraternities, sometimes together but more often on our own. We discussed some of the pros and cons of each as we plodded along.

Our first stop was the Zeta Psi house, which was nearest the train station. Neither of us was particularly interested in becoming a Zet, which was the social fraternity of the University and the most expensive as well, but the blast was cutting us to the bone and we wanted out of the cold. We came to the front door and found it ajar. Nobody was tending it, so we peeked into a large living room. Normally we would be met at the door by a whole host of enthusiastic brothers vying for the privilege of shoving a cigarette in our mouths and filling us with stories about the honor and glory of dear old KDM or whatever fraternity it might be.

We made our way into the room and saw a crowd huddling around a large radio which was blaring out the news. Going up to the nearest guy, we asked him what was up. At first he impatiently hushed us up. Then he turned to us and said, "The Japs have just bombed Pearl Harbor." We were stunned, particularly when we heard reports of how extensive the damage had been. We realized that the attack was a major assault and not just a raid as we had originally hoped. This meant WAR!

We waited for a few minutes until the broadcast was over and the radio turned off. All of us were stunned. For over twenty minutes after the broadcast, Mort and I forgot why we had come and the brothers forgot why they were there. We discussed the ramifications this would have on us as individuals and on the country in general. We knew that war was now inevitable and that it would involve us all.

Finally, things returned to normal and we remembered why we were present. The brothers started their handshaking and butt-passing in a halfhearted manner. Youth is resilient and soon things returned to normal. The brothers attempted to pass on their enthusiasm for dear old Zeta Psi to us and several other freshmen who had entered in the interim. However, my enthusiasm for this type of social grace—never great at the best—was now zero.

No news, before or since, has ever shocked me as did the attack on Pearl Harbor. The few of us who had followed the war were much more concerned with events in Europe and Africa than with those in the Pacific. Hawaii might as well have been on the moon as far as we easterners were concerned. We knew, of course, that the Japanese were fighting a brutal and unprovoked war with China and we were awed by the phenomenal success of the Flying Tigers. We knew that the U.S. had issued severe sanctions against the Japanese, but we were not aware of the desperate situation these sanctions had created there. The few of us who knew anything at all about the situation in the Orient thought the Japanese would be duck soup if we ever had to take them on. Our confidence stemmed from the success of the Flying Tigers, from the small stature of the Japs, and from the shoddy merchandise they were noted for. We didn't realize that the success of the Tigers was due to their being hand-picked pilots, led by a brilliant tactician, Clare Chennault. In our own simplistic minds, we just plain thought that we were better than they were.

It didn't take me long to realize that for better or for worse, things had changed forever. In a short time, my college career would be over, at least temporarily. Math was eating me alive and another big ogre, physics, loomed on the horizon. I knew it was going to be tough to survive as an engineering student, and I was not sure that the Herculean effort would be worth while. I wasn't enjoying either my classes or the university itself and the uncertainties left by the Pearl Harbor attack added to my dissatisfaction.

Turning to Mort, I said, "Let's get the hell out of here."

Since he was a social butterfly and was enjoying himself, he insisted on staying. I hesitated for a minute or two and then headed into the dark by myself, all thoughts of college and fraternities completely forgotten. I took little notice of the weather on my walk to the station. For the first time, I was too preoccupied to engage in my favorite sport, scrounging a secondhand newspaper from a vacant seat.

At the end of the train ride, I walked the mile or so to the house with my mind in a whirl. Although I didn't give it a second thought at the time, the onset of the war was probably a good break for me as an individual. It forced me to make a decision that I should have made on my own—to quit engineering. However, for a lack of a better goal, I continued the unsuccessful struggle for another year.

In the long run, I did profit in several ways from this experience when I returned from the war. First, I realized that a large impersonal college was not my cup of tea, so I had the good sense to matriculate at Haveford College on my return instead of reentering Penn. Second, I dropped engineering and entered other fields of study which were more enjoyable, easier to learn, and more suited to my talents. Three years away from school not only gave me ample opportunity to reflect on what I wished to accomplish with my life, but sufficient time to gain the maturity to make the correct decisions as well.

Like millions of other eighteen-year olds starting college, I had neither specific goals nor any idea of what course of study I should follow. It was by inertia that I went to Penn and by inertia that I took chemical engineering. I had displayed some talent for chemistry in high school, and I thought that engineering would help me in business so I drifted into it at Penn. I was unaware of the vast difference between college and high school chemistry and how important mathematics was to the former. College chemistry had proved to be tough, but taking engineering as well made me realize to my intense dismay that there *were* forms of mathematics more advanced than trigonometry and that those forms exceeded my Peter Principle.

It soon turned out that Pearl Harbor was only the beginning. Several days later, Germany and Italy declared war on the U.S. That did it. Had they not done so, I might have had enough time to restructure my college and thus have been able to complete my education. Their decision broadened the scope of the war about fourfold and my involvement became a certainty. *C'est la vie.*

On Monday, December 8th, classes were in an uproar at dear old Penn. The profs were as confused as we were. Being at war was as new to them as it was to us. They didn't teach and we wouldn't have learned anything if they had. All we could think of was the war and its effect on each of us as individuals. Some students were for enlisting right away, others wanted to keep up their grades and take courses essential to the defense effort and so remain in college. Most of us just decided to hang in there and see what would develop. I had no option of taking special courses and was not upset by this realization. I'd had enough of education for the present so I decided to struggle along and see what would happen.

I finished out the school year, spent half the summer of 1942 as counselor in a boys' camp in Canada, and the other half taking a remedial math course at Penn. I suffered through the fall semester at Penn, and in December, I threw in the towel and quit. I spent most of January working as an apprentice lineman in the family business, awaiting Uncle Sam's pleasure.

Late that month, I went to Baltimore where the company had a large job for the Navy. While I was there, I met some Navy brass who were high on the Seabees, the combat construction forces for the Navy. From their description, I thought that this would be an ideal solution for my military service. I would be able to use my talents and do something useful for the cause as well. They had seen me work and wanted me to join. I got some papers to fill out and sign and to bring back the next day. All looked rosy; my career appeared to be set. Not only would I be doing something I liked, but I would also be considered a volunteer, helping to win the war and learning a trade or two for the future. Who could ask for more?

There is many a slip twixt the cup and the lip. When I got home that evening, I found that my good and faithful friend, Uncle Sam, had already staked his claim on me. Waiting for me was a cordial invitation from the president himself inviting me to report for a physical exam. I talked to my navy friends the next morning and we both shed a tear or two. Their hands were tied—there was nothing they could do. *Que lastima*, but what the hell, easy come, easy go. I was sure that things would work out for the best as they always had in the past.

A week or so later, I went to the Lancaster Street Armory in West Philadelphia for my physical. The bedlam of the exam room had to be seen to be believed. Hundred of guys, attired in their shorts, ran helter skelter all around the huge armory, getting poked here and there by doctors and by what we were later to call "medics." Every branch of the service was represented and all gave their particular branch a fancy boost. The whole scene looked like glorified chaos to the uninitiated.

Gradually, I began to make some sense out of it and managed to get to the right station at the proper time. I swallowed a thermometer, tried on a cuff for a blood pressure check, and went through the other routines of the physical exam. For the first time in memory, I didn't panic when they checked my blood pressure so it came out normal on the first try.

When asked to spread my cheeks, I did what hundred had done before me and put both hands in my mouth. A bored doctor corrected me. The optical exam verified something that I had known forever, I was color blind. I didn't think anything of it at the time, but later I realized that this eliminated me from the navy and probably would have queered my

Seabee career as well.

It is odd how things work out sometimes. While at Penn, I wished to join the Navy ROTC as my first choice but was rejected. Then I tried for the army program. Here I was interviewed by a guy who had coached me in football in high school and who liked the way I could catch a pass, so I was selected. However, the training period for Army ROTC conflicted with one of my important chem classes so I had to pass on it. Our chances of going to war at that juncture seemed to be so remote that it never occurred to me to change my class. So to paraphrase Sammy Kaye, I couldn't make the one I could make and could make the one I couldn't make.

Years later, the idea of switching courses so I could take Army ROTC finally occurred to me. I quickly realized how lucky I had been not to do so. A horrible thought came to me. All who took ROTC were considered as enlistees and they had to maintain a certain grade point average or it was off to the infantry or some other branch of the Army as a private. The idea of my ending up as a cook or an MP struck me with horror. A cook!! Gadzooks.

At any rate, I passed my physical, and in a week or so, I received a note requesting me to report to New Cumberland Army Depot, Pennsylvania, for induction. Not only that, but I was promoted to the temporary rank of corporal and placed in charge of some eighty other recruits. A long list of names came with this added responsibility. I assumed that the army had already detected some leadership qualities in me that I had been previously unaware of. Much to my disappointment, I ultimately found out that this advancement was due solely to the location of my name on the manifest. Had I known at that time that corporal was as high as I ever would get, I would have been more impressed. My orders were short and to the point—bring my command to New Cumberland at the specified time. For some reason, I took this responsibility lightly.

On the day of destiny, a cold blustery day in early February, my mother drove me to the local train station. To our horror, it was completely deserted. I had forgotten where I was supposed to report. There was only one thing to do, try the Suburban Station downtown and hope that this was correct and that the train had not already departed. My duties as temporary corporal started to hang heavy on my conscience. We raced downtown and saw a huge crowd on one of the platforms. The train was still there, surrounded by weeping families and well wishers of all us future fighting men. This was my first experience of the old army game of "hurry up and wait", but this time it saved my neck. I hopped on board amidst cheers of the assembled crowd. For the first time since my arrival there, I heard the music of a band in the background playing a stirring march to celebrate our departure.

The train, heading to New Cumberland Army Depot in central Pennsylvania, was made up of a dozen cars, jammed to the gills with apprehensive recruits, and pulled by an ancient steam locomotive. I tried to find my command but it was impossible to move from one car to another much less check off names. I relaxed and hoped that my boys could make it on their own.

We were an hour late pulling out of the station, and as we did, an interesting thought came to my mind. Suppose I had gotten there too late and missed the train? I didn't think that I would have ended up in Leavenworth, but I'm certain that my absence would not have been appreciated. Years later, it occurred to me that my mother could have driven me to New Cumberland and beaten the train with ease. The only redeeming feature about my mistake was that my mother, who was upset by my induction, was so concerned in getting me to the train on time that she had no time to mourn my departure.

Once we arrived at New Cumberland and had gotten off the train, we cooled our heels in the pouring rain for what seemed to be an eternity. We learned another important lesson—time meant nothing. There were two essentials for adjusting to military life: one is to look out for numero uno and the other is to keep one's calm while waiting interminably. Most of my companions came from working-class families who were familiar with these two truisms, and particularly with the latter. I finally caught on but it took me far too long.

I did learn to watch out for myself. If I hadn't, life would have been miserable because nobody else would have and the army loves those who neglect this basic principle as this narrative will prove. When I realized that Christian charity had no place in the "survival of the fittest" in the military atmosphere, looking after myself became an exciting challenge. I improved in this every month.

At long last, we were led into the supply depot, and slews of clothing, identical in color, were thrown in our faces. After checking each item against the master list we were given, we jammed everything into a large canvas sack known as a duffel bag and were led to a nearby barracks and assigned bunks.

Next on the agenda were immunization shots: typhoid, tetanus, and a vaccination for smallpox. As we walked to the infirmary, bystanders who had already suffered greeted us with uncouth cries of "needle bait." I resented their superior attitude until I got mine. The relief I felt on surviving this traumatic experience was almost physical. Survival also made me bold—I was soon yelling at the unfortunates still in line with the best of them.

At New Cumberland, they had a novel and bizarre way of giving shots. We stood in line (what else?), took off the shirts they had just given us, lined up, and approached the fatal door. As we reached it, we had to turn around, back in, raise our arms above our heads while two sadistic medics, one on either side, stabbed us under the shoulders, behind the arm pit. The involuntary jerk each injectee made was not lost on those still in line. Just to make things more interesting, about one out of every dozen guys would keel over in a dead faint. If this happened before they had been shot, they were rolled over and shot where they lay and then revived. If they had already been shot, they were lugged out of the way and revived. New Cumberland was the only place where I saw shots given in this manner. I guess this was the quickest way they could devise, and there was always plenty of business. Just after we were done and had donned our shirts, another group, as large as ours and pale as lepers, quaking with apprehension, came through the door. No attempt was made to check to see if one might be allergic to those lethal drops. It was just wham, bam, NEXT.

These medics must have done a lot of experimenting before they discovered that this nifty way to belt us was the most efficient. New Cumberland was a huge induction center. No other station I stayed at had even a quarter of the "needle baits" that they did. I didn't envy those poor guys who were doomed to spend their entire career pumping tetanus and typhoid vaccine into terrified recruits. To me, the boredom of jabbing needles into quivering flesh would have been excruciating. Dull needles, long lines which gave the imagination time to conjure up horrible thoughts, and guys keeling over always made shot time a traumatic experience, but New Cumberland took the cake. Unfortunately, getting shots was to occupy an important part of our training time.

After surviving this ordeal, we took our written tests. Cold and wet as I was, I didn't expect to do very well and I am certain I could have done better under more favorable circumstances. However, there were so many people being processed at this time that the army couldn't wait until a guy was at his best. There were plenty of brains being inducted, so missing a genius or two was of small consequence. Adhering to a strict schedule was necessary so it was always full speed ahead.

The most important test of our military career was the Intelligence Test. Our score in this test was one of the two most important factors used to determine where we would serve. The other and even more important factor was where men were most needed at the time of one's induction. I imagine one could tell how the war was progressing by where the majority of inductees were sent. If casualties were heavy, it was the infantry, high IQ or no. If the fronts were stable, the IQ test might very well be the determining factor on what branch an individual would end up. I always enjoyed taking multiple choice tests because of the challenge they offer. Some answers were obvious but it is the ones I am not sure of that are most fun because they offer a good chance to use some common sense. I tested out in the upper third percentile in my intelligence test. My score was high enough to make a difference—I think. I am sure that one of the reasons for my high score compared to the others was my familiarity with this type of test—many others were taking this type of test for the first time. There is something to be said for "practice makes perfect." Theoretically, the higher the score, the more options the placement officers had. I believe that the air force was considered elite and the infantry a lot lower, but I am not really sure. I met a lot of smart dogfaces during my time in Europe, and some of my air force comrades were no mental giants. I only knew that the air force was tops with me. I was delighted to find out that no new unit such as an infantry division or an armored group was being formed at this time. If it had, it would have been dough boy or tanker time for me. I particularly dreaded being in the tank corps since I am more than a little claustrophobic. I would have dreaded pulling down that hatch cover on the top of the tank.

We also took a mechanical aptitude test and a few others I can't remember and I did well in all of them. After that, it was off for some of the usual psychology nonsense which bored the hell out of everybody because we all knew that we had to be nitwits to be there in the first place.

After these tests, we were assigned to barracks and went there to change into our new GI togs. To my surprise, mine fit very well, much better than I had expected. The sergeant in charge offered us the alternatives of sending our civies home or donating them to charity. Feeling parsimonious, I opted to send mine home despite the fact that they were the worst rags in my limited wardrobe and my mother had specifically told me to junk them. I had worn them for so many years that I didn't have the heart to callously pitch them. I was also certain that no self-respecting charity would have anything to do with them. This applied in particular to my third-hand overcoat which was missing two out of its three front buttons. In her first letter to me which I received in Miami, my mother wrote that when that package arrived from New Cumberland, she knew what it was and consigned it, unopened, to the trash.

At the time of my enlistment in early 1943, the Japanese had swallowed up the Philippines, all the islands of the Malayan Archipelago, Indonesia, and Thailand. Even the "impregnable bastion of Singapore, the symbol of white supremacy", had fallen to forces under Yamashita, soon to be known as the "Tiger of Malaysia (Basil Littell-Hart)." This was serious, but the war in the Orient at that time was primarily a naval contest so there appeared to be no need for a massive army buildup there in the foreseeable future. We had a few ground forces under General MacArthur in New Guinea, and the Marines were at it hammer and tongs in Guadalcanal in the Solomon Islands. Losses in the army were light, so the demand for ground-force replacements was slight. The big ground pushes in that area were in the distant future.

In Europe, the last German forces in Stalingrad had surrendered during the previous week, Africa and Sicily had been cleared of Axis troops, and the Allies had invaded Italy. Overexpansion had finally caught up with Germany, and Hitler's idiotic military decisions had brought on some colossal defeats and huge Axis losses in men and equipment.

The course of the war at this time called for a massive buildup of the Army Air Force. There were three reasons for this: the strategic bombing of Germany, support of the navy with long-range bombing of Japanese bases in Rabaul and other fortified outposts, and last but not least, to supply massive ground support for the titanic land battles that lay ahead against both Axis countries. Ground-support squadrons were also being formed to replace Navy aircraft which were supporting the few army contingents in New Guinea and Guadalcanal where army units were replacing the Marines.

Following a short rest, six of us were called up for KP (kitchen police), and I got pots and pans. For twelve hours, I washed literally thousands of huge aluminum colanders while my old high-school buddy, Ken Beardsley, shoved trays of raisin tarts into a many-tiered oven and then pulled them out when they were finished. Most of my pots had a two-inch layer of gooey raisin residue stuck on the bottom and it took some muscle to scrape this gunk off. The fumes got to me so much that I detest cooked raisins to this day. Cleaning these monsters was bad enough, but it was real torture to see a pot on which I had worked so meticulously immediately filled with another fifty pounds of raisins. I felt that I had a lifetime job—I would never be finished. For each one I cleaned, two more were unceremoniously dumped at my feet. However, not even that torture could last forever and at last I reached the end of my ordeal. All pots and pans were sparkling clean and hung up on their racks.

I looked forward to a nice long rest. However, our friendly mess sergeant had other ideas. He set me to cutting slabs of dough into eight-inch squares and dumping a handful of slimy raisins into each square, folding it over to make a triangle, placing it on a large aluminum tray, and handing it to Ken who put each in his oven. This operation buttressed my dislike of cooked raisins. The only satisfaction I got out of this caper was watching a bored Ken slide in one tray and yank out another for hours on end. This little adventure stuck in my memory for my entire army career and colored my view of KP forever, despite the fact that none of my subsequent tours in the kitchen were half as bad. I dreaded KP until my final discharge.

I had no way of knowing at the time that this was the nadir of my KP career. Even the greasiest pots I had from then on were child's play compared to the gooey monsters I wrestled with that night. Pots and pans no longer have the power to intimidate me. There is an old saying, "Eat a toad for breakfast and nothing worse will happen to you all day," I have modified this to "Wash a raisin-caked colander and all other kitchen duties will be a cinch."

Memories of this ordeal at the New Cumberland sink have stayed with me even to this day. At the soup kitchen here in Salt Lake City where I now serve as a volunteer, I am thought of as a masochist since I willingly wallop many of the big, greasy stainless-steel pots and pans of all sizes and shapes that the chef dumps into my sink. So far, nothing has come even close to the horrors I endured that first night of my army career. My motto has been that time goes fast when you're having fun.

Enough of that, at some weird hour, we finished at last and we plodded our weary way back to the barracks and to bed with heavenly thoughts of a long and late sleep.

We had been told that exercise minimized the effects of our shots. As far as I am concerned the jury is out on that. KP did take our minds off our sore arms, which was a plus of sorts. Some of our comrades really suffered, but I had always been lucky about things like shots and medicines. I have no known allergies so I am not sure the twelve hours of heroic effort did any good. However, this whole KP episode was a harbinger of things to come. On my return to the barracks, I faced another unpleasant aspect of army life, I went to the latrine and faced at least a dozen hoppers with no barriers between them. They were just inside the door so that when the door opened, I was in plain sight of any passerby. The potties closest to the wall and away from the door got ten times as much play as the others. I was happy to realize that I was not the only modest person in the army. With typical army logic, the urinals were placed behind a wall so they were invisible from the outside. Initially, this lack of privacy when answering nature's insistent call was enough to give me constipation. This same situation existed at Buckley Field, Colorado, as well. However, the fight I had to secure a hopper when our whole squadron had diarrhea, or the "GI's" as they were called, cured me of what little modesty I had left.

Ken and I, as KP veterans, were entitled to sleep until noon. However, it was impossible to sleep very long with all the excitement going on around us. Our barracks mates who had been awake since dawn were making a hell of a din. Finally we gave up and hustled over to lunch, just beating the deadline by a whisker.

Since we were just about the last in line, we were able to pile chow on our aluminum trays. When we came to dessert, there were those #@&% raisin turnovers. The smiling attendant who was passing them out told us brightly that since we were just about the last in line, we could each have two! We overcame the urge to punch him out and politely declined.

We retired to a quiet corner of the mess hall and ate in silence.

We both had slight fevers from our shots, so we returned to the barracks and hit the hay fully clothed. Sleep was impossible. The noise in the barracks was beyond belief. At first we were furious but soon grew philosophical. All of us were in a strange environment. We were strangers to one another and very few had ever been more than a hundred miles from home. I was a real traveler—I had been as far west as South Bend, Indiana, as far south as Norfolk, Virginia, and as far north as Boston, Massachusetts.

My hometown of Philadelphia is made up of small ethnic neighborhoods, each proud of its heritage. Working for the company during the summers had exposed me to all types of nationalities and races. My father always said that our home was "a half house on the wrong side of Germantown", since it was west of Germantown Avenue and the better neighborhoods were on the east side. We lived in a predominately Irish neighborhood, but we were near an Italian enclave chuck full of immigrants. The nearest black settlement was a few miles closer to center city.

During the summers, my brother and I worked in crews made up of Irish, Blacks, Italians, and a smattering of Polish, so I was exposed to different nationalities at an early age. They were all older and stronger than I was and hence did more work. Each man had a wisdom of his own and I learned to respect each one. They all knew their jobs and they did them well. It was with them that I learned the most important lesson of my life—there is true nobility in any job well done. These guys taught me how to pace myself so I could do more work without tiring quickly. I appreciated the patience they took in showing me the tricks of the trade instead of letting me find things out the hard way. During lunch hour, they expounded their diverse views on current events. Their politics were far different from the Republican views I had been brought up on. It was always fun to argue with them since nobody got uptight. Many of the older ones had acquired a homespun philosophy based on common sense and experience that would have impressed Aristotle himself. Knowing how to mix with different nationalities proved to be a big plus since the army was so diverse. It made my transition to army life much less difficult.

The army was a great equalizer. In New Cumberland, I quickly made friends with a huge Italian steel worker named D'Mico from a hamlet called Donora. I'm not sure that he had a first name because he never used it. He was not only big and tough; he was fearless as well. Like most of the big and strong, he was an amiable type, but when a fight broke out, standing next to him gave me a pleasant feeling of security. It did not take me long to realize that big friends were more useful than small ones. There were several short fuses among the inductees present. They hit first and asked questions afterwards. No fuse was short enough to tackle D'Mico.

At this time, the army was still segregated, so there were no blacks in our barracks. There were all kinds of Eastern Europeans, Pennsylvania Dutch, and scads of Irish. Virtually every white nationality was represented. It was hard for me to believe that Pennsylvania had such a diversity of people. Every degree of education was also represented, from college students such as Ken and myself, to some who were virtually illiterate. There were even a few hard-bitten old timers (Similar to Kat in *All's Quiet on the Western Front*) who knew the ropes and were therefore the ones to know. However, the mesh of the net of some draft boards must have been narrow as hell to admit some of the oddballs I met in New Cumberland.

It was here that I was introduced to the one aspect of the army that left an indelible impression on me—the language. Never in my sheltered life had I been exposed to such a torrent of oaths, obscenities, and crudities. It was almost as bad as the lingo in today's movies. I was fascinated. It was awe-inspiring to see a guy goof off and then hear the sergeant take off on him. The one word that predominated was the four-letter word for intercourse. I soon found out that accurate army communications were impossible without using that word or its many derivatives.

At this time, the highest rank we had been exposed to was second lieutenant. Naturally, I assumed that officers, being gentlemen by definition, were above this sort of thing. Not by a jugful! Their language was as picturesque as any noncom. I didn't know at first whether they liked to use this type of language or felt that they had to use it in order to communicate. I soon realized that they were so adept at its use that they had to enjoy it. I imagine that it gave them a reassuring macho feeling. I was determined to stay above the herd and remain pure in heart. This kind of talk was not for me. All my comrades were impressed until one day in basic training, I broke a shoe lace at a crucial moment and before I realized it, I really took off. My roommates were both shocked and impressed. Constant exposure and a difficulty in communicating finally took their toll. Unfortunately, this was only the beginning. These "bleeps" (as Nixon was to classify them) became ingrained in my psyche so that I still use some of them in times of acute stress. I did draw the line on saying "Jesus Christ" and waited for lightning to strike those who did.

I learned another important GI truth—everything happened to or was caused by one's rear end. Thus a poor card player never lost his money, he lost his ass. It didn't take me long to realize that when a noncom told me, "Henkels, get your ass in your hand and grab that mop," he meant two hands on the mop, not one on it and the other on my derriere. I also heard more often than I cared, "Henkels, your gd ass is in a f—

34

—— sling." I knew then that I was in deep trouble. One irate sergeant once told me that he was going to eat all around my poor little posterior until it fell out. I always thought that it was unfair to blame everything on the least offensive part of my anatomy. After all, just what can an ass do on its own? I developed a habit of manually checking my posterior to make sure it was still in place. Obviously, the gluteus maximus can take care of itself. Mine is still in place, without a mark on it despite the many threats made by so many to work it over. I have neither a scar nor a Purple Heart to show from all the bluster of noncoms too numerous mention who made so many and such picturesque threats against it.

It was always fun to buck the system. By trial and error, and some observations of human nature, I found a few chinks in the army monolith which were fun to exploit. I learned how to get around noncoms and thus avoid some of the ass-chewings I might have otherwise had to endure. There were just a few of us who looked for openings to gum up the works while in basic and in specialized training. This was harmless, although it upset some of the brass. The challenge of following the system verbatim when it did not apply provided me with some real fun. Any reader who has the patience to read this opus to its conclusion will see what I mean.

Whenever we were in the barracks, someone pulled out a deck of dog-eared cards and started a poker game. Gambling was endemic in the army. At every opportunity, cards would appear and six guys would huddle around and dig out their money. I quickly noticed that those who played their cards the worst always bet the most and were always welcome to participate in any game. Guys gambled on troop trains, in the barracks, and at any interval that occurred during the day.

One entrepreneur had the temerity to start a crap game. Evidently, our CQ didn't know the rules of this harmless game or perhaps he had been burned playing it, because he quickly broke it up. I was sorry when he did so, because I had not the foggiest notion of how it was played and was anxious to learn. I did get the opportunity to "roll dem bones" on our boat ride to Europe. I quickly learned that it was a lot more complicated than it seemed. It was the best way I knew to lose a bundle because it is very easy to get wrapped up in the game without realizing it until it is time to pay up.

In New Cumberland, I was too frightened to play for any large stakes. My father's horror stories about the Great Depression had scared me so much that I had no stomach to bet on which card might turn up. Later on, I got into some of the smaller low-pressure games with some friends who thought as I did. We had lots of fun, won enough to feel important, or lost a small amount that we could well afford to, and still had enough money left over to do what we wanted to. I learned the odds in straight poker and steered clear of games featuring wild cards since winning or losing in them was strictly a matter of luck.

On my second evening at New Cumberland, I ate a meal I had no part in preparing or cleaning up after. Unfortunately, it featured hot dogs which I could barely tolerate under the best conditions. I took only one of the two I was offered, smothered it in mustard, and eked out an existence on it, plus creamed corn and some kind of potatoes and bread. I forgot what we had for dessert which means it did not contain any raisins. We returned to the barracks to the news that we would be shipping out the following day. We packed our duffel bags and retired for the night, full of anticipation.

We were all excited, wondering where we would be sent and which branch of the army would be graced by our presence. Few of us were heroes, so the air forces was the choice of the vast majority since it was safest and the chances of advancement were greater there since virtually everyone in the air force was a technician.

I thought I had a serious problem—no killer instinct, I detested one thing worse than shooting at some stranger and that was some stranger shooting at me. At Penn, I had enrolled in boxing in order to learn a little about the so-called manly art of self-defense. Of course, sparring with a partner was an important part of the course. One of my sparring partners was beating me to a pulp. All I did was counter his right crosses with a left jab. I was getting creamed. Finally, in desperation, I threw my right as hard as I could. For some reason, it caught him right on the button and he staggered backward. Instead of pursuing my advantage, I put my hands at my side and waited for him to recover. He started to pummel me again but not as hard as previously since he kept a wary eye on my right. This bout was my swan song to an indifferent boxing career. If this was my best response to such a golden opportunity, I had no business in being a boxer. This adventure also gave me some misgivings about my value as a fighting man in war. I wasn't worried about my running away, but if I didn't shoot, what good would I be? After the war, I talked to some veteran infantry guys and they reassured me that Uncle Sam would have made a killer out of me. I am eternally grateful that I never had to make that adjustment.

We knew that we were heading out in the morning but nobody told us where we might be going. We naturally assumed that this secrecy was to keep those nasty Germans and Japanese from knowing our destination and perhaps derailing our ancient train. As I look back, I don't think anybody except the guy who threw the switches had any idea of our designations. The army was paranoid about giving out any scrap of information. If enemy spies had nothing better to do than worry about our comings and goings, it is no wonder they lost the war. I, for one, was really annoyed about the lack of information. "Reecroots" as we were called, were the low men on the army totem pole and expendable to boot—there were lots more where we came from. We were not yet accustomed to being numbers on some brass hat's checkerboard, but it was the name of the game and another thing we had to get used to.

Although we were too preoccupied with our initiation into the army to be aware of it, lots of history had been made in a short time. The German Sixth Army had just surrendered at Stalingrad and Rommel was being hotly pursued across North Africa. The Japanese had taken their lumps at Midway, so the Axis were retreating on all fronts.

We had no access to newspapers and would probably have less at our next destination. We knew very little about current events and did not really care all that much. There was nothing we could do about any of it so why worry? All we desired was to get on with it so we could enjoy the next little treat the army had in store for us.

Chapter Four

Basic Training

We must march, my darlings
-Walt Whitman

Having completed our introductory proceedings—gotten our shots, our uniforms, and taken our tests, we bade aloha to New Cumberland and hustled off to basic training. Each branch of the army had its own special area for basic training. The infantry had Fort Bragg, North Carolina, the armored corps, somewhere in Texas, and the air force at Miami Beach in Florida. Unfortunately, the army was too preoccupied to let us know our destination. There was lots of speculation and weird rumors abounded.

We were all babes in the woods in a strange and impersonal environment, and at every new station as we progressed on our military careers, we made friends easily for the comfort we gave each other. This was particularly true at New Cumberland when we were the greenest of the green. Many were more concerned about whom they went with than where they went. Although I had lots of friends, I still wanted to be in the air force, no matter who came with me.

The morning of our departure, the entire camp was a mad house. Hundreds of GIs loaded their belongings in duffel bags, lugged them from the barracks and toward the train they were assigned to where they milled around like a bunch of loco sheep. There were several trains lined up, each consisting of a dozen or so cars with an impatient choo-choo in front. With typical army disregard for time, we had breakfasted at six to prepare us for our eleven o'clock train. I saw my friend D'Mico head for a different train, so I hurried over to bid him a tearful farewell. I knew I would miss his comfortable bulk in the future.

Ken Beardsley and I were assigned to the same train. Instead of milling around outside, we entered immediately so we could get good seats. I latched onto a window seat opposite the sun and Ken joined me. This started a rush to board and chaos reigned supreme for the next half hour as hundreds of rookie soldiers battled for position. All who came with us were strangers—not one of our newfound friends came with us. We both felt a wrench as we bid them a silent farewell. We knew that our parting was permanent. As soon as we were loaded, we were off, bounded toward the unknown.

We rode pullman class, in ancient and uncomfortable cars, pulled by an ancient locomotive. I made a great hit when I stated that these were the same cars that had carried Union soldiers to the battle of Antietam during the Civil War. Youth is very adaptable, however, so the ride to our destination became one rollicking good time with many a coarse joke about how the railroads were screwing the government. I don't remember how many cars were on our train but it was impossible for the few noncoms on board to police them all so we enjoyed a wonderful anarchy for the entire trip. Occasionally, one would pass through our car and all would be peaches and cream for a minute or so but as soon as he departed, we returned to our lawless ways. We were so glad to be on our way from New Cumberland that we really went to town. Occasionally on the first part of our trip, our iron horse stopped to catch its breath, and some cars were detached for other destinations. Normally, I was restless and traveled from car to car on troop trains but on this particular trip, for reasons unknown, I remained in the same car for the entire time.

It didn't take us long to realize that the climate was rapidly warming up. On the morning of our fourth day out, we made one of our frequent unexplained stops. A lineman was working on a signal pole nearby. We asked him where in tarnation we were. His reply was "You're in Fort Lauderdale."

"Yeah," we replied, " But what state are we in?"

When he responded that we were in Florida, we let out a tremendous cheer. We were in the Air Forces! He pulled out his induction notice and waved it at us. We all yelled, "Needle bait." He grinned and went back to work.

Two hours later, we detrained in the main station of Miami, standing in slipshod ranks, sweating profusely in our winter uniforms. The trucks sent to pick us up were "on their way." After an hour's wait a fleet of six by sixes pulled up and we loaded our equipment on some of them and boarded others, heading for Miami Beach, which was our basic training base. We were enthralled at the beauty of the Venetian Causeway as we went along it on our way to the beach. If this was the army, we had it made!

When we arrived at our hotel, a stone's throw from the ocean, we were assigned rooms in one of the smaller hotels and mercifully allowed to change to our fatigues, as the army working uniform was called. They were far more comfortable than our woolen od's which we had worn during our trip. Next was a six block march to the mess hall where we were introduced to "Miami chicken" or pork spare ribs. We got them so often that I wondered if the army had developed a special pig that grew only spare ribs, and if not, what happened to the rest of the pig?

After our repast, we marched back to our hotel and settled in. This involved selecting roommates. Ken and I were a definite duo, but we needed a third for our room. We were approached by a redheaded guy by the name of "Red" Henzelman from the Pittsburgh area. We accepted him with alacrity and the three of us got along very well. Ken and I were excitable but nothing could upset Red. He was unflappable. He could, and did, commit misdeeds and smile his way out of retribution. We had lots in common but we were still our own persons, which made for a good combination. We all enjoyed a good time and didn't take the army too seriously. We were also more adventurous than most and thus had some great times on our Sunday holidays which we used to explore the beach.

Our hotel, as I mentioned was one of the smallest on the beach, belying its pretentious name, "Ocean Grande." It was seven stories high and we drew the top floor. Naturally the elevators were off-limits to us but this was no hardship. They were inadequate and far too slow. It was much easier to climb up the stairs than it would have been to wait for the elevator.

At six P.M., we were called out to the front of the hotel where we were introduced to two charming noncoms who were to be our instructors. One of them, Sergeant Di Mola by name, talked tough and I disliked him immediately. This was living proof that first impressions are not always reliable. He proved to be both fair and competent with a waspish sense of humor. We got to know each other pretty well before I departed for other climes. The other bird was a corporal whose name forever escaped me. It seemed to me that he spent a lot of time preening himself and showing us his best angle. This was acceptable behavior—after all, if you have it, why not flaunt it? For all this, he was fair, did a good job, and was not near as tough as Di Mola.

On our first trip to the drill field, early next morning as we were marching down Indian Creek Avenue, a lovely road that ran along a salt water canal, a pod of enormous dolphin chose that time to put on a spectacular display of leaping clear out of the water. None of us had ever seen a fish larger than an eighteen-inch trout, and these things were monstrous by any standards.

Di Mola hollered, "Company halt. Company dismissed." We raced over to the bank of the canal and watched them frolic. When they departed for other parts, after perhaps five minutes of cavorting around, Di Mola shouted, "Company fall in. Company forward march." This incident was the talk of our squadron, and Di Mola became a hero.

Our CQ was cut from a different cloth. He was a royal pain in the ass. He was known as "Chicken Shit", a term I heard for the first time but which required no definition. A "book man", he was great at enforcing the letter of the law with no imagination whatsoever. He was constantly gigging us for trivial, and to us, sometimes fictitious offenses. I was an object of his thoroughness because I liked to stargaze at night and occasionally missed the curfew by a second or two. Whenever I did, it was wham, right in the orchestra pit and I would be gigged for a week. We always hoped he could look the other way once in a while but this was not his way. It was more his method than his wrath that we objected to.

It puzzled me how some guys got ahead in the army. I wondered how a jerk like that could get such a cushy job. A certain amount of conformity was essential, but other mysterious ingredients were also necessary and I didn't know what they were, but I was soon to learn.

When I got into the business world after the war, I found that many of the same traits that made for success in the army worked pretty well in the corporate world as well. Ability is important, but flattery and knowing how to use the rules to your advantage still pay off. Playing with the power is a vital ingredient for success everywhere. Our esteemed CQ must have known someone, somewhere, who greased his path.

It was about this time that another significant crisis occurred in my life. I got fed up with all the crap the army stood for. A volunteer, instead of being a hero, was an idiot; goof-offs got ahead. Playing the army game and shirking your duty were rewarded. Endless time was spent doing "make work" projects which were built today and destroyed tomorrow, and a host of the other idiocies that armies have been doing since time immemorial. It seemed to me that virtue, hard work, imagination, and enthusiasm were regarded with ridicule. Seeming idiots gave us dopey orders. I became infuriated with the whole stinking mess.

For almost two weeks, I went around in a surly rage. Inexperienced as I was, I did not realize that what I was going through was just a microcosm of growing up, something that everyone must go through. The bitter letters I wrote home only made the family feel bad and gave me no satisfaction. I was headed for eternal misery.

One morning, I missed our breakfast formation because I was in my customary snit, so I had to walk the five or so blocks to the mess hall. On my way, I thought about the "ass-chewing" I would get, what a miserable life I had, etc., etc., etc. I was on the point of blowing my top. Suddenly, about halfway there, I got disgusted with myself. All my sniveling, bellyaching, and feeling sorry for myself seemed petty and childish. I was no worse off than any other recruit and a lot better than most. What about the guys who had to take the risks and do the killing? Just who the hell did I think I was, carrying on like a two-year-old? Nobody liked what they were doing any more than I, but it had to be done, so why shouldn't I do my share? Just who the hell did I think I was? "Enough of this crap," I told myself. I started to feel good about myself again. I guess I felt like a Inuit must feel on March thirty-first when the first crescent of the sun appears on the horizon after six months of darkness. The rest of the walk to the mess hall was a pleasure. Even the prospect of catching hell and perhaps doing KP couldn't break my euphoria. I knew that I could handle anything they could throw at me and keep my cool.

When I finally got to the mess hall, I tried to be inconspicuous as I snuck into line. I heard someone call, "Henkels." I looked up as innocently as I could, but a hideous knot grew in my stomach. Over came Di Mola, a sadistic smile on his face. "A little late for breakfast, aren't you, soldier?" When a noncom addressed me as "soldier," I had good reason to expect the worst.

However, the game is to admit nothing so I replied, "Gee, sir, I thought the formation left a bit early this morning. Sorry."

I was relieved to see that he was in a good humor and amused by my innocent expression. He said, "You better get in line if you expect to get anything to eat." No ass-chewing, no KP! What a nifty surprise!

My handling of this situation with Di Mola is an excellent example of how to handle every tough situation in the army—*never* admit you are wrong, no matter how wrong or stupid you may be. Telling a boldfaced lie is far better than an admission of guilt. This is basic. Most of the time there is no question that you are lying in your teeth. Sarge knew that I was goofing off when I missed the breakfast formation and it was not my intention to fool him. Even the toughest drill sergeant has his weak moments when he prefers to ignore minor violations and thus avoid the time-consuming rigmarole of punishment and all the paperwork this entailed. Had I admitted guilt, he would have been forced to face an issue he preferred to ignore. This does not always work, but at least you are giving it your best shot. Admitting error is just plain stupid. While I am not a liar, either by nature or by avocation, I am not a sap either, so I caught on quickly. I am more than a bit stubborn and self-willed by nature, so I sinned a lot, but playing the game kept me out of a peck of trouble and gave me some amusement as well.

I have noticed that the armed forces have not changed in this respect. One look at the antics of Oliver North and some of his compatriots proves this. However, the real champs are Congressmen who have fine-toothed this technique to the ultimate. The only difference between Congress, the Norths, and us run-of-the-mill GIs is that we never kidded ourselves into believing that we were *really* innocent.

My normal good humor quickly returned, and my roommates stopped ignoring me. When things went bad, as they often did, I compared my problems with the Vicar of Wakefield or some other literary hard-luck guy, and it didn't take long before the humor in each situation became apparent and took the sting off of things. There is always a bit of humor in each bad situation, and it is always better to dig it out than to get into a snit over something that can't be changed. Some of my most amusing recollections are incidents where things went so bad that they became ludicrous.

I didn't realize at the time, but mine had been a somewhat sheltered life. Sure, I had worked with all kinds of people; I had worked hard and earned their respect, but I still didn't know what it was like to earn a living. My brief experience at Penn was an introduction to the vicissitudes of the real world and I hadn't quite measured up. The army forced me to face the fact that the world didn't owe me a living and that if I wished to succeed, I would have to make it on my own. I quickly realized that this was a challenge which I could either face and conquer or be miserable forever after.

Once I understood the problem, facing it was duck soup. My reaction was a monumental growth in character. It is no wonder I felt so good on my trip to the mess hall. I had taken a big step from youth to adulthood.

To my great relief, I found out that I was not alone in experiencing this moment of disenchantment. Several months after my recovery, I got a letter from my cousin who had been drafted several months after me and was in basic training for the infantry. In his correspondence, he expressed exactly the same views which I had overcome. I assured him that this was a temporary state and that all would be well if he gave his keen sense of humor a chance. While I knew my words of wisdom shortened his days of disillusionment, I am certain that he sooner or later would have recovered on his own since he was low-key and had a great sense of humor.

I realized that this crisis was common in the army. The adjustment from civilian to military life can't be made without pain. I ran into many who had gone through this valley of tears and who couldn't make the adjustment. Most of these guys were high-IQ types who felt that their talents were being squandered. They became chronic malcontents who groused about everything. They may have been right, the army probably did stink, but why bitch about something that you could neither avoid nor change? Better to laugh and accept than to ruin one's life. I, for one, didn't want the powers to have the satisfaction that they could get me down.

Most of these malcontents were nice guys, and I felt sorry for them. All they accomplished was making their lives miserable along with those who had to listen to them. I saw myself in them and thanked my lucky stars that I had seen the light before it was too late. I often wished I had known then a prayer that has helped me since, "Dear Lord, grant me the grace to change what can be changed, to bear what cannot be changed, but above all, grant me the intelligence to differentiate between them." This would have made life much easier in my time of crisis. By the same token, perhaps it was better that I had found this truth out the hard way.

What one learns that way is often well learned.

Everyone knew that military life was different from civilian life in many ways and adjustments were painful. Very few of us completely adjusted or really wanted to. While we accepted military life as a temporal necessity, we were still civilians at heart and did not want to change.

I encountered two career army soldiers during my stint, one a West Pointer and the other a miscast sergeant. Career army men stuck together like endangered musk oxen. There existed a brotherhood in the regular army that was off limits to anybody else. Draftees, "Ninety Day Wonders" (as OCS grads were called), had no part in this lofty aerie. We were accepted by "real soldiers" as necessary evils. West Pointers were constantly concerned about their rank in their class, how long they had been in grade, and their graduation year, although they couldn't change any of them. Evidently these three factors determined their advancement and their social status. Theirs was a society of its own. Their main claim to fame was that they had selected the military life voluntarily while the rest of us had to be dragged in.

During my time in the army, I met only one West Pointer and that was in Miami. We had clashed at one of our big Saturday afternoon extravaganzas. We marched sixteen abreast and I had the misfortune to be on the far right of one line. Since we were a good distance from the band, it was difficult for me to pick up the beat. Sound travels 780 feet per second, so the beat gradually changes by 180 degrees every 390 feet. Our cadence was one hundred and twenty steps per minute or approximately three hundred feet, and we were marching toward the band.

When it first became audible, we were about 780 feet away and I was in step. As we got nearer, it became more difficult to pick up the beat and I was skipping like a Mexican jumping bean to do so. I was trying to follow the band, while the others just followed the guy in front of them. Thus, I was ninety degrees out of phase when Captain Marvel came out of nowhere, walloped me on the shoulder and yelled, "Goddammit, get in step, soldier." His angry face was all the incentive I needed. One more step and I was in sync with the others. I didn't know where this bird came from or where he went. This brief moment of glory represented my entire contact with a West Pointer and that was enough.

As we were returning to our hotel, I mentioned my little *tete-a-tete* with Mr. West Point and found out that others had been victims of his wrath. It was, of course, strictly forbidden for an officer to touch an enlisted man, but where was Melvin Belli when I needed him? Perhaps our hero was a frustrated fighting man who had to train recruits at Miami instead of earning medals at the front. Some guys don't appreciate a good deal when it hits them in the face.

In my business career, I found that the transfer from the military to civilian life was far more painful than ours to the military. The word "profit" doesn't exist in the military lexicon unless applied to their suppliers, but it is the oil that keeps the business world ticking. The few retirees whom we have hired worked best handling our contracts with the military where their knowledge of shuffling the enormous amount of paper engendered in every contract was invaluable. Some also had useful contacts as well. They had very fancy pensions, so there was little incentive for them to really dig in.

The army, colossus that it was, was not noted for its ability to improvise. An innovator who succeeded was a hero, but heaven help the failure. Playing by the book is a hundred percent safe, even under circumstances when something else was required. We had some great times deliberately doing things by the book when we knew it would gum up the works. It made our day when we saw the looks of frustration on the faces of our peerless leaders on these occasions.

This rigid philosophy cost us lots of money and lives. It was my understanding that the German Army gave their noncoms almost complete freedom of action which made them formidable in action. They had the flexibility to act on their own, which noncoms of many other nations do not. Thus, they were able to exploit many opportunities others wouldn't be aware of.

For all that, the book is not dumb; it is the rigid interpretation that caused all the troubles. I don't know whether the authors were smart, but they were thorough and very few circumstances are not covered. I considered myself a self-starter, so I liked to act on my own. This didn't make me popular with the brass. Since I didn't aspire to be a general, and it made things easier for me, I was puzzled by their reaction. Some of the others did the same but most played it safe and took no initiative whatsoever. This took some getting used to.

One of the essentials of basic training was to make us all conform, and things were easy for those who did. I had a rebellious side which prevented me from playing ball one hundred percent. Sergeant Di Mola, our chief instructor, was smart, had lots of savvy, and knew all the answers. He liked guys with "spirit" as he often told us. While it was his main job to make us conform, he had a special place in his icy heart for guys who exhibited a little independence. Training recruits year in and year out must have been a boring routine, and the few who were different broke up the monotony of everyday life. It often occurred to me that he must have been no bargain himself when he started out. I always thought that he knew all the answers because he had asked all the questions when he was in basic. In short, he was a man after my own heart.

I went on sick call with a touch of flu and had to miss breakfast. We had almost an hour before heading for the drill field, so I asked him if I could sneak down to a little eating joint nearby and get a bite. I was tempted to ask for expense money, since the army is responsible for our meals and it was not my fault that I had been forced to miss my GI meal. His answer was, "Hell no. This is the army. It's not my fault you missed breakfast. I'm going to catch up on some paperwork for about three quarters of an hour and then I'll check that dump. If you're there, it'll be your GD ass. Try and behave yourself for a change."

I don't know whether he checked it out or not. If he did, I was long gone. My second thoughts about asking for meal money paid off. That might have made me a "wise guy".

The good sergeant relished sadistic punishment—punishment that suited the crime. When we committed one of our many indiscretions, he had the temerity to yell, "Gas."

This meant that we had to don rubber gas masks after which he made us march double time through the many sand traps still existing on the one-time golf course which served as our training field. Wearing a mask in the hot and humid Miami sun soon brought us to terms. He took a savage pleasure in listening to the expletives that came from the interior of each expressionless mask.

Another one of his quaint tricks was to line us up and then yell, "Dress right, dress! Ready, front" until we were ready to scream. However, he saved his trump card for the few times we were "wise guys." When we returned from the drill field, he said, "Squadron, fall out." We thought we were through for the day. Not so. As soon as we arrived on the seventh floor, he yelled, "Squadron, fall in." Down the stairs we raced and got into ranks. He repeated this procedure until our tongues hung out. After three or four trips up and down those stairs, even the most recalcitrant of us came to terms.

One time our right guide, none other than Ken Beardsley, didn't hear an order to turn right and marched off into space. We enjoyed this spectacle so much that we all kept quiet, hoping that Ken would march clear out of sight. Di Mola hollered at him and Ken replied, "Why the hell didn't you sound off?" The rest of us roared laughing. Di Mola said nothing so we thought we were home clear. However, the good sergeant was just biding his time. When we returned to our hotel, he pulled his little "Fall out- fall in" routine on us. Too late, we realized that we had been "wise guys" and were now paying the price. Although he never stated it in so many words, "don't get mad, get even" was his *modus operandi*. This dampened but did not extinguish our enthusiasm, and I'm sure he would have been disappointed if it had. Getting the best of him was a challenge well worth the effort.

Sarge was not all fire and brimstone—there was the incident of the porpoises and also occasions when our drills went so well that he permitted us to march back to the hotel at ease, and finally, there was the big incident.

We were headed toward the drill field one morning and approached the 41st Street bridge. All of us knew that we were supposed to take a left turn and cross over the bridge. For some reason, Di Mola forgot to give us the proper order. We went straight ahead, singing at the top of our lungs so we would drown out any orders he might give. After we had progressed almost a quarter of a mile uptown, he managed to get in front of the squadron and halt it. He was absolutely livid and we trembled at the thought of being "wise guys" once more. He stood there panting for about two minutes, just staring at us, and then to our relief and amazement, he started to laugh. He realized he was at fault and we were just taking advantage of his mistake. We went back, crossed over the bridge, and had one of our most successful drills.

Basic training consisted, for the most part, of close order drill. We were required to march in formation the mile or so to the drill field and perform close order drill when we got there. We got a ten minute break every hour so we could get out of the blazing Miami sun. At about eleven thirty, we marched back to the mess hall for lunch.

We enjoyed an hour break and then it was back to the field for more of the same. While we were not overworked, five days of the same old thing with a chicken shit inspection on Saturday morning and a formal parade in the afternoon did little to broaden our minds.

In the air forces, we were permitted to sing as we marched. This was great. Singing made the long march to the drill field each morning a pleasure and really helped to relieve the boredom of our existence. Our entire outfit came from Pennsylvania, so we specialized in songs from the Keystone State. I taught the outfit to songs from of the University of Pennsylvania which was about all I learned in my ill-starred career there. Each outfit had its own repertoire, and it must have been quite an impressive show to bystanders as various units marched by.

When I met some infantry types after the war, I asked them if they had done any singing while in basic training. When they replied to the negative, I ask why they hadn't. Their reply was that they might forget and sing while in combat. I thought that this was ridiculous. I think that the real reason is that singing seemed feminine to them and to do so might ruin their macho image. They should have tried it. They might have charmed the Germans and Japanese into surrendering. At any rate, to each his own. I know that we all enjoyed it, and it made our marching a lot more pleasant.

One happy day, instead of the drudgery of the drill field, the army decided to introduce us to guns. We were trucked out to a rifle range for weapons orientation. Fortunately for all concerned, we shot over the ocean. Few of us had ever seen a rifle, much less fired one, so we had some anxious moments as we flexed the hoary muskets they gave us. These blunderbusses were fugitives from the "war to end all wars", British castoffs known as "Enfields." They were as heavy as lead and had been "cleaned by others", so they were rusty as hell.

Seeing that Sarge was in a good mood, I was tempted to ask him if I could go into the nearby jungle and cut a forked stick to rest the muzzle of my gun on while I shot. To my intense regret, I lost my nerve and never followed through. This was surely a picayune incident, but I still recall my not doing it with regret. It was one of my few (?) incoherencies in the crisis.

The targets we shot at were so decrepit we were unable to tell a hit from a miss, and some of the fun went out of the shoot. Just at that moment, a huge, low-IQ pelican came gliding along, parallel to our range and just above the targets. Life suddenly took a turn for the better. We drooled at the prospect of creaming this delectable bird. Without looking up, sarge said, "If that f——— bird gets hit, your asses will double-time it all the way to the hotel." We realized that Sarge and his cohorts had gone to a great deal of trouble to have trucks available to us, and we didn't want to disappoint them, so we let *rara avis* alone. We banged away at our moth-eaten targets while that damned bird continued its serene glide all the way down our entire target area without even breaking his flight pattern. Our rusty old firing irons were so inaccurate that it was lucky for all concerned that Mr. P. didn't get hit by accident.

Next on our agenda was the completion of the series of shots we had begun so auspiciously in New Cumberland. When I went to get mine, I found to my chagrin that they had lost my records—I had to begin from scratch. I was amazed at the poor record keeping. From that moment on, I kept own personal record. By keeping my own records, I saved myself a lot of misery and the government lots of serum. I found at this time that it paid to be first in line. Evidently, needles were scarce. The few available were in constant use and got dull rapidly. After each use, they were soaked in alcohol to sterilize them and then reused. Everybody thought I was a masochist as I ran to be first in line. Sharp needles hurt less than dull ones. As I recall all this, I am thankful that the age of AIDS was still in the distant future.

The shot we feared the most was typhoid. While the tetanus shot burned like fire for a few minutes after the injection, typhoid gave us a real painful arm for some four days afterward. Some "authority" told me that the carrier for the typhoid antibug was some kind of rabbit fluid which was incompatible with human blood. I think I could have avoided all this misery, but if the shots felt so bad, the real McCoy must have been hideous. I preferred the devil that I knew to the one I didn't.

48

The one illness we dreaded was spinal meningitis. During my tour of duty, I was aware of some five cases. These unfortunates were hospitalized posthaste and never seen again. We heard grim tales of excruciating headaches, agonizing back spasms, etc. I think that the medics dreaded any occurrence of it so it must have been contagious. I heard that there was no cure for meningitis, either you lived or you didn't.

I didn't realize until I reread this chapter that I have exalted Sergeant Di Mola to the skies. This was not intentional, it was just how things turned out. As I thought about this, I concluded that the good sergeant was the best person for his job I encountered in my entire army career. It was unusual to encounter a really competent person in the army, but Di Mola was an outstanding exception.

Chapter Five
Sabbath in Miami

Files on Parade
-Rudyard Kipling

Saturday was our day of agony. We wore our suntan (khaki) uniforms, our summer dress uniforms, to breakfast and shortly after our return from the mess hall, we had an inspection of our rooms. Fledgling officers, i.e. OCS trainees, armed with clipboards and nasty dispositions, descended on us en mass to fine-tooth our humble abode for all sorts of microscopic infractions that their fertile minds could conjecture. They had a lot of fun telling us how filthy things were and that they would be forced to gig us etc., etc. ad nauseam. After several weeks of this abuse, we just ignored their comments. We had a mutual regard for each other. They thought we were dullards and we thought they were chicken shit.

We took turns doing the bathroom, which was the key to the inspection. One of us worked on it while the others did the bedroom. One fine Saturday, Ken did the bathroom, finishing just before our inspector arrived. When he entered, one of us yelled, "Ten HUT," and we all popped to. After his majesty had put us at ease, he started his inspection. The room passed muster and he proceeded into the bathroom. After a microsecond, he bellowed, "Who the hell did this bathroom?"

Ken replied that he had.

"Well, come in here, soldier. Would you use this bathroom?"

Ken was a rather sensitive type so he replied, " Hell, yes, what's wrong with it?" Fortunately omitting the usual GI expletive before "wrong."

"There's a hair in the bathtub. I'm going to have to gig you guys," said the Great One.

Ken was speechless with fury. Red and I looked at each other and grinned. None of us said anything. There was nothing we could do except let his nibs make his run. We didn't want to paint him into a corner by bitching which would just have hardened his position. Red and I realized that all this bluster was just for show and we would be okay in the long run.

He came out of the bathroom, looked around the room again, opened some drawers and then our closet. All was shipshape. He looked at Ken, paused, and said, "Well, I guess things aren't so bad at that. As a matter of fact, they're pretty good. Have a nice weekend." He threw us a salute and left. Red and I had a ball telling Ken that his slipshod ways had almost killed our weekend and that he must remove that offending hair before we could take a shower. Like Queen Victoria, he was not amused.

The following week was Red's turn. When he had finished, Ken and I examined it and found scores of imaginary hairs in the sink and shower. Red was unflappable and just grinned through it all. At times like that, he was no fun at all.

Following our inspection, we marched to lunch and on our return, we donned our leggings—glorified spats which laced about halfway up our shins. I think we had to wear these Neanderthal appurtenances either because they were in stock or as a concession to "real soldiers". This done, we reported to Di Mola out in front of the hotel and every unit on the beach marched to the parade grounds for a massive show of military might.

I missed the first two of these extravaganzas because I was missing a buckle on one of my leggings. When I asked Di Mola what I should do, he replied that it looked like I would miss the parade. I spent the entire afternoon on the beach and was greeted by a bunch of tired and dusty comrades on their return, some five hours later.

Nut that I was, I felt left out after two Saturday afternoons of concentrated beach time. On my own, I went to the supply sergeant and replaced my faulty leggings. This bit of insanity was greeted by hoots from all my peers. I had two problems. First, I felt that any kind of misery would be better than the guilt feelings I got when the others departed for Parade Land. The second reason was even worse; I had, and regretfully still have, an altruistic streak which continually got me into all kinds of trouble and probably will until I depart this world.

As I look back, I am puzzled by Di Mola's attitude in this particular instance. I have never been able to fathom why he let me miss two parades when it would have been a simple matter to send me to supply to replace my defective leggings. Did he like me? Was he checking me out to see if I had the initiative to correct this situation on my own, or didn't he give a damn one way or another? This would have been completely out of character so this incident will remain a minor mystery forever.

The only time I regretted my decision was on my first parade. From then on, I took masochistic pleasure in suffering the same torture as my compatriots. Perhaps I suffered just a bit more than they did, after all, I had brought this misery on myself. My action in this case was suitable for a saint but just plain idiotic in the army. A break like that is "The tide in the affairs of men that, taken in the flood leads on to fortune"—(Apologies to William Shakespeare). Some people never learn and I am certain that, given the same opportunity, I would do the same thing. Gadzooks!

Naturally, I was curious to find out just how bad these parades were. We marched out to the parade grounds where we formed into ranks of sixteen. Establishing this formation was a major logistical problem since most groups were quite small—ours was about one hundred and sixty people. These groups had to be combined to make a company of perhaps a thousand. After we were organized, we drilled for about an hour until we got our maneuvers down pat and then awaited the arrival of the legendary Colonel Kimberley, who was rumored to be the headman of this entire assembly.

This wait was the worst part of the entire ordeal. The dust was incredible, and standing still as it swirled through our ranks was rugged. Occasionally the monotony was broken by a guy passing out. Two medics came in and hauled out the corpus delicious and life continued as the gap was filled up. On one occasion, the guy right behind me collapsed, brushing my shoulder as he fell. I started to reach down when I was reminded in no uncertain terms that I was at attention.

Our drill masters were nervous as kittens during this whole shebang. Watching them stew was some compensation for our misery. None of us appreciated how massive a job it was to organize a spectacle of this magnitude on such short notice. It was no wonder that they were jittery. In the army, each guy had his own problems and he never gave a damn for the other guy's. Anyone doing an erg of extra work was either a ka or a nut and qualified for derision and/or ostraization. It was remarkable to me how quickly we all picked up this *modus operandi*. I guess it went with the territory.

Although we would never have admitted it, and may not even have been aware of it at the time, we took a certain pride in the small part each of us played in what must have been a very impressive ceremony. None of us knew how many paraded but we did hear the number "fifty thousand" bandied about. Every basic training unit on the entire beach took part and that was lots of people.

While we all maintained that the aim of these parades was to satisfy the ego of one person, I am sure they really served as a progress report so that the brass could see how well we were doing. Using hindsight, I think that they were also a big factor in building *esprit de corps.*

When Kimberley finally arrived, we were called to attention. The band started to play a Sousa march, the front ranks began to move, and after an eternity, we also started. When we neared the reviewing stand, we were ordered, "Eyes left." We looked toward the reviewing stand and passed it. Two hundred yards more and it was all over. We were dismissed to return home on our own. It seemed like a lot of work for a few seconds of glory. We made many caustic comments on how hard thousands had worked to satisfy the ego of one individual. I am sure that the good colonel disliked these parades as much as we did. There are many more exciting ways to pass a Saturday afternoon than watching some fifty thousand yo-yos march by. Even golf is more fun than that.

As I have already intimated, I think we all really enjoyed them in the long run. They gave us something to bitch about and we took a certain pride in not passing out. Watching our drill sergeants sweating out our ability to march correctly and not humiliate them was compensation of sorts. I am sure that these parades were very impressive if the size of our audience was any criterion. Perhaps the army *did* know what they were doing when they scheduled them.

Enough of parading and back to the real world of soldiering. We had a cohort who was the champion manipulator of all times and successfully ducked out of all duties. We looked forward to his Armageddon. When that day finally arrived, he was slated for KP next day. We could hardly wait to see him walloping pots and pans or dirtying his hands in some other way.

When we arrived at the mess hall, full of anticipation, we found that our bird had flown. He had worked out some deal with the mess sergeant and gotten off scot free. We never had the pleasure of seeing him do a lick of work. We realized that we had a genius in our midst and probably a future general to boot. One of the real regrets of my life was losing track of him. After basic, he went his way and I went mine. I had visions of his being carried in a luxurious litter, a cluster of grapes in his hand, a few good-lookers brushing imaginary flies from his face, and a twentieth century Cleopatra by his side as he ordered his troops into battle. He was my idea of Marc Antony. We admired his talent, but none of us were jealous. We were satisfied to do our share because we knew that if we shirked, it was our friends who picked up the slack.

Another facet of our training was taking three written tests, math, mechanical aptitude, and communications. The math test was on elementary algebra and was a snap. I finished in half the allocated time and got a perfect score. I did almost as well in the mechanical aptitude test. I made sure to flunk the communications test, because I had heard that radio work in the air forces was a crashing bore. Later experience confirmed this view.

After we finished our tests, each of us was interviewed by a couple of staff sergeants who went over the results of our tests. The ones who interviewed me were impressed by my scores and predicted great things for me, such as ASTP (Army Specialized Training) or even OCS. Neither of these pipe dreams came true, although I continued to hope until I was shipped overseas.

As I look back, I realize that I was not qualified for either. For one thing, I was only nineteen at the time and not the most mature nineteen at that. This was pretty young for an officer, even in the air corps. As for ASTP, had I gone to college under the auspices of Uncle Sam, I would have faced the same math that had torpedoed me at Penn. I was actually very lucky. One of my high school classmates who was drafted at the same time made ASTP. During the Battle of the Bulge, he was yanked out, given hasty infantry training, and shipped overseas. He was killed in what was supposed to be a quiet area. My sleep was unimpaired by the failure to make either program as was my disposition. At nineteen, one tends to bruise easily but heal quickly.

I didn't realize until late in the war that when I was assigned to armament school, my chances of going either to OCS or ASTP were nil, and I should have withdrawn my application. When I was inducted, there was a concerted drive to build up the air forces. The Air Corps was dedicated to daylight bombing, and the losses of heavy bombers over Germany were heavy. Thus, the need for fighter escorts was acute. Trained ground crews were far more important to the war effort than putting guys through college.

Plans were being drawn up for a colossal campaign against ground targets in occupied France. Fighter bombers were to strike at German communications, important bridges, rail yards, etc. to isolate the proposed invasion area. An entire new air force, the Ninth, was organized for this effort. Literally thousands of mechanics and armorers were needed for this buildup. Since both crafts were in such short supply, it was impossible for anyone to transfer out. *Sic transit gloria mundi.*

So much for my ambitions and back to reality. During my stay in Miami, I pulled three tours of KP, each lasting for three days. Most of it was routine misery. Most mess halls were standard GI buildings which had been shoehorned incongruously between existing hotels. One, however, was in a posh hotel, six blocks south of the Ocean Grande. KP was supposed to be a luxury there. This, of course, was pure poppycock. KP anywhere is KP, and all of it is hard and unrewarding work. The only consolation we had was that the permanent staff worked as hard as we did and they had to do it every day. These guys had a bad habit of foisting off some of the more distasteful jobs, such as cleaning grease traps, on us transients. While we hated this, we had to admit that we would have done the same had we been in their shoes.

We regretted that we didn't get to peel spuds. The army used either mechanical peelers or dehydrated potatoes. The peeler was introduced because the average GI started out with a spud the size of a grapefruit and ended up with one the size of a marble. Missing out on peeling potatoes was unfortunate. In the ancient days, this was a KP's only chance to sit down. KP had two things going for it, we got lots to eat in the brief time that was available and we had no insomnia when we retired for the night.

One of my tours was at this ritzy hotel. I reported to there at the usual crack of dawn. For once, KP deviated from the hideous norm. To my intense surprise and pleasure, I didn't draw pots and pans. It was my duty to transport coffee cups on a dolly from the washer to the front of the chow line. This seemed simple enough, but I quickly found out that the hotel kitchen was not designed to feed twenty-five hundred hungry GIs in two hours, nor was it designed for my particular job. I had a blind hairpin turn or two to negotiate and several narrow corridors to traverse. This would have presented no problem except that several obese mess sergeants, chomping away on some goodies, insisted on congregating just where the corridor was the narrowest. Trying to avoid these portly ones delayed my delivery of cups and the chowline was held up, an unpardonable sin for which I got a royal ass-chewing.

Something had to be done. When polite requests were ignored, I took the law in my own hands. As I approached the critical area, I pretended to trip and roared right through them, making certain I didn't score any direct hits, and scattered them like chaff. The sound of the collision reverberated along the corridor and thence to the entire dining room. The usual mealtime chatter ceased abruptly. A piece of pie flew into the air, cups of coffee crashed to the ground, and a plate or two skidded across the narrow corridor. I didn't break stride, apologizing over my shoulder as I hustled along. I wondered what welcome would await me on my return. When I did return, they had dispersed. I soon caught up and the line moved smoothly from then on.

When things quieted down, the head man of the chow line called me over and said, "Nothing like a little ass-chewing to get you going, is there, soldier? You done real good there at the end." I just smiled.

After some five or six weeks in Miami, we had completed all requirements of basic training and were ready for either mechanic or armament school. I preferred to be a mechanic because the work was more interesting and would have a future after the war. We had no idea how selections were made, but we suspected that openings occurring at the training schools played a major part. We had no idea what part—if any—our test scores played. We all knew that the mechanics had the best and most prestigious job of any craft in the Air Corps. They were responsible for the entire plane except for the armament. Two mechanics and an armorer made up the ground crew for each fighter with the senior mechanic being the crew chief.

As per usual, we never knew what fate had in store for us until we arrived at our new base. Ken got his orders next day, and Red the following one, leaving me as the sole occupant of a luxurious hotel suite. Later I found out that Ken became a mechanic, but I lost track of Red for several months when I received a letter from Ken saying that Red had gone to MP school, that he had some good connections because he was headed for OCS. I am sorry that Red never got in touch with me. It would have been fun to follow his career. He was the only person with whom I served who made it as an officer.

At long last, I got my orders. My best friends had long since departed, so I was surrounded by strangers once more, many of whom were from different companies than ours. Some of them had been hanging around Miami for over a week awaiting an assignment.

I was disappointed to miss out as a mechanic. I've since consoled myself by thinking that armament school took less time and produced a finished product sooner so we would be ready for overseas action sooner than the mechanics. This was certainly true in the case of Ken and myself. I went overseas long before he did and thus saw lots of historic action which he missed.

In retrospect, what did we get out of basic training? Was it worthwhile or should we have gone straight to craft school? Although we never did any formal marching again, I think that learning how to march was a definite plus. We learned a lot about teamwork, the necessity of some conformity, and, above all, we learned about the military. We completed our immunizations without missing any class time. The most important thing I learned was to keep my own shot records. Starting typhoid shots all over again was too horrible to contemplate.

As I have mentioned, we also got an opportunity to shoot a rifle, although I'm sure that had we gone into combat on the basis of this one experience, German insurance rates would have dropped sharply. Parkinson's Law, "Time needed to perform a task expands to fill the time available," certainly personified the army way. We just didn't have enough to do to fill up the time allotted to us. The result was interminable waiting in lines under the hot sun, being called out hours before it was necessary, and spending hundreds of hours at make-work projects. I imagine that the brass believed that an idle mind is the workshop of the devil. This was okay, but our poor minds began to vegetate for lack of mental stimulation. We tried to compensate for this lack by doing some high-class reading, but the early curfew stymied us.

Nevertheless, I am sure that we absorbed more than we imagined. We found out how a big bureaucracy functioned and we developed a loyalty to our comrades which is vital in war and not all that bad in peace either. To quote Herman Wouk in his book, *The Caine Mutiny*, we learned the "camaraderie of the downtrodden for each other." We learned to face adversity with humor and courage.

Of course, the old adage about the stupidity of volunteering was as true as I had been warned about since my induction. This really teed me off at first, because it favored goldbricks and kiss asses, known otherwise as KAs. Once I realized that it was not my duty to teach ethics to the military, I learned how to play the game. I had volunteered for KP my first day in the army and got royally burned doing pots and pans. From that time on, I made it a point to fade into the woodwork when the duty sergeant made his rounds. The more inconspicuous you were, the less fatigue you pulled. Of course, KAs made out like bandits and I guess they always will. Being restless by nature and not stimulated by the usual dull barracks conversation, I found out that once in a while it was better to work than to sit on my duff. This was not acceptable military behavior to my peers. However, life could have been lots worse. I got lots of beach time.

Once I got squared away and started to roll with the punches, life became tolerable. I met lots of nice guys from every environment under the sun. We has some great times swapping adventures and a lie or two. To my amazement, some of them actually had it far better in the army than in civilian life. Most of them came from working class backgrounds and filled me in on what it was like to mine coal or work in a steel mill. My college stories paled compared to theirs. Some of the farmers were homesick. I guess that their insular lifestyle didn't prepare them for the hurly-burly which inundated them like a tidal wave. Once they adjusted, they mixed right in with the rest of us.

Fortunately, we lived in an innocent age. As we moved from base to base, we acquired many guys of diverse nationalities. None of us took life seriously and ethnic jokes were taken as lightly as they were intended.

For some reason, many of my friends in Miami were Jewish. Most were from The Big Apple and did not know that anyplace else existed until they were drafted. One of them had a Brooklyn accent, hard "g" and all. He never ceased to rhapsodize over the wonders of the world that the army had exposed to him. While at POE near New York, we told him how dirty the city was, how everyone was out to take us, etc. He listened quietly to all our complaints and then said, "On me it looks good."

The one big drawback at Miami was being perpetually broke. After we had been there for two weeks, they gave us ten bucks apiece. This evaporated overnight. We could eat dinner out on Saturday nights, but lack of funds cramped our style. Luckily my folks sent me some money so I took my roommates out several times. Since we were too young to imbibe, we could eat for ten bucks if we left a skimpy tip and had a cheap dessert.

I, for one, had no desire to "kill Huns", as some of my more warlike companions did. I didn't hate anyone. I was no hero, but I started out a bit idealistically and wanted to do my part. When I finally landed in a permanent outfit, my new pals and I had a chuckle over how naive we had been in basic. They also had forgotten to duck when the CQ was on the prowl. I think that this was true of all us beginners. A few gifted recruits caught on at the start and we held them in awe while we did their work.

When my female friends learned that I was off to war, they all promised to write faithfully. This was fine, but I think in the flush of patriotism, they made the same commitment to many others. For the first six weeks, I got letters from them all, but then the well dried up. My female correspondence dropped like a rock. One girlfriend, Margaret, stuck by me faithfully throughout the entire war. She wrote monthly, and her letters were always light and cheerful. She was the ideal correspondent for a lonely GI. The nifty bottle of first-rate perfume I gave her was just a token, but it was the best I could do. All my family wrote regularly as well, so I seldom drew a blank at mail call.

Drawing Miami Beach for basic training was a huge plus. We had comfortable rooms with nice hot showers. The weather was warm every day and a big ocean was at our beck and call. The beach was a large town, and while it was overrun with soldiers, there were still a plethora of good places to eat and lots of movie theaters. It may not have been the best introduction to the vicissitudes of military life, but none of us complained. As I was leaving, I took comfort in the thought that while the rest of my army career might have to be spent in hell holes, they could never take my six weeks in Miami.

Chapter Six

Learning to be an Armorer

Purple Mountain Majesty
—From "America the Beautiful"

A day or so after Red departed, I got my orders. Most of my close friends were long gone and I was among strangers once more. We loaded our equipment on one truck, hopped on a six by six, and bid "aloha" to Miami Beach. We drove over the Venetian Causeway for the last time and headed to the depot. We boarded "Pullmans" once more for a trip to the unknown.

After the usual interminable wait at the station, our train finally pulled out. Trains leaving Miami went only north, so we passed Fort Lauderdale and Palm Beach before it grew dark and we hit the hay with no idea of our destination.

When we awoke next morning, we were passing through the metropolis of Birmingham, Alabama, indicating that we had taken a turn to the west during the night. Next we passed through a town with the intriguing name of Tupelo, in the state of Mississippi, and crossed the Father of the Waters at Memphis, Tennessee. After baking for two days and freezing for three more, we ended up in Denver, Colorado, where we were taken about fifteen miles east to Buckley Field and reported for duty. While we were being assigned to ancient wood barracks, we learned to our disappointment that we were to be trained as armorers and not mechanics.

Colorado introduced me to real mountains for the first time. Our view of the Rockies, some sixty miles to the west, was fantastic. Since it was early spring, they were covered with the whitest snow I had ever seen. Beautiful as they were, I never really had time to enjoy them at close range.

We put in a six-day week, starting classes each day at six A.M. Although we only had class until noon, we still had little time for recreation and even less to negotiate the sixty some miles to the foothills. Also, after six weeks in Miami, it took me several weeks to get acclimated to the cold weather and the altitude of mile-high Denver. Due to the altitude and the desert climate, every morning was nippy. It warmed up rapidly during the day but I never got used to those cold mornings.

Buckley Field was the hard luck station of my army career. My stay was a classic case of Murphy's Law—if it can happen, it will happen. First

I caught the German measles and had to spend a week in the hospital, which permanently separated me from the friends I had made on our transcontinental trip. This was a minor hardship, since I enjoyed meeting new people and making new friends.

However, while I was in the hospital, some nutty pilot noticed that the doors of a huge hangar were opened at both ends and proceeded to fly right through it at top speed. This scared the hell out of everybody and got him canned. What a way to go! What a thing to miss! From that day forward, one door of the hangar was always closed. Excitement like that occurs only once in a blue moon and it is a tragedy to miss it.

Before we started classes, we had a few small details to take care of. First they checked our shot records which were inaccurate, as usual. Luckily, I had my own records and was up to date. Some of the others were not so fortunate and had to start all over again. Then we checked out our newly issued gas masks.

As an embryo chemist, I liked the smell of chemicals such as chlorine, ammonia, etc. Years before, as a kid, I took some Chlorox and poured battery acid in it. Green fumes of chlorine gas poured out of the container and the whole room took on a greenish-yellow tinge. Since I had a cold, I sniffed it for a time and then opened the window to air out the room. My cold got better and I suffered no ill effects.

They put us in a small room where an itty-bitty candle was burning and a faint aroma of chlorine was in the air. Everyone donned their masks except me. It was customary for someone to yell "GAS" before we were supposed to put on our masks and since no one had, I didn't put mine on. I didn't realize that the tiny taper was emitting the gas that I smelled. I thought that the faint chlorine odor was the residue left over from the last group who had gone through just ahead of us. I was waiting for them to turn on the real McCoy before donning my mask. The guy running the show was horrified and ran up to me, banged me on the shoulder, and hollered, "Put on your f——— mask, soldier. Do you want to get killed?" I put it on but was disappointed by this whole operation. However, it did give us exposure to a lethal gas at a safe concentration so perhaps I learned something after all.

A few weeks later, we had a similar drill using tear gas. Our charming instructor threw an open canister of tear gas in our midst. Pandemonium set in. This time I didn't wait for the magic word. I put mine on pronto but not quite quick enough. My eyes burned like fire and tears streamed down my cheeks. My first whiff made a believer out of me. This lethal stuff not only made me cry, it soaked into my clothes and took forever to evaporate. I had traces of that stuff in my fatigues for at least ten days. We had the option of keeping on our masks despite the blazing heat or taking them off and having another good cry before it evaporated—a bad no-win situation. I think our instructor took a particular delight in my plight after he had seen my reaction to chlorine.

Once we started school, our daily routine started with classes at six A.M. and finished at noon. After lunch, we had PT (Physical training), but nothing was really set up for us. Sometimes we did setting up exercises which we termed "callawooptics." Mostly we went out into an open field with some yo-yo who knew nothing about exercising and cared even less. Even the most active of us were lukewarm to organized exercise. We spent these afternoons horsing around or sitting in what shade was available and shooting the bull.

At one of these outings, I introduced a game we played in grade school called "Thirty." One unfortunate was designated as "It." He had to catch the others individually, saying each time he caught somebody, "Thirty once, thirty twice, thirty three times for all." Once caught, the catchee had to help round up the others until all were caught. The first one caught was "it" for the next game. Since we had some thirty guys, one game usually took most of the exercise period. Many of the guys caught early drifted away in the confusion, so we usually ended up with perhaps two-thirds of our original compliment when the game was over. These were the hard-core ones who were into physical activity, so the second game was always more fun.

Exercise for our last week at Buckley was a lark. Our captain scraped up a corporal from a bush or cave somewhere and put him in charge of our program. This gent's name was Grover. He was a real winner. He disliked organized exercise as much as we did. As a result, we spent most of our time in bull sessions and sneaking to and from the PX. He was so low key that we nicknamed him "Chicken Shit", since he was anything but.

After we shipped out to Drew Field in Tampa, Florida, and he had gone to MacDill Field, some twenty miles away, he came over to visit us. As soon as I saw him, I yelled, "Hiya, Chicken Shit," at the top of my lungs.

He replied good-naturedly, "I knew you were going to call me that."

Embarrassed, I resolved never to make that mistake again. We met several other times before we both shipped out to different locations. We were kindred spirits in more ways than one—we both had nasal pharyngitis at the same time in Colorado and neither of us went on sickcall.

While in Denver, I celebrated my twentieth birthday. Birthdays in our family were second-class feast days. We got a few presents, some cake and ice cream, and after the candles on the cake were blown out and the dessert was consumed, the party was over.

This was not so for my twentieth in Denver. My parents called up the Catholic USO and asked them to give me a cake or something. I got a call from them telling me that they had arranged to have a party for me on the Saturday night nearest June 19th which was my birthday. They told me to invite eight or nine of my friends.

What my parents and the USO didn't realize was that none of us had any real friends since we were fully occupied at school. This was particularly true in my case since I had been separated from my original group and had just started making new friends. After much arm-twisting and being politely turned down by half a dozen people, I finally got eight reluctant volunteers. I was grateful to them since I realized that each had other things to do which were a lot more fun than attending an old-fashioned birthday party.

The last one to show up had a hooker in tow, racy dress, inch-thick makeup and all. This put a strain on everyone—my hosts, my companions, but most of all on the tart. The guy who brought her was blissfully unaware of the consternation he had caused. Right after dinner, she excused herself and both departed to complete what they had met for.

We had a nice, if desultory, meal of steak, ice cream, and cake, and then all but I quickly departed for the pleasures they had postponed. Before my departure, my hosts insisted that I call my parents. As upset as I was, I didn't know what I would say to them. Fortunately, all lines were busy. I thanked my hosts and then I, too, departed. By this time, all my fellow party-goers had scattered and I was alone. I took the first bus back to the base, wrote thank you notes to the USO and my folks, and then retired for the night, my earliest bed time in history.

The story of "John's birthday party in Denver" has become part of the Henkels family lore and has been told, embellished, and retold a thousand times. I have been wary of surprise parties ever since.

At armament school, I met the real army for the first time. Prior to this, all my acquaintances had been recruits like myself. At Denver, however, many of the students were washed out cadets, those who had tried to become pilots and didn't make it. Many of these birds were corporals and sergeants and had been in the army for quite some time before going to cadet school. Washing out must have been a traumatic experience. Although they got back their previous rank, they were now on equal footing with green recruits and had no chance of ever becoming officers.

Virtually all of them claimed that reckless flying was their downfall. While this was obviously not true, we accepted this reason without question since we had lots of sympathy toward them. Most of them were volunteers who looked down their noses on us draftees. They felt that they were more patriotic than we were. The first thing that came to my mind was Samuel Johnson's famous remark that patriotism was the last refuge of scoundrels. Needless to say, I never mentioned this to anyone. Of course, none of us cared a rap about what they thought since we had answered the bell when called. Gradually this simmered down and we became a cohesive group and all this pettiness was forgotten.

My first encounter with these vets occurred just after I got out of the hospital. I was in limbo, waiting to be assigned to a new class. All of us in this state were available for various extracurricular activities such as KP, policing the grounds, etc. Since the units at Armament were quite small compared to those in Miami, KP was not the horror I had become accustomed to. We actually had a moment of rest between lunch and dinner, although we were not permitted to leave the mess hall.

During one of these breaks, we were given a rare treat. The use of hyperbole to describe one's adventures in the army is a time-honored custom. There is, of course, an unwritten law that if you are going to tell your adventures and be believed, you are honor-bound to believe the other guy's yarns as well.

On this particular occasion, two of the vets decided to give us recruits a real introduction into the world of army hyperbole. The result was one of the most entertaining afternoons of my life. Fantasy after elaborate fantasy poured from those two eloquent mouths. They proved to be the greatest storytellers since Sheherazade. For over two hours we listened to these two birds with utter fascination. About every twenty minutes or so, a young Irish kid and I had to go outside, roar with laughter and then return for more. We didn't dare laugh inside the mess hall lest we break the spell.

After about an hour and a half, sex reared its ugly head as it invariably does in all army bull sessions. That really got our birds in high gear. One of the young boys there who evidently had some experience mentioned that it was a shame that there were no places where the gals paid the guys for services rendered. One of our heroes quickly retorted that there was a place in Nevada where the gals did pay and, of course, he had been there. It seems that he happened to be in that particular town one night and was on the prowl. On entering one of the local bordellos, he selected a real queen (what else?). When he asked what she charged, she replied—and I quote him—"Oh, we don't charge, we donate to servicemen." To my everlasting regret, I was so entranced by this fascinating tale that I never thought to ask how much she donated to him. Since then, I have sometimes wondered what kept that cathouse in business when they gave away the merchandise to their best customers.

This last adventure was too much. Irish looked at me and we both raced outside and bellowed. We hastened back as soon as we regained control so we didn't miss the coup de resistance. Next on their agenda was the many different races who had bestowed their favors on them. Here the older had a clear advantage, since his younger compatriot had foolishly admitted that he had never been in Asia. The older pressed his advantage by going down an entire list of Asiatic races whom he had bedded down and then rated them by race.

After some mundane description of the Chinese and Japanese, he started to rhapsodize on the exquisite abilities of the Indians of Asia. His final words on this important subject were, "Now you take Hindu ass, that's *goddam* good ass." This fractured even the greenest recruit who had previously hung on his every word. Unfortunately, this also broke the spell for good and a few minutes later, we had to return to work. A fantastic two hours ended with a master stroke. Repetition of this yarn was to gain fame and fortune for me when I repeated it at college after my army discharge.

Irish was in a different outfit and a week or so ahead of me, so he was soon gone. We did see each other from time to time before he shipped out and each of us tried to beat the other in saying, "Hindu ass is *goddam* good ass," and then laugh like hell.

Before going to class, I put in another three-day tour of KP that was a comedy of errors. The first to arrive at the kitchen in the morning were given their choice of jobs and the last ended up with pots and pans since this was *never* first choice. On the first day, I woke up fifteen minutes early and was almost completely dressed before any of the others. However, I couldn't find my sock in the dark. Instead of going over with just one sock, I persisted in the madness of looking for it. This made me bottom man on the totem pole and it was pots and pans for good old JBH and one other loser.

There were a whole pile of trays waiting by the sink so we jumped right on them, scouring them with a vengeance. We had just finished the last one when the mess sergeant came over and said, "Goddamit, you didn't do those f——— cake pans did you?" Of course we had. He said, "All you were supposed to do was wipe them off. What the f— is wrong with you guys?" We chuckled wryly over an extra hour's work. However, the worst was yet to come.

Knowing that local policy forbid having pots and pans two days in a row, my cohort and I were in no hurry to report to the kitchen next morning. We worked on the serving line for breakfast, after which we were given rags and told to wipe off the tables. The mess sergeant came around and said, "These goddam table legs are filthy. Better turn 'em over and do the legs." After wiping off the tops, we turned the tables on their sides and scrubbed all the legs and braces. This was bad enough, but looking at the malicious grins on the faces of those working in the sinks made our work doubly painful.

Next day, it was a given that we were back in the sinks so we were in no hurry to get there. When we finally straggled in, our friendly boss greeted us with the news that all the cake pans we had done two days ago were now rusty and would have to be done again. We were shocked and looked at each other in dismay. My alter ego looked so sad that I started to laugh and his reaction to my expression was the same. We spent the whole day wondering what bad news would come next and laughing at every exaggerated tale we invented. Fortunately, I started class the next week and KP, Buckley Field style, was a thing of the past.

I discovered at Buckley Field that the army, despite the seriousness of its main purpose, was not bereft of humor. One fine afternoon after lunch, our CQ told us that we were going to have a GI party. This sounded exciting. Visions of beer and pretzels danced in our heads. First, we were told to move all the bunks to one side of the barracks. While this was underway, several guys entered the barracks with soapy water which they promptly spilled on the floor. Our boss then gave us brooms and mops and told us to scrub the floor and mop it up.

When we had finished one side, the procedure was repeated on the other side. In the army as elsewhere, many hands make light work so we finished in about forty-five minutes, almost before any of us realized that we had been had. I have to hand it to the guy who invented this little caper.

I have used this same ruse on my children with great success. Before they have a chance to complain, the job is done. I also caught a few of their friends who had the misfortune to come visiting too early on a Saturday morning. One father called me up to complain after his son gave him an exaggerated version of his mistreatment that morning. When I filled him in on what had really occurred, he roared laughing and told me, "I got to pull that one on my daughters." Although I have no proof as yet, I am certain that some of my grandchildren will find out about GI parties the hard way.

Our first order of business in school was to learn all the secrets of the Browning machine gun. Our instructor first reminded us that it was always caliber fifty, *never fifty- caliber*. Second, they showed us how to dismantle some thirty calibers which were similar to the fifties but lots smaller. I never got a clear answer as to why we worked on thirties when all our ships would be equipped with fifties. Thirties were too small to be effective on modern aircraft and they differed from the fifties in more than just size. The Browning machine gun was light and virtually foolproof. We found out that the fifty was even better, and we had very little problems in maintaining them. The fifty was the standard weapon of the air forces and proved to be very successful. It was both accurate and had a high rate of fire. Both of these attributes were very important in aerial combat and for strafing ground targets. Since it was smaller and lighter than the twenty-millimeter cannon used by the Germans and the British, our planes were able to carry more guns and ammunition. While the twenty millimeter slug had almost twice the diameter of the caliber-fifty and was explosive as well, our brass thought that the rapid rate of fire and the accuracy of the caliber-fifty more than made up for its deficiency in size. Our fighters were armed with eight of these guns versus our opponents' four twenty millimeters, and we more than held our own. We liked them because they were easy to load and maintain.

The weekend between our classes on caliber-thirties and our start on twenty millimeters, I felt a bit odd. I happened to look in the mirror and noticed I had tiny red spots all over my face. I went up to the CQ, stuck my face about six inches from his, and asked him if he noticed any spots on my face. He gave me a sharp kick in the stomach and replied, "Hell yes, go on sick call." It turned out that I had German measles and I was exiled to the hospital. This was the only time in my army career when I lost any time. It also meant—another separation (ho hum) from my friends of one week.

In my case, measles turned out to be virtually painless, but I was still restricted to bed and not allowed to read. I caught up on my shuteye, but time hung heavy on my hands. I was restless, rolled around, and kept mussing up my bed almost as soon as it was made. Most of the other guys with my ailment were hit harder and were not near as active as I.

About the third or fourth day, a nice-looking nurse saw that my bed was in shambles, clucked sympathetically, and made it for me. She repeated this every afternoon until I was discharged. I am sure that she was just being nice, but I got a reputation as a Romeo which I enjoyed and wished I deserved.

I left the hospital on a Sunday afternoon and had to start school at six the next morning. However, immediately after I left, I picked up a king-sized cold which I was told later went by the name of nasal pharyngitis. This was a horror that caused hideous nasal congestion and made me feel miserable to boot. I knew that there was no cure for a cold, and I had had enough of the hospital, so I just decided to sweat it out and what a sweat it was! This ailment made my measles feel like a day off with pay.

Since I had no fever, I was not officially sick, but my nasal congestion was brutal. I ruined all my handkerchiefs and started to use toilet paper. I have never felt worse in my life. Since we were not permitted to use our beds except at night, I spent my waking hours in what passed for a library. I only stayed alive because I was too sick to die. My new classmates thought that I was a misanthrope and left me alone, which I appreciated.

After three days of misery and total fasting, I decided that I was not going to die and therefore HAD to get something to eat or I'd starve. I went to the mess hall for lunch and saw that they were serving wienerschnitzel and sauerkraut. This was something I normally detested, but I guess my disease was on its last legs, because I tore into those glorified hot dogs as if they were steak or lobster. I was cured.

The only permanent result of my illness was spending the first three days on the twenty-millimeter cannon in a fog. I hadn't learned a thing. The twenty-millimeter cannon was technically known as the Hispano AN-M2C. As I recollect, It was of Spanish origin and had been used extensively in the Spanish Civil War. The action of the twenty was far different from the caliber thirty. Its action was termed, as I recall, "a gas and blow back action." This meant that the exhaust gases of one firing operated the mechanism to recharge the gun for the next, while it was the recoil of the thirty that operated it. I don't recall my having any difficulties with the twenty, but we never fired it. Our instructors placed no particular emphasis on it which made me think that it would not play a significant part in our future. At this time, we were unaware that the Air Corps had already decided to go with the Browning caliber-fifty. I did know that the twenty mm was quite popular with the German Luftwaffe and that it was also catching on with the RAF. The Germans ultimately mounted thirty millimeters on some of their later model Me109's, and the British went almost exclusively to the twenties. However, I still think our decision to stick with the fifty was a wise one. After all, the larger the caliber, the more complicated the firing mechanism—we had a gun that was powerful, reliable, easy to maintain, and had a rapid rate of fire, all one could wish for in an aerial gun.

The best day we had while studying the twenty was the day they showed us a long movie on what made it tick. It was not long after the lights went out that I also went out. The speaker in the movie droned on in a sonorous monotone, perfect as a lullaby. When I finally awoke, every light was on and I sweat out being caught. The penalty for such a transgression could be repeating the course, and I had no desire to go through that boring course again or dropping back a week. I asked the guy next to me why he hadn't woke me up. His reply was that he thought I was dead. I think the thing that saved my little butt was that the instructor had seen it dozens of times and he had drifted off to other climes himself. He didn't like to get up at five in the morning any more than we did.

Life had another cruel blow waiting in the wings for me but this time I didn't suffer alone. We were introduced to an ailment known as the GIs——, usually shortened to the GIs. Civilians call it diarrhea. I was sleeping soundly in the wee hours of the morning, when I was awakened by the sound of a guy pounding down the barracks floor for dear life. Somebody shouted after him as he banged through the door, "Have you got them too?" Just as I started to laugh, hideous cramps grabbed hold of my stomach and then came an overpowering urge to go potty. I bounded out of bed and raced for the latrine, just beating another panting soldier for the last stool. The latrine was jammed with guys in mortal agony awaiting a seat. Some who waited did not make it and returned slowly to the barracks for a change of underwear. Others ran to the neighboring latrines only to find that they were teeming with customers as well. All our latrines did a landslide business that night, but after the first mad rush, it was usually possible to get a seat. This horrible rush had another adverse result—we ran out of toilet paper.

My cramps continued all night. They hurt like hell whenever they grabbed me. I have never had a grenade explode in my stomach but I now know how it would feel. As morning approached, things began to ease up and by lunch I was okay, but from then on, I made sure to avoid any fried food for months to come. Some of the others were not so lucky; their illness lasted all day. We were permitted to leave class whenever we had the urge. This helped but didn't cure. From this time on, there were two things I really dreaded—spinal meningitis and the GIs—in that order. I escaped meningitis but was destined to get hit with the GIs twice more—once on shipboard while enroute to England, which almost became a first class disaster, and then again I had a mild case in France. I was lucky to escape a king-sized attack in Belgium that almost got our cooks lynched. These attacks almost always resulted from our cooks trying to eke an extra meal out of some particularly appetizing-looking gravy. Every attack led to a rush on the PXs for about a week or until we ran out of money.

On one of my early tours of KP, either in Miami or in Denver, I saw a pan of gravy that had been standing for a few hours and the grease had risen to the top, forming a very unappetizing-looking mixture. Just before the chow line opened, one of the cooks stirred it up into a tan colored homogeneous substance which innocent servers ladled out profusely to unsuspecting soldiers. Most of our refrigeration was not all that good, and cooks had a tendency to let some things stand in the open for longer than was prudent. I am also sure that the nice pool of grease on the top of the flour base was such a delectable looking target that even the most benign of germs could not resist. Of course, the evil gravy looked exactly like the innocent. Perhaps the army should have given us kits of litmus paper to check out gravy before we tried it.

After completing our week on the twenty-millimeter, we advanced to harmonizing and synchronizing guns. These two operations proved to be the most interesting operations of our entire stay at Buckley. At that time, the air force still had a few crates where the machine guns fired through the plane of the rotating propeller. Obviously, the firing of these guns had to be synchronized so that the slugs would not damage it. The engine of these planes had a protruding cam which had as many projections as the propeller had blades. The shaft of this cam had two ratchets—one which turned clockwise and the other counterclockwise. One armorer slowly turned the propeller while the other adjusted the cam. As the cam rotated, it pushed a stiff wire which activated the firing of the gun. By adjusting the cam in relation to the position of the prop blades, the gun could be fired safely. Once the gun was synchronized, it was very important to secure the cam so that it would not move.

Since synchronized guns, were right in front of the pilot, they were very accurate. It was fun and a challenge to work on these guns but it involved a lot of responsibility since the margin of error was small. However, their rate of fire was much less than that of the same gun mounted in the wing, and the wire, cam, etc. were high maintenance items so the air force soon abandoned them.

Next on our agenda was harmonization of wing guns. All modern fighters in World War II had guns mounted in the wings. Of course, the pilot couldn't adjust them in flight, so it was necessary to do so on the ground. Adjusting wing guns was one of our most important duties. They took us into the huge hanger where several old war weary P-40s awaited us. At this time, the P-40 was borderline obsolete. It was still in moderate use but was outclassed by fighter craft flown by the Japanese and the Luftwaffe. However, it was fine for our purposes. These planes had two caliber-fifties in each wing.

In order to make a fighter effective, it is necessary to concentrate its fire at a single point. Harmonization is much like using a concave lens to focus incoming parallel light on a single point. Gun mounts were adjusted with set screws so that we could aim the guns at a given point after which the set screws were wired so that they could not move. At Buckley Field, we focused the four guns so that their fire was focused on a single spot about three hundred yards in front of the plane. To do this in the limited space of our hanger, we used a system of similar triangles. We calculated the angle at which each gun had to be set so it all would hit the same spot. Using this angle we could build a line of targets that was only one hundred and fifty feet from the guns or less from the plane, and could boresight each gun on its own little target. When we had accomplished this with the guns, we went into the cockpit and made certain that the little gunsight was in tune with the guns. Once harmonized, it was only necessary to do so again if the set screw was not wired down correctly. In point of fact, I never had to harmonize a plane since they had done so at the factory. However, it was important to know how to perform this chore because it would have been a major disaster if some of our guns got out of kilter and we were unable to adjust them. We had a lot of fun harmonizing these guns and were sorry that they were unable to check our work on tow targets. Our old buckets of bolts were just a little too old to fly.

Next on our agenda was the thirty-seven-millimeter cannon. This was a big gun for a fighter, far too big to be mounted in the wings, and its firing pattern was not reliable enough to synchronize it. So, it had to shoot through the hub of the propeller. At that time, only one plane, the Bell Airacobra, was so designed to mount a thirty-seven. When I first saw this monstrosity, I realized that the larger the caliber of the gun, the more complicated the firing mechanism. The thirty-seven was a complicated nightmare. The many springs involved were strong and a horror to replace. After working on it for a week, I felt as ignorant as when I started. Our instructor took this opportune time to have me explain to the rest of the class just how it worked. I started out stuttering, feeling completely ignorant. As I went along, things fell into place and I realized, by Heaven, that I did know how it operated and that, given enough time, I could make one work.

When our class finished learning about the thirty-seven-millimeter, I was a graduate armorer and just about ready for assignment to a *real* outfit. All that was left were a few odds and ends such as qualifying with a rifle and shooting both a Tommy gun and a carbine.

To my amazement, these little chores took almost a month. First we had to qualify with a rifle. This required two days. On the first day, we went out and made ourselves familiar with our "pieces", as rifles are sometimes referred to. The second day we fired for record. For this purpose, we used bolt-action Springfield rifles, which were a light year ahead of the Enfields we had shot in Miami. They were a cut or two removed from muzzle loaders but were much lighter than any other rifle I had ever shot.

To qualify as a marksman, we had to score over one-thirty out of two hundred. As I remember, a bulls-eye counted five, the next ring was four, and so on. A clean miss—and there were many of them—was known as "Maggie's Drawers", because the guys in the pit who did the scoring waved a large rag attached to a stick for each such miss. After taking a few shots to zero in our pieces, we shot for record from three positions—prone, sitting and standing. We fired twenty rounds from each position, ten at regular fire and ten at rapid fire.

All of us took turns shooting and working in the pit, which was a large depression protected from would-be marksmen by a very tall and thick wall of dirt. The guys in the pits pulled the targets up for the hot shots to shoot at, and then yanked them down to mark the scores. The only hazard involved occurred when some guy just grazed the top of our fort and scattered some debris down on us.

Qualifying was a ball, particularly the rapid fire. I did very well in both the prone and sitting positions, particularly on the rapid fire, but I really tapered off on the standing position since I had difficulty holding my rifle still. I still managed to score over one-forty and thus qualified.

When we started shooting, pandemonium reigned supreme. Our magazines held five rounds of ammo each, and at rapid fire we had to shoot off ten rounds in a minute or less. Guns banged away like crazy and it seemed to me that the only things that were safe were the targets. I never enjoyed anything more than those precious three minutes I had shooting rapid fire. I found, to my surprise, that I scored best at rapid fire because as soon as your sight was on the target, it was BAM. In slow fire, I either held my aim on the target too long or I jerked the trigger. Either of these resulted in "Maggie's Drawers" for sure.

After our two days on the range, I discovered that nobody had been killed and that everybody had qualified. This latter piece of knowledge took a lot of the luster from my accomplishment of qualification. I wondered just how well I had done in reality.

Just before I shipped out, I ran into the sergeant who ran the firing range. I accused him in my best bantering way of having rigged the scores to reduce our fun time on the range. I told him that it was not much fun being in the army and that he had deprived us of a good bit by rigging up our qualifying scores. He gave me a great big grin, slapped me on the shoulder and said, "War is a terrible thing and we all have to make sacrifices. Better luck next war," or something similar.

All of us stalwarts who qualified were entitled to wear a little tin Maltese Cross, similar in shape but not in value to the German Iron Cross. It had a little bar below it saying "Marksman." I only donned mine once—on one of the few dates I had while in Colorado. My date asked me what my medal was for and without thinking, I told her the truth. I couldn't stand the look of disillusionment on her face when I blurted this out. An opportunity of a lifetime had been squandered in five seconds. I didn't take the time to think that perhaps she had no idea what a marksman was. As I look back on this minor tragedy, I recall the second part of Cassius' speech to Brutus when they were discussing opportunity, "Omitted, all the voyages of their life Is bound in shallows and in miseries." Of course, it wasn't *that* bad but it was bad enough. At any rate, back into the box it went and it finally disappeared, unlamented on one of my various moves.

The army, like many other government organizations, was great on awards. We were given different colored bars to pin on the left side of our uniforms, each representing such heroics as good conduct, our victory in Europe, and the other campaigns we had participated in. We accumulated an impressive amount in the short time we were in the army. At our discharge, we were told that it was possible to get the medal itself by writing to the War Department, but I never took the time to do so. One of my friends sent in for his and sent me a picture with this handsome hardware decorating the chest of his uniform. He looked so impressive that I almost relented and sent for mine. I wrote to him and said that he looked like the head honcho of some two-bit principality. Sour grapes?

The next event was firing the Thompson submachine gun and the caliber-thirty carbine. These events took two days, although we didn't shoot for record on either one. We had lots of fun, shot up scads of ammo, and might even have learned a little in the process. The Tommy gun was a treat to shoot, so I could easily see why it was so popular with the mob although I am sure that they liked it for different reason. Tommy guns use .45-inch slugs, the same that are used in the Colt "45." It had a kick like a mule if you didn't press it firmly against your shoulder. We fired at targets against a bank high enough to intercept even our most errant shots. We each got to shoot a clip of twenty-five bullets. Twelve of us shot at one time, and those not shooting amused themselves by smoking or playing cards.

Unfortunately, our targets were as pockmarked as those we had used in Miami, so we had no way to test our accuracy. They were held up by two by fours facing edgewise toward us. Our instructor told us that the guns were more accurate if fired in short bursts of perhaps six shots because they pulled to right as they were fired. Since I was unable to tell how well I shot, I got the bright idea of trying to shoot out the two-by-fours. After my first burst drew out a nice bunch of splinters. Just below the target, I felt certain that I would shoot it down.

At this juncture, Sarge called for a time out and told us that he would take it personally if any targets were shot down. He and I were such good friends that I didn't want to hurt his feelings, so I dutifully emptied the rest of my clip on the defenseless target.

Next day we were handed thirty brand-new carbines and a handful of ammo for same. These guns were standard for AAF ground crews. They were a well-conceived weapon but were mass produced, so there were such things as tiny burrs or other imperfections that not only made them inaccurate, but also caused them to jam at the most annoying times.

Once again our targets were nondescript. However, the slugs of the thirty were thinner and the muzzle velocity greater. The only thing that dampened our ardor was the inability to see the result of our shooting. However, the thirty has a thinner slug and its muzzle velocity was high. This meant that they would leave a very small hole if they went through a two-by-four. I used all my ammo in shooting at the two-by-fours. I missed far more than I hit. Constant jamming took some of the fun out of shooting the carbine, but the Tommy gun was pure pleasure.

The last phase of our training was aircraft identification. We went to the base theater, where an expert explained the differences between various types of aircraft, both ours and theirs. He used the same method later made famous by Roger Tory Peterson in his bird books. We were taught to recognize at a glance distinguishing characteristics of each plane. This was a challenge and lots of fun.

After his initial lecture, he used slides, and we had to identify each plane in the second or so it was on the screen. Most were easy, i.e. the P-38, B-17 which had obvious unique features, but when it came to the P-51 and the German Me109 or the P-47 and the Fw190, it was a horse of a different color. We didn't know it at the time, but these were the identifications we might have to make when we went overseas. We learned everything about enemy planes except what to do if we ran into them or, perhaps more correctly, if they ran into us.

July 10th, 1943 marked the end of our schooling, and we were fledgling armorers. All we needed were some airplanes to hone our skills on. To our surprise, we didn't receive any diplomas. This was contrary to normal army practice, but it was okay by us—one less thing to cart around.

We were now in Limbo, waiting for our assignments to permanent outfits. We had a lot of free time and the weather was good, so we spent lots of time in Denver. One of the real treasures there was an amusement park called "Elliche's Gardens." Scads of young ladies flocked there, so it was a great place to meet some nice girls, dance to first rate music, go on the rides, and even steal a peck or two if you were bold and the girl willing. Most of these young ladies came from farms or ranches and were really fine kids. Of course there were the usual guys who wanted more and they made out, but the vast majority of us, both GIs and girls, were there for a good time and each departed on his or her separate way when the park closed. I went there six or seven times and always found a date who was fun and innocent. The "Gardens" was first rate and I have fond memories of it to this day.

As it must to all, Duty's clarion call came, and we bid "Aloha" to Buckley Field and Colorado. On our last night, some of the boys broke out a guitar and sang sentimental cowboy songs. I joined them for a while and then opted for a good night's sleep. I forgot, of course, that there would be scads of time to catch up on my shuteye on the train.

Just as I started to doze off, a mouse ran right over my face. This little surprise dampened my desire to sleep so I rejoined the singers. We saw lots of these little beasties in and around the barracks but this was the first time one had the effrontery to do anything but run for a hiding place. His appearance was proof positive to me that it was time to move on.

At about two A.M., our songfest broke up and we all retired. After a restless half hour of anticipating a return of my furry friend, I finally fell asleep while visions of working on *real* airplanes danced in my head.

Next morning they woke us at five A.M. as usual. We grabbed our barracks bags and ran outside, where we were quickly loaded on trucks and hustled off to the train depot. I felt a pang of nostalgia as we passed through the main gate for the last time. I was just getting used to the cool mornings and the great view of the Rockies. I had premonitions that our next stop would be hot and humid. We had left cold for hot, hot for cold, so why not cold for hot this time?

Chapter Seven

Tampa - Joining a *Real* Outfit

Nothing quite new is Perfect
—Cicero

Five A.M. breakfast was filled with excitement. We all wondered where we were headed and which of our friends would accompany us. We realized that at our destination, we would be part of a combat squadron, although we had not the foggiest idea whether it would be heavy bombers, fighters or any of the various intermediate craft. We knew that there would be many destinations since there were far too many of us for one outfit.

Once again we boarded rusty, dusty Pullmans for a seven-day trip during which some cars were detached at various points for other destinations. True to my foreboding, I ended up where it was hot and humid— Drew Field near Tampa, Florida. We had two eight-hour layovers on our trip, one in Kansas City, Missouri, and the other in Jacksonville, Florida. In each case, we were allowed to hit the towns for some six hours each. In Kansas City, fifty percent of the guys got roaring drunk and suffered miserable hangovers next day. Since I was not into booze at this time, and getting drunk was never one of my goals anyhow, I was on my own. I roamed the streets of KC and poked my head into a few shops that sold stuff I couldn't afford until it was time to reboard. KC was the first Midwest town I had ever seen and I thought I was in the Wild West. It had an aura of lawlessness that appealed to me. The real plus for this stopover was a chance to get some very welcome exercise.

Jacksonville was a horse of a different color. I persuaded three of my friends to head for a beach and a nice swim in the ocean. We hopped a local bus for free and took a scenic twenty-mile ride to the beach. We changed our clothes at a cabana and raced into the ocean. The water was refreshingly cool. This worked out spectacularly. We had a long, cool swim and a nice, freshwater shower to rinse off the salt. Getting rid of the grime we had accumulated during six hot midsummer days on a troop train was sheer luxury. After we had changed, we ate supper in a cheap restaurant overlooking the ocean, latched onto another free bus, and then returned to the train refreshed and invigorated.

By the time we had returned, the sun had set and things were much cooler. We reboarded our rusty cattle car and enjoyed the envious looks of our companions, many of whom had repeated their Kansas City misadventure. We were tired from our vigorous afternoon, so we had the best sleep of our entire trip. Even the off-key melodies of the inebriated failed to keep us awake.

Riding troop trains was always uncomfortable because the equipment was ancient, we had zero priority, they were slow, and we were cramped for space. There were some compensations: discipline was lax because there were too few officers and noncoms to police each car. They came through our car occasionally, almost always at the same time every day. At first we thought that this was pretty dumb, because we were always on our good behavior when they came. In time, we realized that what they didn't know wouldn't hurt them. They could readily detect anything that was really amiss, and anything else didn't matter.

We learned to live like kiwis or other night animals. Every train had its inveterate gamblers who played cards all night long. It would have been pleasant if they had done so quietly, but that was not their *modus operandi*. After each stop such as Kansas City, an illicit jug was often passed around which increased the decibels considerably. I got some sleep at night, but when it got too hectic, I got up and read and caught up on my sleep during the day. Paradoxically, it was often quieter during the day than at night. Of course trains varied, some were quieter than others, but gambling was common to all of them.

The morning after we left Jacksonville, our train pulled into the Tampa depot. Several six-by-sixes were there. We hopped on board and headed to Drew Field, which was to be our home for most of the summer. Most of the guys were dropped off at permanent barracks, and twelve of us remnants were looking forward to similar accommodations. To our dismay, we were shunted across the huge runway to a remote wooded area next to a swamp and into ancient swayback wood barracks set on cinder blocks. This was a bad start!

Inside these rustic ruins were double bunks in two rows leaving a narrow aisle running down the middle. There were two pitch-black potbellied stoves at each end of the barracks, near the entrances. We were issued sheets and blankets which we used to cover decrepit straw mattresses. We were assigned beds so we could be identified easily. We made them up and then sat down and commiserated with each other on the rude blow dealt to us by a cruel fate.

We felt like the outcasts of Poker Flat when we looked across the runway at the luxurious-looking accommodations occupied by the others. However, there is a ying for every yang. I recalled from Miami days that the better the accommodations, the more GI (disciplined) the living conditions. In our bucolic environment, we had neither retreat nor reveille and we were spared visits from faultfinding brass. Most important,

76

though, was the universal feeling that we were really toughing it out.

Only twelve of the fifty guys who came to Drew ended up in the swamp. The others were part of our group, but we never saw them again until they rejoined us at our permanent U.S. base in South Carolina. Our ragtag outfit had the impressive title of the 626th Bombardment Squadron. Ultimately we became the 511th Squadron of the 405th Fighter Group. The birds across the runway from us became the 509th and the 510th Squadrons of our Group. This august bunch was part of the Third Air Force.

In the swamp, six of us were put in one barracks and the others in the neighboring one. We were separated so we would not hang together. George Sibley, first sergeant, then gave us the facts of life. He was so low key that he was able to use the most frightful army expletives in such a way that they sounded almost proper. After this brief orientation, we had the rest of the day at liberty to gig frogs in the swamp or wander around and to get the lay of the land.

We thought that we had been given the day off out of the kindness of their hearts. The real reason was that they had no idea what to do with us. Some guys went to the PX, but most of us just wandered around to look for our airplanes and to get the lay of the land.

At this time, we were part of a dive bomber group modeled after the German ground support squadrons which had helped make their infantry so successful. Our pilots flew such ancient wrecks as the Douglas Dauntless and the Curtiss Helldiver. These crates were designed to do the same job as the German Stuka dive bomber, and like it, they were slow, cumbersome, and lacked firepower. Once they had dropped their bombs, they were a liability since they were virtually defenseless.

Our outfit was just forming, hence we had a bunch of greenhorns such as us new arrivals, and some savvy vets who had been around for several years. Since they were out on the "line," which was where our planes were parked, we didn't meet them until almost dinner time. I expected the usual verbal hazing when we met them, but they were cordial and glad to see us.

Before dinner, while we greenhorns were in our barracks exchanging experiences, an odd bird by the name of Spence made his appearance. He was the first and only regular enlisted man I met during my entire career. He'd evidently had a checkered career of ten or so years, and somewhere in antiquity, he had conned some weak sister into making him sergeant. He was one of those guys who didn't deserve to be discharged but whose talents, if any, were such that nobody knew what to do with him. He entered our barracks drunk and proceeded to pick a fight with Bob Loitz, the biggest guy in the place. Bob fended him off good-naturedly, saying that he was too drunk to fight.

Spence retorted, "I'll make you a bet." He proceeded to put a twenty-dollar bill on the floor in the middle of the barracks. He then told Bob, "You put a twenty on top of this, go to the one end of the barracks and I'll go to the other. We run at each other and the one who knocks out gets the money." Bob laughed and declined. I would have put my life savings on Spence even against the Liberty Bell.

We were sorry when old Spence left us to become some other outfit's problem. He had added something special to our first afternoon in Mosquito Village. Genuine characters were far too scarce in the army, so the few one gets should be treasured and not cast into exterior darkness.

I liked the old guy who was ignored by most of the others. He filled me in on what life was like in the regular army, and I didn't envy his life. Life was the same for regular army guys yesterday, today, and tomorrow.

Next morning, we all met formally and we newcomers were assigned to one of the four flights. My boss was a Lebanese from California named Deran V. Isakoolian, known as "Dee", who was in charge of "C" flight and who always wore a nonregulation pith helmet. He took us out to the line, a short walk on a narrow path through the jungle, and showed us the few decrepit planes we had to work on. There were several Douglas Dauntless dive bombers and a few newer Curtiss Helldivers. Both of these types were really designed as dive bombers for use on aircraft carriers. The Dauntless were of the same vintage as those used at Midway and were really obsolete.

It appeared to us at this time that the ground support planes of the Air Force were to play the same role that the Stuka dive bomber played with the German Luftwaffe. These crates were a far cry from the sleek P-51s or P-38s we had expected to see.

Our faces must have fallen when we looked at the fleet because Dee laughed and said that we should be getting more modern planes in soon. Unfortunately, soon was not quick enough, and we spent almost a month working on obsolete ships. We became sentimentally attached to the Douglasses, which had performed so valiantly at Midway, but we were wary of the Helldivers which looked like overgrown aluminum boxes with a propeller in front. They were so big and bulky that we compared them with bumble bees and wondered how they could fly.

The first day out, I proved that I could synchronize a gun. We first made certain that the gun to be synchronized was not loaded. The previous week, they had neglected this little chore and the gun went off with a hideous bang, scaring the two technicians doing the synchronization half to death as the slug ricocheted off the prop blade and whined off into space. Nobody knew why the gun was loaded, since it had never been fired and planes are not supposed to have any ammo aboard. Even in the army, it was the unloaded gun that was the most dangerous. I often wondered whether some fun-loving guy loaded it on the sly or whether the navy did not check the chamber of the gun when they removed the ammunition prior to sending the plane to us.

We had been in Tampa about two weeks when we received all our back pay. Prior to this, we had survived on several partial pays of ten bucks each, and I would have starved without some financial help from home. Some guys were lots worse off than I. They were in serious debt. I was okay since my parents were generous and my wants were few. With the bonanza we received, I paid off my parents and sent home some money for my savings account as well. From this time forward, I made certain that I sent a little something home every pay day.

Drew Field was an inexpensive base. On our day off, we hitched rides to Clearwater on the Gulf of Mexico and spent the day bathing in the warm water there. Wearing our uniforms made hitching a ride to Clearwater a cinch. First-run movies were about thirty-five cents, cokes and other drinks were a pittance at the PX, and books at the library were gratis. The only real expense occurred when I went downtown. Since I was not into babes and booze, I only went downtown once, just so I could say I did. Tampa was a big loser compared to the rest and relaxation we enjoyed on the Gulf beaches. Watching the girls cavort on the beach reminded me of happier days on the beaches of New Jersey. Unfortunately all the girls were all spoken for.

We had few planes in our squadron at this time and even fewer pilots, so we had lots of time on our hands, which we spent listening to the old-timers tell us about how things were when they first joined up. They had worked on all kinds of weird planes. They all liked the Douglas and disliked the Helldivers, but their pet hate was a monstrosity which had long since passed into oblivion. This beauty was called the "V-72," more properly known as the Vultee "Vengeance", a bizarre dive bomber.

From all I heard, it took out its "vengeance" on those who either worked on it or flew it. It evidently looked like the piece of junk that it was. Usually, when the air force was stuck with a turkey, it rhapsodized to one and all about its many virtues. This happened with both the P-39 and the B-26, but evidently the V-72 was so bad that they couldn't even lie about it. All of us newcomers felt cheated that we never had the opportunity to skin our knuckles on this freak. I finally found a picture of one on page seventy-four of David A. Anderson's *The History of the U.S. Airforce*. In the picture, it is all dressed up for the ball, so it looks quite respectable.

Since ours was an existing squadron, there were only a few armorers on board when we arrived and all were old-timers by our standards. Our arrival filled the squadron's complement. Thus the veterans were cadre, that is, on the ground floor, and they became the enlisted brass of the squadron and received all the high ratings. There were no high ratings left for us newcomers. Once again this was the luck of the draw. Some of my "classmates" at Buckley Field joined outfits which were brand new, where they became cadre and got the high ratings. However, they had to train longer and hence missed out on much of the overseas action.

As I mentioned, our pilots preferred to fly the Douglasses and it didn't take me long to find out why. We were all dying to get a ride in an airplane. Due to shortage of pilots, we had little opportunity to do so, although all the pilots were happy to have our company when they flew. All it took to get a ride was to be johnny-on-the-spot.

One evening, I was there at the right time. A pilot came out to check out in a Helldiver. I asked for a ride and he told me to get a chute and hop in. The take off was a real thrill and the view of Tampa harbor from the air was spectacular. I noticed an odd kind of vibration but thought that it went with the territory. We flew around for an hour or so and then landed uneventfully. The pilot approached the plane's mechanic and mentioned feeling a vibration in the right wing.

Since the Helldiver was designed for carrier flying, it had an appurtenance on the front of the wing to give it more lift on takeoff. The mechanic went out, gave this gadget a shake and it almost came off in his hand. The pilot stalked off saying," I never did like those f——— crates." I did a lot of speculating that night.

Several days later, I hitched a ride in one of the Douglasses. It was a bit slower but more maneuverable, and since the pilot was a fun-loving guy, he put the old bucket of bolts through its paces. The open cockpit made me feel as if I had gone through the sound barrier. Fortunately, he did no loops or rolls but what he did was lots of fun. While the first ride is always unique, this one was almost as good and I was spared the worry of having a wing fall off.

Prior to our arrival, the bored pilots did a lot of clowning around. Some of our old-timers flew with them, and they had a ball buzzing cattle on the nearby dairies. The passenger had a better view, so he pointed out the herds to the pilot and down they dove, driving the poor cattle nuts. When the farmers began to complain that their cows were drying up, orders went out to cease and desist this type of harassment. Of course all this was done in the Douglasses—nobody had enough nerve to try any fancy stuff with the Curtisses.

Our ancient Douglasses had one big fault—they had to be started by hand. Since the engine was far too stiff to be cranked like a car, it had an inertia system. This consisted of a series of enclosed gears which were cranked manually until they reached the proper velocity. The system was then engaged to the engine to turn it over. It was necessary for the crankers to keep at it until the engine caught. Occasionally, the pilot would overprime the engine and large yellow flames came out of the exhaust, engulfing the cranker's head. This was not particularly dangerous, since the flames had little heat in them and the backwash from the propeller quickly extinguished them, but it was not a situation we looked forward to. On other occasions, the engine backfired hideously, scaring the poor cranker half to death.

At first, I had fun helping the mechanics start these planes, but my first backfire resulted in a permanent cure. From that time on, I was unavailable until all planes were merrily chugging away. Our newer ships had electric starters which eliminated all the cranking and the risk of backfires as well.

It is said that an idle mind is the workshop of the devil. That certainly applied to us armorers when we first came to Drew Field. We had scads of free time and lots of energy. For lack of any other form of entertainment, we started to mess around with the planes. Gerald Mackey and I took turns blowing in the pitot tube of a Douglas. This is a thin, tubular projection in front of the wing and is used to indicate air speed when the plane is airborne. Just as I was on the threshold of four hundred miles per hour, the crew chief came up and really ate us out. Gerald and I winked at each other and looked for another plane to experiment on. We were disappointed that our maximum speed was only about three-hundred-seventy-five miles per hour.

Being a smoker, Gerald never went as high as I did. Luckily, the Guinness Book of Records was not in existence or we would have really felt badly. Four hundred miles per hour was at least one hundred fifty miles per hour faster than any Douglas had ever attained in actual flight.

Much to the chagrin of the other sections, each armorer was issued a fancy tool box crammed with all kinds of exotic instruments which we had to try on anything with wings. We were tooled up for every conceivable emergency. I think that over eighty-percent of these tools were never needed and were gradually lost through attrition, but at this time we had to experiment with all of them. We ultimately learned to use them correctly, but drove all the other sections nuts in the process.

All of us free-spirited armorers cut a mean swathe through our staid outfit. I quote from one of my letters home concerning our shenanigans:

> One guy was in the front cockpit industriously pumping up the flaps, a second was smashing a stuck fastener with a hammer. Two other guys were under each wing, skillfully wielding enormous screwdrivers. There was another pushing the ailerons up and down as vigorously as he could, his hands partially covering up a large "Hands off" sign.

While this is a slight exaggeration, we got to be such pests around the planes that the other sections called us "gremlins." It was a name that stuck until we went abroad. We had lots of fun, but no matter how we tried, we couldn't do any real damage to those buckets of bolts.

On the serious side, we familiarized ourselves with the caliber-fifties and with the aircraft in general, but we still had time to burn. We caught up on our sleep and read lots of books. Even when more pilots came aboard, we still had little to do because they had to qualify on each type of plane before they did any practice combat flying.

At about this time, we had several weeks of interesting diversion. Hollywood made a movie at MacDill Field, just across town from us. At first we were startled to see what appeared to be Japanese bombers flying around, but our identification course paid off and we recognized them as B-26s masquerading as Jap planes. These bombers flew around and were pounced on by P-38s. After each pass by a P-38, one of the bombers peeled off, trailing smoke as if shot down. This was fun to watch. Unfortunately, the movie, "A Guy Named Joe," starring Spencer Tracy and Van Johnson, was eminently forgettable as most war movies are. I saw it while on furlough and conned the family into going with me. I wriggled and writhed through the entire movie. My family was too polite to comment on it.

Sunset was our hour of misery. Enormous mosquitoes from the adjacent swamp descended on us like the proverbial plague of locusts. These monsters had an insatiable lust for human blood—our blood. Mosquito repellent, available in short supply, seemed to enhance their already voracious appetites. We had two recourses, go to the base theater, or hole up in the barracks. At ten P.M. or so, they were either glutted or exhausted from their efforts, so we could come out of hiding.

One of the things that exacerbated this unpleasant situation was pulling early guard duty. Our officers were as green as grass and felt that the only way to avoid trouble was to go by the book. This meant that we had to protect our swamp from any Nazis who chanced to be in the neighborhood looking for an opportunity to blow up our planes or ancient barracks. One officer per night was selected as OOD (Officer of the Day) while we EMs pulled the duty throughout the night.

On the second night after our arrival, I was selected on the first shift. As luck would have it, my post was at the camp's only intersection and was also farthest from the OOD's barracks. One of our newer pilots was the OOD for the evening. He posted us at about eight in the evening and gave us the sign and counter sign, leaving us with strict instructions that nobody but nobody could pass without giving us the countersign. He then departed for parts unknown. I could smell trouble ahead.

He hadn't been gone for more than fifteen minutes before the gas truck pulled up at the intersection on its way to the line to fuel up the planes for a night flight. I stopped it and asked the driver to give me the password, knowing full well that he had no idea what it was. I recognized him and knew that neither he nor his truck posed any threat to the security of the United States. However, in accordance with my instructions, I refused to let him pass. This created a sensation.

The gas was urgently needed on the line to fuel up the planes for their mission. Everybody, including my partner, urged me to let him through. Finally the CO came out of the orderly room and asked me to let him go. No soap, I had my orders and I intended to obey them. Since a guard is responsible to the sergeant of the guard and the OOD, period. There was nothing they could do except find one of them.

After almost a half-hour, they located the OOD playing poker with the medics. When informed of the crisis taking place, he rushed out to my post and started to give me hell. When I repeated the orders he had given me, he gave me a funny look, admitted that I was right, and sheepishly told the driver of the truck to proceed. By this time, it was too late and the mission was canceled.

This incident created quite a stir. At that early stage, no one knew my name, but everybody knew who I was. Within a day or so, the officers had a meeting and it was unanimously decided that the Axis menace to our area had been grossly exaggerated, so guard duty in the barracks area was not necessary and it was canceled. This announcement was received with universal joy, not only by the enlisted men who had to pull the duty, but also by the officers who hated to have their social life interrupted by the drudgery of pulling OOD. This decision made everyone happy except the mosquitoes, who were forced to forage farther afield to obtain their sustenance. We still pulled informal guard duty on the line but this was not strictly enforced and we guards got together and passed our shifts yakking away while lying in the warm grass.

Sometimes, guards were isolated due to the position of the aircraft. This was my favorite duty, provided the tours weren't too long. Most of the other guys hated the isolation at night, but I loved it. Tramping through the moist grass in the moonlight, looking at the stars, and listening to the chirp of a million crickets cured all my ills. I met the Southern Cross for the first time during this era. Orion and the other northern constellations I had been familiar with since childhood were visible from a different angle. Every once in a while, a shooting star blazed across the sky. Our blackout condition made star watching spectacular.

Officially, we had a complicated routine to follow—passwords and counter passwords and all that trivia, but in point of fact, all we really had to do was keep awake. The sergeant of the guard visited us at specific times, sometimes by himself but more often with the OOD. Since we were not concerned with sabotage or any other type of enemy action, our OODs took their responsibilities lightly. They were pooped from a day's training and concerned about the day ahead. OODs gave the official watch to the sergeant and told him to wake him at a specific time. Often the sergeant in turn gave it to the nearest guard and told him to wake him up if he wished to be relieved on time. This made for light duty. Next morning was free for those who pulled guard duty during the night, and the sergeant of the guard had the entire next day off. We ate a late and hearty breakfast, since the cooks were glad to get rid of excess grub. Sergeant of the guard under these conditions was the cushiest job in the army. Unfortunately, it was late in my career before I had an opportunity to attain this nugget. I got to sleep between guard changes and then got the next day off.

After the war, I told one of my ex-marine friends about this and he replied that had we been marines, we would all have all been court-martialed and shot for our naughty behavior. My response was that I now knew why they were called Leathernecks.

As time went on, all the rigmarole about passwords was dropped and things became even less formal. To my knowledge, we never had the occasion to stop a single unauthorized person throughout the entire war. *Deo gratias.*

While in Tampa, I found out that people really did get killed in war, even while training. We were on the line early one morning when we heard the engine of a P-39 which had just taken off begin to sputter and then conk out. The plane crashed about a hundred yards from us and the pilot was motionless in the cockpit so we rushed out, unstrapped him, and yanked him from the plane as gently as we could.

Moving a wounded person sounds like bad safety procedure, but crashed planes have a bad habit of exploding, and the aroma of 100 octane gas was strong. The pilot had just come to when we arrived and was struggling to free himself from his harness. His face was bloody from contacting the instrument panel. We laid the poor guy on the ground and made him as comfortable as we could until the meat wagon came along and picked him up. We later heard that he died from internal injuries that night.

Soon afterwards, we started getting P-39s of our own. This was another jolt. We had expected to get something more exotic such as P-51s, the glamour plane of the air force. This would have meant a trip to England sometime in the future to fly escort to heavy bombers—the most prestigious duty in the air force as far as we were concerned. We had no idea what the future held in store for us when we got the thirty-nines. We were virtually certain that we would not go overseas with them, since they were too slow for escort flying and not much good for flying ground support since they had only two machine guns, one in each wing, and didn't have sufficient lift to carry a decent bomb load. Its only claim to fame was the thirty-seven millimeter cannon which shot through the propeller hub. This seemed formidable but in the latter part of the war, most tanks were so heavily armored that the thirty-seven was ineffective against them.

When we moved, it occurred to me that the army had no intention of sending us abroad with these crates. They had already failed against the Japanese Mitsubishi and would have been sitting ducks for the Me109s and Fw 190s of the Luftwaffe. Since they were available, they were used as trainers for outfits like ours until combat aircraft became available. We ultimately foisted them off on the Russians who loved that big gun.

One of our good pilots was Joe Marr, who had the respect of his peers and all the ground crew members as well. Besides being a nice guy and a first-rate pilot, he had a sense of humor. Every plane was equipped with a flare pistol and several flares. The gun was kept in a special holster in the cockpit with a guard strap around it to hold it in place. Since these guns kicked like a mule when fired, there was a small port in the fuselage where it was placed when fired. This gun was our responsibility, but since it was never used, it never occurred to us to see if it was fastened securely. Marr took off one morning and did some acrobatics just overhead. We watched his antics with fascination until he suddenly stopped, headed for the runway, and landed. As he taxied over to his hardstand, he stuck his hand right through his canopy as if making a Fascist salute. His flare pistol had broken loose during his acrobatics, and while he was upside-down, it flew right by his head, shattering the canopy on its way to its gravitational destination. The armorer who worked on his plane expected the worst, but all he got was a smile and a pat on the shoulder. Marr then hopped into a waiting jeep and took off. From then on, all flare pistols were periodically checked, and many, including mine, had to be refastened.

We had many pilots killed during the war, both in training and in combat both before and after him, but Joe Marr's death hit me the hardest. Although he never flew my plane, I regarded him as the ideal fighter pilot and as such I considered him invincible. I am only sorry that this was not the case.

Gradually, we accumulated more pilots but few more planes. This made it more difficult to keep busy. There was just so much make work we could do. Finally, we got word that we were leaving good old Drew for Walterboro, South Carolina. This was the only time in my career when I knew beforehand where we were headed. Some of our pilots who ferried our planes there spilled the beans. We found that in the long run, they were ten times worse than enlisted men at keeping a secret.

85

Prior to our move, "Sheepie" Larson, a ranch type from Laramie, Wyoming, and I decided to have our teeth checked since we knew that it would be impossible to do so in South Carolina. We left early one morning and trudged across the field to the dental office. After a short wait, we got into adjacent chairs.

While awaiting my dentist, I saw a dental orderly who served the next chair idly cleaning his fingernails with a drill. This began to get on my nerves, so I finally told him to knock it off. He looked up in surprise, put the drill bit away, and left the room. This did little to ease my tension.

At long last, a dentist finally appeared, gave me the once-over and then started to drill on about six teeth, one after another. During all this, I heard grunts of pain coming from Sheepie's chair. However, I had too many problems of my own to pay any attention to what went on next door. GI dentists had a lot of work, so they kept a drill in a tooth until it smoked. This guy followed standard procedure and drilled all my teeth before filling them. He drilled with such intensity that I though for sure that he was using a jackhammer.

Just before he put in the mercury filling, he had another thrill in store for me. He blasted a jet of cold air on my open and defenseless teeth, ostensibly to dry them. I had to hold on to the chair with both hands to keep from hitting the ceiling.

When the worst was over, I noticed with surprise that Sheepie's chair was vacant. I wondered why he had finished so quickly. I had little time, to dwell on this at the time since my dentist was doing some touch-up drilling.

When all the drilling was completed and my teeth jammed with mercury, I was released and went outside to meet Larson. His jaw was swollen and blood trickled from the corners of his mouth. His dentist had drilled his teeth and then decided that he couldn't save them, so he pulled them. This would have infuriated me, but Larson was more realistic. Whenever a guy had a tooth pulled, he was given the rest of the day off to recuperate. For reasons of his own, Sheepie felt that the loss of two teeth was a small price to pay for a day off. To each his own.

GI dentistry might have been unpleasant, but it was well done. Virtually every filling I had done in the army is still in my mouth today, almost fifty years later.

Drew Field was fun and I enjoyed my stay there. The big plus, of course, was the vicinity of our swamp to the beach town of Clearwater. On my days off, I hitchhiked the twenty or so miles to the Gulf and spent the day bathing in warm saltwater. Occasionally when we had a little money, we ate dinner in Clearwater and then took an evening dip just before leaving to camp. This kept us cool for the entire night.

Hitching rides was a cinch since we wore uniforms. Often a bird colonel or some other higher-up would pick us up. It gave me a feeling of power to ride in the front seat of a nifty car with a bird colonel as my chauffeur. We reached our zenith in this regard when a former Flying Tiger, who was stationed at MacDill Field to check out in P-38s, picked us up.

I spent much of my leisure time catching up on my reading. The library on the main base had all types of paperbacks which we didn't have to return. Although not many of my cohorts were readers, we still managed to acquire a substantial library of our own, consisting of classics, technical books, whodunits, and even some drama and poetry. Since I still had hopes of going to ASTP, I had my folks send me some math and physics books and I spent some of my time perusing them.

Due to chronic lack of planes and pilots, virtually all our time at Drew was wasted as far as combat training was concerned. We had no gunnery or bombing practice, and our pilots had barely enough flying time to maintain their requirements in this respect. Since all combat aircraft are hot, it is essential for pilots fly frequently so they won't lose their touch. There was such a demand for combat aircraft from our allies and on all fronts that none could be spared for a squadron in training, so it was back burner for the good old 405th Group. This was tough on us enlisted men. We were all dressed up with no place to go. Fortunately, this was to change when we got to Walterboro.

While we were isolated in our swamp at Drew, the war moved on without us. Rommel was finally driven out of Africa; Sicily had been invaded and conquered. The Anglo-American navies had eliminated the U-boat menace, so supplies could flow freely from the U.S. to England and Russia. The air war on Germany intensified. Colossal air battles were fought over the Fatherland, as Allied bombers hit German cities around the clock and one thousand bomber raids increased in number.

At first, our B-17s flew unescorted, but the Germans soon found weaknesses in them and started to shoot them up. They were then escorted by short range fighters, but the Luftwaffe waited until the escorts had to go back and then they inflicted heavy losses on the 17s once again. At last, long range P-51s and 47s were equipped with auxiliary belly tanks and were thus able to escort the bombers for the entire mission. The air battles were spectacular and slowly the Luftwaffe was beaten back, but they were never driven completely from the skies until their sources of fuel were destroyed.

The RAF, dedicated to night bombing, also took their lumps from German night fighters. They were forced to use their Mosquito bomber as escort in order to reduce their losses. Night fighting must have been an eerie experience. All planes were invisible and had to be found and shot down using radar.

In September, just as we were in the process of moving to Walterboro, Italy itself was invaded and the southern part of the boot quickly conquered. This put the Ploesti oil fields in Rumania within range of the B-24s of the 15th U.S. Air Force.

In Russia, the Germans suffered a staggering loss of tanks and infantry in a titanic battle in the Kursk area, and the Russians went on the offensive. The ultimate defeat of Germany now seemed inevitable.

There was still a fly in the ointment. Either our reporting was inaccurate or the recuperative powers of Germany were superhuman. Every day, our publicity people reported that hundreds of German planes were destroyed, yet on the following day, hordes of them arose and attacked our bombers with their usual vigor. I think our intelligence used the formula $Y=X$ cubed, where Y is the number of planes reported shot down and X is the real number.

I was always puzzled as to the reason behind reporting German losses as so high as to strain all credibility. The Germans may have had many faults, but the ability to count was certainly not one of them. They surely knew what their losses were, so who was kidding whom?

It must have been discouraging for the bomber crews to read about the terrible losses their enemy had sustained and then encounter as many fighters as they had the previous day. Admittedly, it is difficult to make an accurate count when as many as five guns may be trained on a single enemy plane, but our figures were ridiculously high. As an example, David N. Anderson mentions in his book, *The History of the U.S. Air Force*, that on the second air strike on the German ball bearing center at Schweinfurt, U.S. gunners claimed 186 German fighters destroyed when the actual number was thirty-eight.

It was actually the destruction of the German fuel supply that ultimately eliminated the Luftwaffe, although as the war progressed, German losses in the air exceeded ours by a good bit as our pilots got better and many of the best German pilots were killed.

Our squadron was also successful in the few encounters we had with the German Air Force. There were three reasons for this: Our P-47 was better than any German fighter at that time, many of the pilots we faced were inexperienced since the best were sent up against the heavies who pounded the daylights out of the Fatherland, and last but far from least, our pilots were first rate.

Unfortunately, we were not aware of all these Allied successes since our contact with the outside world was almost nil. We were isolated in our little enclave at Drew and at Walterboro as well. We never saw a newspaper and our radio contact was also minimal. We knew about the main events but were really short on details. We did attend several "why we are fighting" pep talks and propaganda movies at the main base. These masterpieces were supposed to explain to us just what the war was all about. The only problem with them was that they were so garnished with exaggerations that they lacked credibility. These claims were often so preposterous that they insulted our intelligence. It really annoyed me that whoever came up with these jewels did not think we were smart enough to handle the truth. More on this later.

We were too concerned about our daily lives to worry about things we couldn't change. We were quartered in primitive barracks, remote from the war, so we were far more interested in our problems than about the war. My big concern was Notre Dame's quest for an unbeaten season and the national championship.

For all the annoyance of skeeter bugs and the high humidity, we liked our backwoods living. Being isolated from the main base had definite advantages: nobody bothered us and we were spared the saluting and other frivolities which were the curse of those who lived in a civilized area. Our isolation also made us self-sufficient and dependent on each other rather than outside forces. It was far easier to solve our own problems than go clear across to the base for help.

We honed our skills on the few caliber-fifties available until we could strip them down and reassemble them while blindfolded. We were looking forward to playing a more active part in the war and we hoped that our presence in Walterboro would be a step in that direction.

Chapter Eight

Walterboro and the Entrance of the P-47s

In the Land of Cotton and Surviving in the Big Apple

The trip to South Carolina was an uneventful trip of some six or seven hundred miles. Walterboro was a small southern town with all the disadvantages thereof. It was a dusty farming community with no outside entertainment, not even a movie theater. It had a tiny USO manned mostly by elderly ladies where my friends and I played Ping-Pong and enjoyed coffee and doughnuts. Despite its small size, this USO was an example of southern hospitality at its best. Every time we entered, we were greeted warmly and given a cup of hot coffee and some homemade cookies.

We wondered how the army had found this remote place and why they picked this particular spot for an airbase. It was so small that our group of three squadrons were the sole inhabitants. As usual, the other two squadrons occupied one side of the runway and we were on the other.

Southern towns, with their different type of vegetation always seemed like semi-desert to me. The trees seemed to be more straggly and were not as green as those in Pennsylvania. There were fine stands of southern yellow pine which were handsome trees, but the oaks and other deciduous trees appeared to be stunted and the live oaks were a particular disappointment. They couldn't compare with the fine oaks that grow in the North. The soil was lighter in color and sandy and therefore did not appear as fertile. The area around Walterboro was agricultural, heavy on cotton, tobacco, and corn. While it was not a depressed area, neither was it affluent.

Many of the South Carolinians were still fighting the Civil War, and certain topics such as Lincoln and Sherman were taboo. When we first arrived, southern hospitality outside of the USO was conspicuous by its absence. They had to learn about Yanks and we had to learn about Rebs. This slowly changed, and by Christmas time, we were welcomed into their homes with open arms.

The town had two restaurants, a posh one in the center of town where a guy lucky enough to have a date could dine in comparative luxury. The other one, on the outskirts, was less pretentious and looked like a greasy spoon from the outside. It served good, clean meals at soldiers' prices. This became our off-base hangout. There were so many of us eating there all the time that we gradually drove most of the local trade away. This restaurant was famous because it introduced us Yankees to an old southern favorite, known to us as "Georgia Ice Cream", and to the locals as "grits." This exotic concoction was made from ground, dried corn and was served with every meal regardless of the time of day or what else was served. However, the big time for it was breakfast. At first, most of the Yanks refused to eat it, but hollered like hell when the management got tired of throwing it away and decided not to serve it to us. By the time they had made that decision, many of us had acquired a taste for it and were eating it like natives. The only thing I disliked about it was the big gob of melted butter that was placed smack-dab in the center. For some reason that dates back to my prehistoric past, I have hated butter all my life and melted butter most of all. It was impossible to get it served without butter, so I ate around it and left the goo alone.

The management of the South Side Cafe made certain that we were well taken care of. They only slipped up once. My good friend and fellow "C" flighter, Len Hitchman, Sheepie Larson and "Limie" Nash and I came in one evening and ordered our usual, which was steak, french fries, and a local vegetable. Hitch got stuck with a steak that was fifty percent gristle, forty-five percent fat, and five percent meat. He was aghast when it came in and didn't know what to do. However, Limie started to raise hell, so the boss came over, took one look at it and gave him another. Once again the squeaky axle got the grease.

The barracks at Walterboro were the similar to those at Drew Field but were newer and hence a lot tighter. However, the coal stoves saw a lot more action here than in Tampa and the odor of burning coal was prominent all winter. We found that South Carolina got quite nippy in winter after sunset.

Bed check was ten P.M. but was not enforced at first, since we had no CQ. This was quickly rectified when Ralph "Bed Check" Cheever took over the assignment. Vermonter Ralph appeared very mild-mannered, but that was just a facade. None of us paid any attention when he politely told us, "Ten o'clock, lights out." He made it stick in an unique way. At ten sharp, he paraded down the length of the barracks impeccably clad with a money belt around his waist. He said that it was ten P.M. and then turned off the barracks lights. As Pepys said, "And so to bed." Ralph's peculiar uniform made any resistance impossible.

Several P-39s and a single Helldiver came with us. The engine on the latter had just been replaced, so one of the pilots took it up for a test flight. An assistant mechanic asked for a ride. He put a chute, hopped in the back, and it was up, up, and away. Unfortunately, a oil hose came loose and the engine heated up and froze. The pilot told his passenger not to worry, they were near the runway and he would deadstick it in. For reasons unknown, the guy in the back bailed out. When he jumped, he was so low that his chute didn't open and he was killed. He was our only enlisted man fatality before we went overseas. Since the engine on the Helldiver was ruined, it was junked. Adios and good riddance!

Shortly after our arrival, we started taking gunnery practice. One of the 39s pulled a long sock and the other planes took turns shooting at it. We armorers dipped the tips of the ammo in different colored paint so that each ship had a uniquely colored bullet. When practice was finished, the tow plane dropped the sock over the field and we counted the different colored hits. At first there were very few, but it was not long before we knew which pilots were the better shots. One unfortunate pilot was so intent on hitting the target that he ran into the sock, tangled up his prop and had to bail out. Since all our gunnery practice took place over the ocean, he fell into the drink. One of his comrades flew around him, hoping for the arrival of the Coast Guard, but shortage of fuel forced him to leave before they arrived and he was never found. He was our first pilot casualty and his loss threw a pall on all of us. Luckily, the tow plane pilot was able to jettison the sock or he would have crashed as well.

The crew chiefs hated the P-39 because it was small, was difficult to work on, and had lots of sharp edges. We hated it because both machine guns were under the wing and we had to bend way over to work on them. We got all kinds of aches and pains working on them.

Each morning, the mechanics checked out every plane by starting up the engine, running it up to two thousand rpm, and checking out the magnetos and the propeller. They then "redlined" it, which meant that it wasn't fit to fly. The pilot had to sign a release before taking off. I noticed that every plane was "redlined" for some picayune reason and I asked one of the mechanics why not just fix it up and be done with it. He filled me in on the liabilities occurring to both the mechanic and the army if it was not redlined and the pilot was injured or killed. All of this was technical in nature. No pilot was ever forced to fly a plane that was not in tiptop condition.

Since the pilot was unable to charge his two machine guns in the air, we did so on the ground as near to takeoff as possible. Both guns, one under each wing, were pointed straight forward and were about waist high. Once charged, these guns were hot. All the pilot had to do was turn on his gun switch, bend his trigger finger, and BANG. We all avoided walking in front of a plane with hot guns. A caliber-fifty slug could cut a man in half and there was always a slight chance that a gun might fire as soon as it was charged. If a sear was slightly worn or the tip of the solenoid protruded, it was Katie bar the door. If one started to fire, it was virtually impossible to stop it. This did happen to one of our sister squadrons, and we heard the bullets whiz overhead before we heard the noise of them firing. Fortunately, we were in a slight depression when this occurred or some of us might have been injured.

The alleged big feature of the P-39 was its thirty-seven millimeter, which fired through the propeller hub since it was far too large to be mounted on the wings and its rate of fire was too erratic to be synchronized. To accomplish that, it was necessary to place the engine behind the pilot. A drive shaft ran from the engine under the cockpit, connecting the engine to a gear box in front of the cockpit. The gear box, in turn, drove the propeller. This Rube Goldberg arrangement made the plane unstable and made it difficult to keep the engine cool. This instability caused it to go into a flat spin on occasion, from which there was no apparent escape. If the pilot bailed out, the plane either caught his chute or it landed on top of him. If he elected to remain in the cockpit, he was killed in the crash. We lost at least two pilots in our squadron due to these flat spins.

The fact that the engine was behind the pilot made it difficult to keep cool. All in-line engines such as those on the P-39 and the P-51 had large airscopes which forced cooling air over the radiators for the liquid coolant and the engine oil. Those on the P-39 were small, so they had to be taxied above thirty miles per hour to avoid overheating the engine.

As soon as a plane reached the runway, it had to take off as quickly as possible to prevent the engine from overheating. Whenever it did overheat, the pilot had to shut off the engine and let it cool or it might stall in the middle of his takeoff. When the runway was clear, the plane was restarted and it then took off. Luckily, the P-39 had tricycle landing gear, which enabled the pilot to taxi fast enough to steer with his rudder and not with his brakes. This generated a good blast of air which kept the engine cool. The low position of the guns and this tendency to stall were two reasons why the P-39 was not popular.

On one occasion, a flyer took off and just as he left the ground, the engine started to sputter. He was committed to take off, so all he could do was turn as quickly as he could and land. Luckily, he landed without incident. We gave him a big cheer when he parked at his hardstand. A pilot from a sister squadron was unable to put down his landing gear. For almost an hour he went through all types of gyrations to force the gear down without success. Finally, he retracted his gear which was halfway down, and came in on the belly. This appeared to be more dangerous than it actually was. There was lots of airplane between him and the runway. However, the propeller was bent and both the gear box and engine were ruined.

The word came from Group Operations that our squadron had to cannibalize a thirty-seven millimeter from an old junker to replace a defective one on a newer plane. To my horror, I was one of the two guys selected for this chore. Bob Loitz from another flight was my partner. We started out slowly, but soon got into the swing of things and did a fine job in a short time. This qualified us for the dubious distinction of being the thirty-seven millimeter experts of our squadron. When another cannon had to be replaced and test-fired, we were chosen again. We did such a good job that we were allowed to do the bore-sight firing. I lost the toss so my roommate-to-be got to do the honors. The three rounds he fired were the only thirty-seven millimeter rounds ever shot by our squadron. Not a single pilot ever fired his thirty-seven millimeter gun.

One happy day, one of our flyers who had been missing for several days landed at our base in a P-47 Thunderbolt! This was the first of many. Gradually all our P-39s went the way of all flesh and we became a P-47 outfit. These ships were ideal. They were large and reliable with an enormous air-cooled engine. They were armed with four machine guns in each wing and a bomb rack on the belly and one under each wing. They were safer, easier to fly, much faster, and far more rugged than our P-39s. The name, "Thunderbolt," suited them to a "T." The morale of the entire squadron went sky high and the pilots were in seventh heaven.

As I recall, we had no more fatalities while training with these ships, and gunnery accuracy increased exponentially because the guns were easier to aim and fire, and there were eight instead of two. We really started to get our act together as a fighting squadron with the arrival of these planes. For the first time, the prospect of going overseas became very real.

As our complement of planes filled up, each armorer was given the responsibility of a single aircraft. Each plane now had a three man crew—a chief mechanic who was the crew chief, an assistant mechanic, and an armorer. I can't recall who was part of my crew at Walterboro but overseas, my crew chief was a Polish lad by the name of Wasowski. His assistant was a quiet good-natured chap named Semple. I always referred to him as "Semple Simon," eliciting a big grin from him each time I did. We formed a good team and worked well together. Since their job was more responsible and difficult than mine, I kept out of their way as much as possible and gave them a hand whenever possible.

For the first time, we had sufficient planes and pilots to operate efficiently. Each flight operated as a single unit and learned to work well together. We formed friendships which lasted throughout the war. Four of us became particular friends, Len Hitchman from Seattle, Washington, Sheepie Larson from Laramie, Wyoming, Bob "Limie" Nash from Maine, and myself. Bob's Maine accent sounded oh-so-British, so we called him "Limie." He was a feisty guy and lots of fun when we went to town. It was his protest in the restaurant that saved Hitch from eating a lot of gristle.

Just before we gave up our 39s, my crewchief let me preflight the engine. This fulfilled a long-time ambition, but it was a little trickier than I had imagined. First I had to put both feet on the brakes and pull back on the stick so the airflow would keep the tail down and the plane wouldn't move. Next step was to prime the engine so that it would start promptly. Then I activated the inertia starter and set the throttle and mixture controls at "start." I also put the propeller control at low bite so the strain on the engine would be minimal.

When the starter motor reached the proper speed, I engaged it to the engine which started almost immediately. Judging the proper time to engage the starter to the engine takes a little practice. If it is engaged before reaching the proper speed, the engine will sputter and stall. The faster the starter motor rotates, the higher its pitch. Since I had observed this ritual closely, I had no trouble starting up the engine. My success evidently went to my head, because I had some real problems starting up the aircooled P-47 engine later on.

When the engine caught, I set the throttle at two thousand rpm and pushed the mixture control forward to "full rich." The mixture control regulated the ratio of gas to air going into the engine—the richer the mixture, the better the engine performed, but fuel consumption goes up as well. Full rich was used only on takeoff. Once the plane was airborne, the pilot leaned out his mixture as much as possible in order to conserve vital fuel.

When the engine attained two thousand rpm, I checked the propeller by putting it into "high pitch." The rpm dropped as the load on the engine increased. I quickly put it into low pitch once more and the engine speed increased to two thousand rpm. Next on the menu was checking the magnetos, which furnished juice to the spark plugs. I increased the rpm to twenty-seven hundred and then turned off one magneto and checked the drop in rpm. This drop should be less than two hundred rpm and in this instance, it was well within acceptable limits. I turned the mag back on, waited until the rpm increased, and then turned off the other one. Once again it checked out well. All this had to be done rapidly so that the engine would not overheat. The use of two magnetos is a sample of the lengths that the air force went to make certain that all planes were safe. Every engine had two magnetos although it could operate on one.

The mag check completed the preflight, so I eased the rotations per minute back to fourteen hundred and put the mixture control to idle cutoff so that the inertia of the propeller would keep the engine turning until all inflammable gases were drained from the cylinders. This was important since any gas left in the cylinder could ignite and give the prop a sudden kick. Exhausting the gas virtually eliminated this danger, but all of us kept clear of the propeller as much as possible.

Being assigned to a particular ship changed the ball game for us since we could now be evaluated individually for promotions. All of us newcomers were PFCs, and our table of organization called for all of us to be corporals and some of us to be sergeants. We knew that promotions would be staggered and those who made corporal in the first round would be odds-on favorites to become sergeants. The camaraderie of the good old days was replaced by various displays of ambition. I was aware that my boss and I were not on the same wavelength and I think he took my ASTP aspirations as a personal affront. This was my fault. I should have realized earlier in the game that armorers were far more important to the army than students, so I should have withdrawn my application. My chances of going were next to nil. It was not very intelligent on my part to buck the system when there was no chance of success and it just upset my peerless leader. I had some hope that my success with dismantling the two thirty-seven millimeter guns would improve my position, but this was not the case.

Bucking for promotion set the stage for some very interesting infighting. Although I remember about the goings on of this time very well, I still got some good chuckles rereading one of the letters I sent home on this subject while in the throes of doing some bucking of my own. The extract below is taken from a letter I sent my family at the height of the competition:

> At promotion time, attitudes change and two types of personalities evolve. First are the ever-present KAs who flatter all the brass and ingratiate themselves as much as possible. Then come the "eager beavers who are always industriously at work whenever a wheel is in the vicinity. Promotion time is commotion time and the time for the above to strut their stuff. It is only fair to point out that virtually all of these guys were good armorers and deserved any promotion they got. However, the world was not limited to the above. There were two more categories, and they were: first, the Calibans who did fine work but were not smart enough to realize that success in the form of promotion only *began* at that point and that some self-promotion was necessary to get ahead. Second came the drones who did nothing, cared about nothing, and attained nothing.

This was an exciting time in the army. The only thing lacking was pari-mutuel betting. Everyone's chances were assessed at length. Odds were quoted by, "He's a cinch", "Naw, he'll never make it", "Well, I don't know, he's pretty close to Sergeant X." Six or so of us were in a separate category—seemingly in Lt. Hodges' doghouse. I thought that like Abou ben Adam, my name led all the rest in this unenviable class. This, of course, put all six of us in the "Naw, he'll never make it" category. As it turned out, our guesses were pretty accurate, about seventy-five "cinches" made it; twenty percent of the "possibles", and five percent of the "Naws" made corporal.

I was disappointed but not surprised when my name did not appear on the list. What did hurt was that the newly crowned corporals were excused from KP!!! I knew that I would ultimately make it since my job called for, it but any sergeant aspirations I had were dashed. *Sic transit gloria mundi!*

I finally made it in November, tops in the last group which is being damned with faint praise. The big letdown was a note at the bottom of the promotion sheet informing us that, due to shortage of eligible personnel, corporals would now have to pull KP!! However, the timing was exquisite since I went on furlough the following week, which allowed me to spend Thanksgiving Day at home. Half of us armorers thus spent Thanksgiving on furlough and the other half got Christmas. I had my stripes on quick like a bunny, but it was a case of love's labor lost since my parents could not tell a PFC from a general and were not impressed at my explanation. However, I enjoyed the extra money.

As soon as we got our furlough papers, four of us hired a guy with a car to take us to the railroad depot in Charleston, S.C., a drive of some fifty miles. We just missed a train that would have gotten me into Philadelphia at two A.M. instead of at eight o'clock. Don't ask me what prompted this insanity. All I can say is that it looked like a good idea at the time. Perhaps we had subconscious misgivings that our boss might change his mind. We did catch the right train to Washington where some guys got off and headed for different destinations. I remained on board since the train continued on to Philly.

I was greeted at the station by my family, including my younger brother who was wearing one of my suits, an unpleasant surprise for both of us. I spent ten days at home, went fishing in the ocean for winter flounder, did some Christmas shopping, and told everyone how tough it was in the army. It was nice being the center of attraction after some eight months of the anonymity of the army.

At first, I wore my uniform because I was used to it. Then some chickenshit officer ate me out for not saluting him at a street corner, so I tried my civvies. This was worse because I got dirty looks from "patriotic" civilians who didn't serve themselves but wondered why I was not "doing my bit." It was axiomatic with some people that anyone of the proper age who wasn't in uniform was a draft dodger and a coward even if he were on crutches or was carrying his head under his arm. All I could think of was Samuel Johnson's famous remark that patriotism was the last refuge of scoundrels.

This was worse than saluting some officer, so it was back to the old uniform. This changed my status immediately from "draft dodger" to "hero", although I was neither. A lot of perks came with heroism and I played them to the full lest I be unmasked as just plain GI Joe—free rides on the subway, a free meal here and there, and lots of attention. Best of all was the way civilians hung onto my every word. Everybody needs fame once in a while to inflate fragile egos and my cup overflowed. My furlough was too short for any of this adulation to cause permanent damage.

My ten days were up and it was back to Walterboro. Parting from my family was sweet sorrow. On my return, my "furlough blues" were not assuaged when I found that I was posted to KP.

While I was gone, our training had been accelerated. Pilots flew several gunnery missions every day and the air was rife with rumors that we were headed overseas shortly after the new year—something we had considered impossible only two weeks before. Going overseas only happened to the other guy.

In addition to gunnery practice, our pilots started making bombing runs. We loaded one hundred pound "blue jays" on the bomb racks. These were tin bombs filled with sand that were bright blue in color. They had a spotting charge of black powder which exploded when they hit the ground. Pilots dropped them on preselected targets which required some navigation to locate. This went on for some six weeks. Finally, just prior to our departure for port of embarkation, they dropped some honest to goodness five-hundred pounders. Loading and fusing them created quite a sensation for us armorers. At this time, we handled the bombs with kid gloves. Later on we were not so respectful of them.

Our squadron in November of 1943 was overloaded with enlisted brass for some reason or other. We knew that some had to transfer out. Some were very competent—others must have gotten their stripes for longevity. One of these was a master sergeant who occupied the bunk next to mine. I have no idea what he did since he never appeared on the line. Early in the game, I had determined that breakfasts served near the end were at least as good as those served at first and I had a chance to get seconds if any food was left over. For this reason, I was in no hurry to get up and this annoyed the sergeant no end. He finally could stand it no longer and started to rout me out of bed. When he did, I took my time getting dressed, arriving at the mess hall just before it closed. My *vis-à-vis* with him went on for some six or seven weeks with neither of us giving the other guy an inch.

One happy day in early December, his name was on the list to transfer out. Next day, I leaned on my elbow, still in bed, and watched him dress. He scowled at me but made no attempt to rout me out since he knew that he was defanged as far as I was concerned. At the last moment, I got up quickly, hustled over to the mess hall, chuckling all the way. All of a sudden, I realized I had played things too close. They shut the door of the mess hall in my face. I raced around to the exit, sneaked into line and managed to get fed. One of my pals, Wisnoski by name, was just a step behind me and got nailed and put on KP. He was not a happy person when I came through the chow line with a great big grin on my face at lunch time. When I returned from breakfast, my sergeant friend had departed, so I was unable to wish him bon voyage and best wishes on his next assignment.

Christmas of 1943 was my first away from home. As it approached, I was apprehensive because I came from a close family and Christmas was our big day. I needn't have worried, the local people went all-out to make us feel at home. Any GI who wanted to was invited to some local home for dinner. I decided to go with several friends after I attended Mass at Walterboro's tiny church.

When I arrived at the local rendezvous after Mass, they were gone. The only person there was an old farmer, dressed to the nines, who had been stood up by his GI guest. I accepted his invitation and enjoyed a sumptuous repast of roast wild goose, some wild duck, and wild rice with cranberry sauce—a super meal. He said that he had a son at the Philly Navy Yard. My folks had told me that they had invited some sailors from the Yard and I wondered if my farmer friend's son might have been one of them. Unfortunately, this was not the case.

When I returned to camp late in the evening, I ran into my friends. Their host was a nice guy who could not get his mind off the Civil War. A few of the Game Cocks were good at that sort of thing. At any rate, this got so tiresome that they had enough and told him they were posted for guard duty that evening and had to return to camp at by seven-thirty. I lucked out—no Civil War, just some nice conversation, a huge meal, and an invitation to go squirrel hunting in the future.

Most of the guys we had from the Big Apple hated the outdoors. Some even considered cows and sheep to be wildlife. I finally persuaded a Jewish friend from Brooklyn to go on a nature walk with me. It was early autumn and evidently lots of migrating birds were in the vicinity, filling the air with their songs. This even impressed my friend. He turned to me and said, " Listen to them boids."

I retorted, "For heaven's sake, they're not boids, they're birds."

"Well, they sure sound like boids to me," was his reply. He kept such a straight face that I never knew who was kidding whom.

Mid-January came and our favorite uncle felt we were prepared to defend his good name overseas. We received this news with mixed emotions. We were excited about seeing some action and going overseas to strange countries, but none of us wanted to get killed. It didn't take long before the prospects of an exciting boat ride, a nice raise for serving overseas, and the thought of some action overcame our fears and we were raring to go. We packed up all our personnel gear, the planes took off for the unknown, and we started to get into physical shape for the rugged days ahead. We took long hikes with full packs and spent several days on bivouac, sleeping in pup tents and eating warmed up "C" rations. Most of us youngsters enjoyed this thoroughly even though the nights were cold. We had to attend evening Taps when the flag was lowered for the night. We had never done this before in our entire careers and would never have do it again.

On one of these reveries, I was caught without my dog tags. These were little identification tags made of some unknown metal which we had to wear around our necks at all times. Our administration officer put me on restriction for a week. I could not leave the base during this time. This was small loss and I think he knew it. Walterboro in winter was not exactly the Great White Way.

Next day, Sam Weinberg, our company clerk, called me in from the line. Not knowing what to expect, I came in post haste. He gave me a form to sign saying that I had waived my rights to a courtmartial. I said, "Suppose I opt for the courtmartial instead?"

He looked at me, yawned, and replied, "Henkels, just sign the f——
— thing and can the bullshit, will you?" I often thought that a courtmartial might have been more exciting, but I somehow think that it would not have been a smart thing to do. Small stakes would have suddenly become large stakes.

We hiked and camped all around the area for almost a month and then, early in February, we boarded a train bound for POE camp near New York City and an unknown overseas destination. The only thing we were reasonably sure of was that our destination would be somewhere in Europe, since our planes and the type of training we had undergone were not suited for action against the Japanese and Roosevelt had said that the defeat of Germany was first on the Allies agenda.

There were many destinations in Europe; the most likely were Italy or England. Since I spent lots of time reading English literature and history, I hoped that we would be sent there and I would have the opportunity to visit many of the places I had read about.

At POE camp, we were ensconced in the best barracks we had seen since leaving Miami. All us EMs had to take a physical exam which consisted solely in a check for VD. We had to march in formation from our barracks to the infirmary with nothing on but a raincoat and shoes and socks. We had to carry a spoon to be used as a tongue depressor. Everybody knew where we were going and why. This opened us up for the derisive comments of numerous bystanders, including quite a few WACs. At this moment, we were beyond humiliation. We all felt resentful and our officer leader knew it. In an attempt to alleviate our feelings, he shouted, "In cadence, sing." One of the front men had the inspiration to start singing one of the nonsense songs of our generation, "Mairsie Dotes", and we all joined in with a will. While this increased the catcalls and cast doubts on our virility, we were past caring and we had the satisfaction of mortifying our peerless leader.

We had some free time, so our New York natives went home and I managed a trip to Philly to visit my folks. We had a very pleasant Sunday dinner and then I returned to camp. My folks were understandably reserved at the thought of my going overseas, so it was a wrench to leave.

While at POE, we managed to get into New York City for a few evenings. Because we didn't know any better, we hung around places like Jack Dempsey's and other well-known clip joints. Since we were only off duty in the evenings, museums and such were out even if the idea might have occurred to us. None of us gave a thought to the Met or the Philharmonic.

Some of the clip joints we visited had the slick habit of having pretty girls in low-cut dresses sidle up and say that they were thirsty. The bartender served them pink water and charged us for an expensive drink. Some of the less sophisticated guys in the outfit thought that these shills were really interested in them, and they opened up their wallets. When they went broke, they were dumped with a thud and the sweetie pies hunted up another live one. With the huge number of GIs floating around, they didn't lack for victims.

Knowing the tendency of GIs to exaggerate, I am not sure whether the following is true or not but I sure hope so because the ending is so good. Two guys from our barracks, but from another outfit, went into one of these dens of iniquity one evening and one of them was picked up by a sweetie. The other just watched and kept track of how fast the money was flowing. The first guy was a nice looking guy who thought he had a way with women and that this chick was ape over him. He couldn't spend enough on her. As the bill mounted, the other guy became apprehensive and finally urged him to go to the gents' room.

When they met there and went over their expenditures, the sober one pointed out that they were already in debt. Fearing the consequences of being unable to pay the tab, they looked for an out. There happened to be a dinky ventilating fan in the small window higher than their heads. Somehow they managed to remove the fan, squeeze through the window, drop some eight feet to the ground and run like hell. We all had a great laugh next day and wondered how sweetie pie felt when her fat commission turned to ashes. That was aloha to Jack Dempsey's and all the other clip joints for our entire barracks.

Some of the other guys went taxi dancing. At these stands, it was possible to dance with a middle-aged gal trying to look like a teenager at so much per dance. Their makeup was about a half-inch thick and the music was furnished by scratchy records. I guess their rates were reasonable because some of our stalwarts danced all night with the same girl and still had some money left over. I came away from the Big Apple thinking it was a tough place for a gal to make money and an easy place for a GI to drop a bundle.

My mother loved New York so we used to visit it occasionally prior to my enlistment. We went to good restaurants, visited art galleries, went to High Mass at St. Pattie's, took in an occasional play, and rode the Staten Island Ferry. This was a friendly New York that a person could love. When I visited the city as a GI, I acquired an entirely new slant on the Big Apple. Nursing overpriced cokes in clip joints and people-watching were different but still lots of fun. I never saw such a collection of odd balls in my life, each trying to outhustle the other for the GIs' bucks. We considered it part of our education to visit the city and engage in mortal combat with all the Times Square vultures. Our adventures in New York provided lots of fuel for conversation on our boat ride across the Atlantic. Everybody except the natives agreed that "New York is a great place to visit but we wouldn't want to live there."

My Jewish friend was in his element. He went home to Brooklyn almost every night and came back with stories about the beauties of "Greenpernt" as he pronounced it. He took a beating from the rest of us about the clip joints, the high prices, etc., etc. After several days of constant abuse, he told us, "On me it looks good." To each his own.

We spent most of our time in camp reading or playing cards. We did have one sobering training exercise—practicing to abandon ship. We went to the top of a forty-foot wall, decked out with full packs, and had to climb down a rope lattice into a small boat. The accent was on speed. One poor guy lost his grip and fell into the icy water. Since there was no changing clothes for several hours, he was frozen stiff. His misadventure added a little spice to things but it also slowed the rest of us down quite a bit while they were fishing him out of the drink.

At camp, we were introduced to censorship for the first time. We were told what we could write—which was practically nothing—and what we could not which was everything that remained. Normal procedure was to black out any offensive material and then send the letter to its destination. Our censor decided it would be better if he returned our letters so we could correct them and then resubmit them. Thus we would learn what was acceptable and what was not.

This was fine, except I had a girlfriend at Manhattanville College in New York, and I wrote and asked her for a date. I had the temerity to mention that I was near the city, so the censor sent my letter back for correction. It was okay to ask for the date but not to mention that I was in the vicinity. The logic of why I would ask for a date if I was not near the Big Apple was lost on this bird. At any rate, by the time I had eliminated the offending material and resent the letter, we were long gone. I got my acceptance from her when we were in England, a month later. I was furious that the idiot censor didn't black out the part he objected to and then send out the letter since time was of the essence. Every German who gave a damn knew we were near New York City because it was no secret that I had gone to Philly and that all the locals had frequently gone home.

This fiasco was not the only problem we enlisted men had with our censors. When we arrived in England, some of the pilots were pressed into service to screen our outgoing mail. Many were younger than any of us and got a kick out of some of our letters. We found out that some of them were passed around for laughs. This caused lots of resentment and a corresponding loss of morale. Our executive officer called a meeting of all EMs to find out what was troubling us. One of the old-timers told him that we were aware that some of our letters were passed around for ridicule. We could sense immediately that he knew of this problem but wasn't aware of the fact that we also knew it and were very upset by it. The offending pilots were chastised, and the guilty ones were dropped from censorship duty.

Censorship was and still is a sore spot with me. I will never get over the feeling that it was an unnecessary violation of our civil rights. We were told that the Germans were so smart that they could piece together every tiny bit of information in each letter they read and know all that we were up to. This was blatant nonsense. How would they know which letters to read and how would they gain access to them if they did? If the Jerries had about ten million spies, then perhaps rigid censorship may have been necessary. However, the few agents that the Axis had in the States had much better sources of information than what little they could glean from our letters. I was certain they knew far more about our plans than we did. The problem was that the brass were paranoid about what the Axis agents could accomplish. It was odd but true that officers' mail was not censored. They knew far more than we did, since they had access to classified information and many of them were far looser in telling what they knew than most of us.

After some ten days in Camp Shanks, it was time for the 405th Fighter Group to go to war. We were told one afternoon to prepare for a long boat ride. All my belongings except a paperback went into my duffel bag. Others kept decks of cards handy. I always marveled at the ingenious ways some of the guys could find to play a little poker—a deck of cards was their security blanket. Once packed, we waited patiently (?) for whatever fate had in store for us.

Chapter Nine

The HMS Mauritania

There was a ship quoth he.
—Samuel Coleridge

I returned to Camp Shanks from my Philadelphia visit early in the evening, and after a bit of gossip with some friends, I hit the sack. I had a premonition that big doings were in the works for next morning. They woke us up the following morning at the crack of dawn, and right after breakfast we were told to make up our packs and load them onto one of the many GI trucks awaiting us just outside our barracks. There was a lot of "this is it" talk going around but our destination proved to be the grounds of a large convent, evidently the only place near enough to our camp for us to stretch our legs a bit. We hiked for a mile or so , took a breather resting on the grass, reboarded the trucks and headed back to camp. What a letdown! Much ado about nothing!

When we returned to camp, we undid our packs and headed for the mess hall for an early dinner. This was the only mess hall I used in my entire military career where I didn't pull KP so it is still a little special in my eyes. One of my pals said that the army was giving us a break before we had to risk our lives in combat. I don't think the brass gave that a moment's thought. I am sure that the transient nature of those at camp was such that it was far easier to have permanent KPs than going through all the hassle of assigning units and then having them pull out just when they were needed the most.

On our return to the barracks, the big boss was waiting there for us in order to spring the good news that this was indeed IT. We remade our packs, loaded our belongings in our barracks bags, and awaited further developments. They were not long in coming. A bunch of no-nonsense guys entered our barracks, told us to grab our guns and barracks bags and load onto some canvas-topped trucks which had just arrived. We knew that there were big doings because we had to take our bags with us instead of throwing them in separate baggage trucks. This could only mean one thing—a long boat ride. The army didn't want to take any chances on our being separated from our gear while on the ship and more importantly, when we reached our destination.

We jammed onto the back of one of the trucks and put our bags on the floor in front of us. The trucks fired up without more ado, and we zoomed out of camp for an unknown destination. Unfortunately, I was in front of the truck where visibility was practically nil. We went through a tunnel and headed north. When we finally stopped, our tender nostrils were assailed by an aroma that could only mean "waterfront." We were told to disembark as quickly as we could and make double sure we didn't leave anything behind. We needed no urging because we knew what we left behind we would do without for a long time. No sooner had we jumped off than the trucks took off and one more cord connecting us to home was severed.

By this time, it was pitch dark, but we could still distinguish the outline of a huge ship which we thought might be one of the "Queens." We formed loose ranks, our packs and bags at our feet, and awaited orders to board. While we were waiting, a steady stream of soldiers went up the gangplank and disappeared into the cavernous void of the ship.

At long last, it was our turn. We were told to fasten on our helmets, grab our gear, and head up the gangplank. This proved to be higher, narrower, steeper, and longer than we had anticipated. Our bags continuously caught on the uprights of the gangplank and we had to pull them off and keep moving at the same time so we would not slow down the steady flow of troops behind us. The air was blue with muttered curses and I muttered a few myself.

On entering the ship, we were met by an English sailor who told us that the ship was the *Mauritania* and not one of the "Queens" as we had hoped. We were told to follow him to our quarters. We plunged into the depths of the ship at a rapid pace, going through what seemed to be a hundred small doorways and companionways where bags and packs continuously got stuck. This wretched ship must have been built for midgets since we had to turn sideways to get through the narrow openings.

At last we reached a small room where hundreds of hammocks looking like so many enormous bats were hanging from the ceiling. A whole row of long tables stuck out from the bulkhead some twenty feet into the room. Our sailor friend told us, "Well, 'ere you are mateys. Ere's your 'ome for the next week. Any questions?" When I asked him what we should do if we were torpedoed, he answered that our problems were over because sea water would come down on top of us. He told us not to fear, our ship was over forty thousand tons and its speed was almost thirty knots and it could out run any U-boat afloat. As I recall, he told us that we were almost thirty feet below the water line. Before he left, he said that some delicious food was on its way. We gave him a cheer and he took off to herd more cattle on board.

We tried the hammocks with disastrous results. Almost everybody did a flip and hit the floor with a resounding thud. Most of the guys persisted and finally got the hang of it. They were reasonably comfortable for the entire trip, since hammocks didn't sway with the ship. This was great in preventing seasickness but took a lot of practice. I tried several times and flipped over each time, the last time landing on my shoulder with a wicked smack. That was enough for me. I slept on top of a table for the entire trip. Lots of others followed my example, so half the hammocks were empty for the entire voyage.

The promised food soon arrived, but it was a big disappointment. There was lots of cheese and some hot-dog-like meat which was greasy as hell. I had been unable to eat any grease since my attack of the GIs in Denver, but I was so hungry that I had some anyhow. I was to pay dearly for that indiscretion.

After an hour or so of milling around in our tight quarters, we settled down for the night so we would be bright-eyed and bushy-tailed to greet the morning up on deck and watch the Statue of Liberty and the Ambrose Light go by.

While we slept, thousands more soldiers continued to board. We could hear the noise of those nearby as they settled down. We chuckled when we heard an occasional crash followed by an oath as their hammocks flipped on them. We were not the only ones allergic to hammocks.

I awoke next morning with hideous cramps in my stomach which was quickly followed by an urgent need to go numero dos. Seventeen guys were already in line at the head and it was still too dark to go up on deck. I was hit with a despair that has never since been equaled. Why, oh, why hadn't I passed up that rotten meat! Finally, in desperation, I went up to the first in line, a mechanic by the name of Charles and asked him if I could *please* cut in front of him. I didn't have much hope since we had never been particularly friendly, but I had to try. He looked at me, read the desperation in my eyes, and let me go in front. This was an act of mercy I will never forget.

After this crisis, I had some porridge. When I had finished, it was light enough to go on deck so up I went. There were plenty of outside toilets on deck which more than made up for their discomfort by being always available. Much to my disappointment, I found that the Statue of Liberty and the Ambrose Light were far astern since we had started our voyage during the wee hours of the morning. I remained on deck all day until darkness forced me below. By then, my GIs were gone.

I could tell from the constant noise that we were close to the engine room and thus were farther below than I had originally supposed. At first, I imagined that we were rock bottom, but further research revealed that a black outfit was below us. Since we were close, I talked to some of them and found out that they were in good spirits. I don't know why, because they had the worst quarters on the ship and it was not because of the luck of the draw. I'm glad things are better these days.

I fell into a pleasant routine on shipboard. I ate my breakfast of gruel and dried fruit as quickly as I could and then headed up to the deck where I spent the entire day until darkness sent me below. I am not sure whether we were served a lunch or not, since I never left the deck to find out. In the evenings, I ate any part of our dinner that was palatable and then went to sleep as soon as the tables were cleared. I tried to persuade others to go topside and get away from the fetid air, but not many did.

Our dining table seated fifteen per side, and the grub was given to those nearest the inside aisle. I was almost against the bulkhead, fourteenth in line to eat. Most of the guys tried to be fair when they helped themselves, but others took more than their share of the good stuff. This made things tough for a few days, but relief came as I shall relate.

When we left New York, it was evident that our course was southeast which meant either England, via southern Ireland to Liverpool or perhaps even Italy. We had a hunch that we would end up in England since we knew that the invasion of mainland France had top priority with the Allies. All us armchair experts were certain that our type of plane, the P-47, was ideal for ground support, which an invasion of France would require. We thus eliminated any thought of ending up in Italy.

As a result of our course, the weather was great, and the ship plowed through the waves at top speed. Early on, I went to the bow and watched it cut through the waves. Whenever we went through a swell, the bow would split it and create a wave of its own that varied from deep blue at the bottom to aqua marine and then snow white at the top. The spray from this wave created all kinds of fantastic rainbows. I watched this display for hours on end.

During this good weather, we had an emergency drill to show us where our lifeboat stations were. We were assured that there were not only ample lifeboats but slues of life rafts as well. I personally made certain that I knew how to get to mine from anyplace on the ship. I made a mental note to get on board a raft if possible. They looked more stable than the lifeboats and were sure to be less crowded. They did have the disadvantage of being low in the water so that medium-sized waves would break over them.

After this drill, we were sent below while the crew had gunnery practice with the eight-inch cannon on the stern. The reverberations of each shot penetrated every corner of the entire ship. I came to the conclusion that cannon were very noisy animals and I rejoiced once again that I had not been assigned to the artillery.

I walked all over every inch of the deck, enjoying the views from every vantage point and getting some good exercise as well. Pelagic sea birds surrounded us, performing acrobatics while chasing fish or playing tag with our ship. Several gulls, who had evidently hitched a ride on the ship from New York, flew around hunting for refuse. I don't know how they existed since it was a strict no-no to throw any trash overboard. Submarine skippers were experts at picking up discarded trash and then wiring the information ahead so others could ambush the ship. Gulls are unable to catch fish on their own as the shearwaters, terns, and other pelagic birds did, so I wondered at how they made a living. It was a treat to watch the shearwaters live up to their name by flying several inches above the water and then glide along the surface of a wave for hundreds of feet. On the first day out, a pod of dolphins kept up with the ship for a quarter of a mile or so before they evidently got bored and sough entertainment elsewhere.

After several days of this nirvana, the ship changed its course abruptly and headed north. We heard rumors that some German subs were in front of us on our southern course, somewhere off the coast of Ireland. As mentioned before, they could not hope to catch us but they could ambush us.

At any rate, we headed north and the weather changed from sunny and warm to blustery and cold. This forced me to go below and dig out my wool jacket. I was able to stay out for a while but then I got cold and went inside to warm up. Inside, I had posh salons virtually to myself.

All this euphoria ended with a bang about the fourth day out when we hit a genuine hurricane. My deck days were over for almost two days. The wind was so fierce that it was impossible to go out on the windward side of the ship. There was a strong possibility of either being washed or blown overboard and I realized that troop transports *never* turned back.

The waves were mountainous and it was a real thrill to see these monstrous mounds of water approach the bow with terrifying speed. As these almost vertical walls of water came toward us, it appeared that we could not possibly go over them, but somehow the ship rose up and they roared under us. We went over most of them, but about every fourth or fifth wave, the bow would be in depths of a trough and the huge comber smashed into it with tremendous force, creating a spectacular wave and virtually stopping the ship in its tracks. Some eighteen to twenty-four inches of water roared down the entire length of the deck and the screws came out of the water, spinning frantically. The entire ship vibrated from bow to stern. When they reentered the water, the ship charged ahead until the next wave hit us.

On one occasion, I was outside on the leeward side of the deck when this happened. A cascade of water soaked me to the skin almost up to my hips and I staggered down the deck, nearly losing my balance in the process. That was enough deck for me. I hastily retreated to one of the salons and watched the Mauritania battle the storm from there.

Although I couldn't prove it, I think that the ship changed courses in order to battle the storm head on. It appeared to me that we hit all waves at right angles and the wind was right in our teeth. Thus, while the pitching was tremendous, there was very little roll. This was a godsend to those below.

This horrible storm created havoc below. Half of the squadron were sick as dogs. They made contributions to the already fetid atmosphere and steeled my determination to stay up on deck as long as possible. The only positive result of the storm was that for the first time since we had left New York, I got enough to eat. About twenty percent of our squadron were so sick that they would have welcomed the Grim Reaper with open arms. About three quarters of the remainder were at least queasy. Virtually all were horizontal while the storm raged around us. While the few of us who were not sick enjoyed getting enough to eat, we would have gladly gone on half rations again rather than see our comrades suffer.

After almost forty-eight hours, the storm abated, but the seas were still rough for another day or so until we turned south and passed the northern coast of Ireland and entered the Irish Sea. Here the water was calm. Some of the less sick recovered, but the ones who really ailed didn't recover until we hit terra firma.

After six tumultuous days at sea, we sighted Liverpool Harbor one morning and expected to land forthwith. This was not to be—another case of so near but yet so far. Evidently we had just missed high tide and the *Mauritania* had such a deep draft that we had to wait until it came in again to land. While this was a hardship to most of us, it was a lot better than lightering in. With the help of several tugs, we finally entered the port and docked. By this time, many others joined me on deck and watched the landing operation. As soon as we moored, they started to empty the forward hold. They lowered a cargo net into the hold and brought out some small and fancy barrels which they lay on deck. Ever the wise guy, I asked one of the longshoremen what they contained. When he replied that they held gold, I asked if I could have one. He laughed and said that if I could lift it, it was mine. I gave it my all but couldn't budge it. He then told us that each one weighed about seven hundred pounds. Since the barrels were so fancy, we had no reason to doubt his word but we were surprised at the apparent lack of security.

While all this was going on, thousands of GIs were disembarking in the reverse order from how they had boarded. Those topside were the first to leave and the guys in the pits were last. Our time finally came, and I hastened below and grabbed my gun, put on my pack and helmet and bid a fond adieu to our gallant hostess, the *Mauritania*. I made a mental note to take another trip on her after the war, but when she finished bringing the last GIs back to the U.S., she was melted down for razor blades.

Que lastima!

The trip down the gangplank was far easier than our entrance had been. When we reached the ground, we formed loose ranks and marched to some "lorries" that awaited us. I found out that "lorries" were just trucks which drove on the wrong side of the road. We had a short trip to the railroad depot where we boarded a train with all window shades drawn to prevent its being seen in the remote case of a sudden air raid. This was our mild introduction to the realities of war. Some of the guys started a poker game but most of us caught some shuteye in preparation for a big tomorrow.

In the morning, we arrived at Southampton where we disembarked and boarded lorries once more and drove through some very pretty country until we arrived at the little town of Christchurch, some twenty to twenty-five miles west of Southampton.

All our baggage came with us and we started to make camp. First order of business was setting up pyramidal tents, each of which was living quarters for six of us. We set up the kitchen tents next and then those on the line that were necessary to make us operational. All we needed after that were some airplanes and the 511th would be ready for war.

Chapter Ten
Christchurch Army Air Field

Oh, to be in England
—Robert Browning

After setting up camp, Hitch and I took a quarter of a mile stroll to take a peek at our runway. It was a grass strip covered with wire mesh to prevent the planes from sinking into the ground but allowing the grass to grow through it. Also on the property was an ancient mansion, which evidently had been abandoned for many years. It was surrounded by tenacious briars and vines so we were unable to explore it.

Ultimately, some of this growth was cleared away and a few of our officers set up housekeeping in it. However, after my first attempt, I never had occasion to visit it so I had no idea what the interior looked like. From the exterior, it looked a lot like "Wuthering Heights."

First Sergeant Sibley called a meeting of all EMs and sketched out our *modus operandi*, which was similar to what we had been doing. A big difference was the change from sixty man barracks to six man pyramidal tents. Although I was unaware of any serious animosities in our squadron, I was still surprised that this change was effected with so little turmoil. The other big difference was our hanging 500 pound TNT bombs instead of "Blue Jays" on our planes, and our pilots now faced targets that shot back.

We were given a day off each week and could leave the base at any time when we were not needed on the line. Thus we could eat in town if we so desired. The British had been fighting for almost four years, so the food on the base was better and more plentiful than anything we could get in town. We also found that gourmet cooking was not an English forte, and the shortage of food exacerbated an already bad situation.

Four of us went into Christchurch a day or so after we had set up camp. We entered a small restaurant and ordered fish and chips. The fish was breaded to a fare-thee-well, more bread than fish, and the chips were greasy. The preponderance of bread was due to wartime shortages, but the effect of this venture made Cookie's food seem like pure ambrosia.

The village of Christchurch, like so many other English towns, got its name from a medieval legend. The main church in town was built about the year 1200, plus or minus a few hundred years. In the course of construction, the builders discovered that they had just sufficient big timbers to support the roof. As was the rule in those days, an earnest, hard worker, who was not very bright but had a soul as pure as the driven snow, was assigned to cut the last of these large timbers. In his haste and anxiety to do a good job, he cut it eighteen or so inches too short. The architects were in a quandary, but since it was late in the evening, they decided to quit for the day and face the problem in the morning. When they re-

Bridge across the Seine River at Mantes-Gassicourt, northeast of Paris destroyed by our dive bombers just prior to the Invasion.

turned next morning, the timber was in place, a perfect fit. This and many other legends added a great deal to the charm of an already beautiful country.

None of us had ever been abroad before, so we looked forward to seeing something of England. Train service was still excellent, despite the war, so it was not difficult for the adventurous to do some traveling on their own. Unfortunately, my free day was Sunday and the trains ran less frequently over the weekend. I had picked Sunday because it made things easy to catch a Mass, which I thought would be difficult to do in staunchly Protestant England. This cramped my style severely, but after a couple of months, a Catholic chaplain came and said Mass on the base every other Sunday. I promptly switched my day off and did some exploring.

One evening before our planes had arrived, several of us wandered to a fishing pier in Christchurch where we encountered a young lad of perhaps fourteen. He told us some of the strange laws that England was famous for. As an example, if one of us were to catch a fish off the pier, we were required to give it to a professional fisherman. This dispelled what little desire we may have had to play Isaac Walton.

He took us to the church, pointed out the famous timber, and then took us to his home where we met his family. They proved to be what we considered the classic English family, very cordial in a reserved sort of way but not much given to small talk. They offered us the best they had, which wasn't much. From then on, we took turns making sure that they were well supplied with such amenities as cigarettes, candy, and such.

Since we didn't want to embarrass them, it was I who gave them cigarettes, since they knew I didn't smoke, and Bob Loitz who came through with candy, since he didn't eat it himself. When we got to know them better, we were able to prevail on Sergeant Robinson, head chef, to give us some of the better leftovers. This proved to be a godsend to them since their skimpy rations were less than enough to keep them healthy. We enjoyed visiting a genuine family. Their hospitality was a welcome relief for us claustrophobic tent dwellers.

We made a few bloopers due to a difference in semantics. Bob Loitz told a story in which he called someone a "bum." There was a moment of strained silence before our host changed the subject. We subsequently found out that in Merrie England, "bum" referred to a person's derriere.

Mail call was a special treat for us since we were so far from home. My family always wrote religiously, so I never hurt for correspondence. They were also very good about sending cookies and other nonperishables, so I was a welcome tent mate for my peers. I got frequent letters from my youngest sister and my cousin who were bosom friends. Nothing is as therapeutic as getting mail from fifteen-year-olds and reading about their troubles. I remember chuckling when my cousin wrote," Oh Death, where is thy sting?" over some forgotten crisis.

Getting candy and cookies was duck soup, but getting good booze was super tough for those interested in taking a nip. One of the boys came up with an ingenious idea. He had his brother drain a hair oil bottle and fill it up with whiskey. How his brother managed to do this in less than a year is a complete mystery to me. However, it was a case of love's labor lost. Some thirsty mail clerk intercepted it, drank the booze, and substituted water. The recipient of the whiskey-made-water went off like Krakatoa when he took his first sip. War is hell, indeed.

Since I was one of the early draftees among my acquaintances in Philly, I got lots of mail from many girlfriends. Many of these young ladies used V-mail extensively. This not only prolonged my correspondence with them but enabled them to write more interesting letters as well. I was thankful for whatever letters I got from them. Some of them thought it their patriot duty to write to servicemen and we did nothing to persuade them otherwise. A few even persevered for a long time, and one was kind enough to write to me during the entire war. However, it was a case of all good things coming to an end with most, and much of my female correspondence dried up when their real boyfriends were called up. I took this drop off philosophically. I knew that I had been living on borrowed time with many of them, so I considered whatever I got to be pure gravy.

In terms of quality, letters from girlfriends were definitely *numero uno*. Not only did they impress my peers, but they gave me an opportunity to fantasize on the writer both in a bathing suit and in an evening gown. Of course, they all became prettier in my memory than they really were. "To sleep, aye, perchance to dream."

Our arrival in England introduced us to another of the army's ingenious inventions, V-Mail. This consisted of a one-page letter written on special stationary which was then microfilmed, sent across the ocean where it was reproduced on a four-by-five-inch letter, and then sent to the addressee by regular mail. In the reproduced state, it lacked the intimacy of an ordinary letter, so it was not popular with us nor with our most concerned correspondence such as my parents and relatives. I used it sparingly and then only when I was pressed for time. It was handy though, and enabled me to keep up some correspondence I would have had to drop. I did my best to keep up with all my correspondence but sometimes it was impossible. For instance, when we crossed the channel, we got no mail for almost six weeks, and then we were inundated with it. As active as we were at that time, I found it impossible to answer all my letters.

In going over some of the letters I had written home, I noticed that I never failed to ask for cookies, candy, etc. I had not realized that I had been such a "gimme pig." Much to my relief, I uncovered one of my parents' letters in my pile of correspondence telling me to be sure to ask for something in every letter because they were unable to send anything unless I specifically requested it. Since they were both busy attending to the family business, they were only able to send packages about every six weeks. This worked out perfectly for all concerned. The fact that I asked for so much enabled them to send whatever they had in mind at the time.

In the evening, poker games forced all players to play with a different and complicated currency. Gambling is a real sink-or-swim introduction to a monetary system. Those who don't catch on quickly donate to those who do.

The English at that time used two standard units in their monetary system. The first was the pound sterling, which was then worth slightly more than four dollars. The second was the shilling, worth about twenty cents. Twelve pence made a shilling and twenty shillings made a pound. The smallest coin in common use was the halfpenny (pronounced hay' penny). It was worth a little less than a cent. Then came the penny, the thrupence (three pence), the half shilling, and then, of course, the shilling. The word thrupence was quickly corrupted to trumpence or thrupney-bit.

Two other coins were also in common use, the florin, which was two shillings, and the half crown, worth two shillings sixpence. We had heard of a coin called a "farthing", but it was worth so little that it was no longer in circulation. Our English friends managed to get me a farthing coin, which I kept while I was abroad, but it somehow disappeared from my informal coin collection over the years. I guess somebody liked it more than I did. I remember that it was copper, about the size of a dime, had a cute little wren on the head, and was worth about a quarter of a pence.

This was my first experience with a different monetary system. I made a conversion chart so I could tell at a glance the relationship between their asking price and dollars. After a few days, I had a handle on the ratio of shillings and pounds to dollars and cents, so I discarded the chart. I have used this method successfully ever since and it has saved me money, time, and embarrassment. The English were scrupulously honest and pointed out any errors we made. This has not been true in many other countries my wife and I have visited.

Although the English system was cumbersome, we liked it because it *was* different, and things in foreign countries are *supposed* to be different. The only problem was the seemingly pitiful amount of money we got on payday, since the principal unit, the pound sterling, was worth over four bucks. Ouch!

My base pay as a corporal was about ninety dollars a month with an additional ten percent for overseas service. Since I didn't expect to spend much, I sent most of my money home where my folks put it in a savings account for me. I invested some of the remainder in savings bonds. There was very little for me to buy in England and I wasn't into booze. With Uncle Sam taking care of my living expenses, I was able to live very comfortably on very little. The money I saved was important when I returned to college after the war.

I was surprised at the quality of the food served at our mess tent. We had heard how the English were on short rations and we expected to do so ourselves. However, we were well supplied with lots of good American food and therefore ate very well. All we needed for perfection was a glass of vintage wine at our meals. Our first cook was a taciturn and much tattooed gent who was an excellent chef, so our future looked bright. However, Cookie had an Achilles heel, an addiction for the cup that cheers. Perhaps he brooded over the lack of good wine to augment his super-duper gourmet cooking.

At any rate, he decided to solve the mythical booze shortage all by himself. He took several weeks' supply of dried fruit and a hundred or so pounds of sugar and made a huge batch of home brew, which he let ferment and then shared with his friends. The result was chaos. We outsiders woke one morning to find stupefied guys lying all over the place. How he had managed to hide this enormous cache of moonshine while it was ripening remained a squadron mystery until the end of the war.

The officers were furious—either because they were not cut in or because of the alleged waste of food. The result was that our tattooed friend was transferred forthwith and was never seen or heard from again. What a loss for us and what a gain for the outfit that got him! "We could have better spared a better man."

Our next head chef was Troy Robinson from somewhere in the Deep South. He was not only a good cook but a smart guy, as well. He invented a steam table, which not only saved time and effort for KPs and cooks, but kept the food on the serving line warm. For this and for doing an excellent job under wartime conditions, he was awarded the Bronze Star at the end of the war.

Evidently, the other squadrons in our group had good men as well. Some of my friends were fortunate enough to pull KP at the right time. The three mess sergeants took them along when they went for supplies. They had a ball. They reported that these three rascals went over together and stole the supply people blind. One of them would cry the blues to the man in charge about how his people were starving, and the other two looted the warehouse. When the three rogues returned to camp, they stole from each other. Troy was a past master at this sort of thing so we ate very well.

Since this happened repeatedly, I am sure that the supply personnel were aware of what was going on and either didn't give a damn or could afford to let us have what we were "stealing." Soldiers have a tendency to exaggerate, particularly when there is no one to verify their stories. I am sure that a certain amount of hyperbole went with this fanciful story, but where there is smoke, there is fire, and the story was too good to ignore. Unfortunately, I never had the opportunity to check on this yarn since I usually had my face buried in a sink when I pulled KP. I guess the pay off is that we did eat very well.

Troy was also a considerate guy. Since we had no refrigeration, a lot of good food went to waste. The Book says that when an outfit is finished eating, whatever is left is garbage. Period. Exclamation point.

We had an English garbageman who came around regularly to pick up our garbage. He came one evening when I was on KP, working on pots and pans. We had center cut pork chops that night, and many were left untouched, still in the pan. Seeing the guy drooling, I went up to Troy and asked him if I could give them to the poor guy instead of throwing them out. His reply was, " I don't give a damn what you do with them as long as I don't know." Old English went away rejoicing that night.

The next night, I was back on the line and I wondered what would happen to our edible leftovers. Troy had told my replacement to keep the good stuff separate from the garbage and give it to our English friend. I bet that many residents of Christchurch were the best fed people in England for the four months we were there. Troy was also kind enough to turn his back when three of us stole some portable goodies prior to going on furlough in France.

Most of us were quite content with our grub. One who was not was our Italian gas-truck driver. He filled up his tray to the brim and then said, "I can't eat this shit." When we pointed out to him that his mess kit was chock full and he was gaining weight rapidly, his reply was, "Even a pig gets fat on swill." Normally, a chronic complainer was a pain in the rear, but Joe's answer was so funny that we continued to bait him until the end of the war.

Unfortunately, our supply sergeant was cut from a different cloth. He was a parsimonious pain in the ass. He always acted like a stockholder. We often wondered if he felt that he had to reimburse the government for everything we could pry out of him. The good sergeant was a little guy with a perennial cigarette butt in his mouth that never exceeded a quarter inch in length. Someone jokingly declared that he acquired all his smokes by policing our camp area. I was tempted to give him a fresh butt just to see what he would do with it.

Army regulations were his Bible, from which there could be no deviation. While the rest of the outfit and the entire U. S. Army was wasting money and equipment by the billions, the good sergeant was trying to save it by the penny.

Mobility was the name of the game for us. We had to make many moves in order to keep up with the advances made by the infantry we were supporting. Each move caused scads of turmoil, so it was easy to lose some or even all one's clothing, not only because of chaos but also because of theft, both internal and external. The good sergeant accepted no excuses, so we had to pay for virtually everything we lost. I'm sure this made his bookkeeping very simple, but it was tough on us. Many of us preferred to do without rather than pay for a loss which was not really our fault.

I had several unsuccessful run-ins with him, so I thought it might be fun to fix his little trolley sometime. I felt that my time would come, provided I had the patience and a little luck. It finally did, as I shall relate in due course.

Venereal disease was the curse of the army. We were warned that catching it was a court-martial offense. For some reason or other, this was not enforced. I think we might have had to operate short-handed if everyone who got the clap was arrested. Ever so often, we were awakened at some ungodly hour and checked for this ailment. We were given lectures and shown films graphically describing the horrors that awaited those who caught one of these diseases. Unfortunately, biological urges proved to be stronger than the fear of disease. As usual, everybody thought that only the other guy got sick.

Movies on venereal diseases were affectionately known as "Mickey Mouses" and were scheduled every month or so. They were certainly scary, but I don't think that fear of illness has ever been an effective deterrent and these films did little or no good. The only guys who were impressed by them were the few who didn't indulge.

We had one in Saint Dizier which really backfired. I think that it must have been made to show to WAC's, because it showed graphically how women acquired the various types of venereal disease and what they did to women. As was customary, no officer was present to stop the film and the guy running the projector must have become fascinated by the subject matter because he showed the film in its entirety. I don't think the brass were pleased by the results they got from showing this particular film. Our VD rate skyrocketed. The economy of St. Dizier was also affected when all trucks heading to town were loaded to the gills with panting GIs. Every whore in town worked overtime for about two weeks. In a short time, it was the medics who worked overtime trying to heal all those who caught the clap.

Officers were not obligated to attend any of these pix, although it was far more serious if a pilot got a dose than us EMs. The brass really took a dim view of pilots getting any disease because we needed everyone we had. Of course, they had far more opportunity to meet women than we did and their temptations were at least as great as ours. They were classified as "gentlemen" and hence either didn't need this type of admonition, or they had a showing of their own. I am certain that when they heard about our film, they must have insisted on their own showing, since their VD rate went up at the same time.

As far as sex was concerned, there were four groups in our outfit. First there were those who abstained completely. These were very few. Next came those who were particular and only imbibed if something special was available. They were very discerning on entering a cathouse and sometimes left without contributing. After this group came those who had a little pride in their selection but were far less discerning than the second group. This was probably the largest percentage in the outfit. Finally, there were the lechers, who actively pursued anything in skirts. Their sex appetites were never appeased and sex was virtually all they talked or thought about.

In every tent there was some talk about sex; it went with the territory. However, after it had run its course, the topic of conversation turned to something else. This was not true with the last group. Sex seemed to be the sole thing on their minds. For this reason, they usually hung around together and occupied the same tents while overseas. They were not really shunned, but they were avoided. Overseas, we lived in close contact and I could think of nothing worse than living with these birds. Occasionally, one would visit our tent for reasons unknown, and it was not long before an exodus of the regular occupants began. None of us were puritans, and we all enjoyed a racy story, but these guys were too much. They were a classic example of Gresham's Law in action. "Bad money drives good money out of circulation."

I was one who abstained completely. This was not as difficult as it might seem. I just avoided the cat houses and the seamier bars. Everyone respected my views, and outside of some good-natured kidding, left me alone. By the same token, I didn't criticize those who did imbibe, either verbally or in my mind. They did their thing and I did mine. Sex was something that had to be pursued to be obtained. It was no problem for me not to pursue. There were other things to do and I enjoyed doing them.

While the GI was a good ambassador, he was also notorious for his strong sex drive. I don't know whether this was due to rebellion against the Puritanism of our culture or whether there was just a natural letdown in sexual inhibitions during times of war. I think that we went to greater extremes than the other combatants did. A Cockney tart in Picadilly Square was quoted as saying that she didn't know that she was sitting on a fortune until the Yanks arrived.

We had no homosexuals that I am aware of, but with the number of men in our outfit, it is quite possible that we did. We did have a lanky Southerner from Arkansas who used to pick them up in bars, take them outside and beat them up. While most of us left homosexuals strictly alone, this was an accepted practice by a few in those days.

After each exploit, he would recount his heroics in graphic terms to the few who were interested. I think he equated homosexuality with being a sissy. One sad day, he showed up on the line much the worse for wear. He admitted that he had picked the wrong pigeon. When he got him outside and gave him a belt, his opponent said "There's two things I like in this world, being a homosexual and fighting. He then proceeded to thrash the poor guy. To his credit, our guy admitted what had happened, took the inevitable kidding with good grace, and never bothered a homosexual again.

One of our favorite haunts was Bournemouth, a seaside resort not too far away. The beach was far different from the fine Jersey beaches I had grown up with. The sand was coarse with a few rocks jutting out. There was lots of fog, which was accompanied by bone-chilling cold weather, and a cold, raw wind frequently blew off the English Channel. I guess there were limits to the warming influence of the Gulf Stream. It was still nice to walk on the beach and pick up a shell or two, but the chief attractions were its movie theaters and its pubs. I was not much of a pub enthusiast since I was still on the wagon, but I went in with some of the boys, had a coke, and had mental misgivings when I saw how they "washed" the glasses. They just ran them through a sink of cold water and then used them again. When some of the boys came down with trench mouth, I was not sorry that I was too young to imbibe.

On my few visits to the pubs, I found out that they were male castles and the habitués were from the working class. They were a blunt group who had been at war for four plus years without losing their sense of humor. After talking to them, I felt that they were the rocks on which England had built its empire. They accepted us and were grateful for our participation in the war. However, in their heart of hearts, I think that they felt that their own guys were better soldiers. They were great at darts but their boards had wire divisions which kept a dart that hit on them from sticking. I couldn't figure out why they used this kind of board or how they kept score.

One afternoon, Hitch and I went to one of the Bob Hope-Bing Crosby "road" pictures and roared laughing. I noticed after a while that we were the only people in the whole theater who were doing so and we were attracting a lot of attention. I assumed from this that the English lacked a sense of humor. As we got to know them better, we found out that they had a very good sense of humor but it was more subtle than ours.

Every group has a tightwad who ducks out of paying his share of the tab. The rest pay when their time comes. On my few visits to pubs, I paid for scotches and drank English cokes when I was due. When our miserly friend's turn came up, he would suggest a round of beer. Fortunately, he lived in another tent and was assigned to a different flight so my exposure to him was minimal. Other than that, he wasn't really a bad sort, so we never turned him down when he wished to join us.

We got one good chuckle out of him. We went to Bournemouth one afternoon and met some nice English girls who wished to take in a show. We got to the ticket office and he marched up and asked for twelve tickets. We were flabbergasted at his sudden generosity. After the girls had gone in, he turned to us and said, "You can pay me back after the show." It takes all kinds to make a world. Hitch and I had fun for the next two weeks quoting him after one of us had done a good turn for the other.

Some of the enlisted men took advantage of the good train service to do some local travel. John Higgins, switchboard operator and my favorite source of inside information, went to Exeter and Salisbury, and everybody went to London. Three of us, Harvey Hallenbeck, Len Hitchman, and I took an early train, to London and taxied all over town. Even in war time, it was a great city. We hit many of the historic spots, ate lunch at a Fleet Street restaurant, and ended up at the British Museum. There were two trains back that evening, one at six and the other much later. Harvey wanted to take the later train but London during a blackout had no appeal for me. I told them I was going to take the early train no matter what they decided. Reluctantly, they came back with me.

While in London, we got an insight on the reality of war. First we saw bomb damage throughout the city. The rubble had been cleaned up but there were gaping voids where buildings had been. St. Paul's Cathedral had taken a direct hit from a 1000-kilo bomb which didn't explode. There was a neat circular hole in the floor where it had gone through. No cathedral was designed to take a direct hit from a bomb that size. Had it exploded, St. Paul's would have been in shambles. During our tour of the city, we encountered a Canadian soldier who had been stationed in England for over four years. Four years seemed like an eternity to me since this was May and I had been in the army for fifteen months. This Canadian had married an English girl and intended to stay there after the war.

My big bugaboo in England was my inability to ride a bike. Years before I was born, my father had seen a terrible bike accident so we were never allowed to ride one. This made things tough since biking was one of the best ways to get around and see the countryside. It was not until my oldest son reached the age of twelve that I bit the bullet and learned to ride one. However, I really missed some good times and first-rate sightseeing while overseas.

A common feature in most English towns was a square, right smack in the center of town where it could impede the maximum amount of traffic. In the center of the square was placed a large statue of some ancient hero. These squares proved to be a serious hazard for bike-riding GIs. First, they had to learn to go *left* around the square. This took lots of practice and the learning process resulted in some hair-raising close calls before they got accustomed to it. It was at night, however, that these squares wreaked havoc with GI bikers.

One evening, two stalwarts had played the curfew a bit close and were speeding to the base, heads down and pumping like mad. Their path put them on a collision course with a granite statue. There was very little give in this particular statue and one of them hit it head on, ruining his bike and knocking himself cold in the process.

The noise of the collision routed out several habitués of a nearby pub who went over to investigate. They passed right by the inert GI and went straight to the bike. Their only comment was, "Blimey, look at the bloody Yank's bike."

Somehow the poor biker righted himself and returned to camp, ruined bike and all, but long after curfew. Next day he was exonerated for being late "due to extenuating circumstances."

We had a Protestant chaplain who held regular services and was available for consultation. Some guys did consult him, but he was an officer which proved to be a major restraint. It was always easier to consult with a minister or priest from another outfit for this reason.

In England, we Catholics could attend Mass on the base every other week. When a priest was not available, we had to go into town and hunt up a Catholic Church. This was not easy in Anglican England. Catholics were neither plentiful nor popular. We finally found a small church tucked into a remote corner of town that had a very convenient schedule of Sunday Masses. One Sunday, two of us went to Mass, which involved a walk of some two and a half miles each way. The weather was nice and we both had the day off, so it was a pleasant walk.

On our return, we decided to take a short cut across the runway. A small plane, piloted by two nice-looking young women taxied by us heading toward the beginning of the runway. They turned and headed toward us on their takeoff. We casually moved out of their way but they swerved toward us. Once again we moved, but so did they. Things began to look a mite sticky. Finally we started to run, but again they headed toward us. That was enough for me. I hit the dirt while my companion kept on running. The two witches made a last second adjustment and their wheels seemed to bracket the other guy's head. That ended all short cuts across the runway for me, which might very well have been the lesson those fair damsels tried to teach us.

While we were too far off the beaten track to attract Bob Hope or any other really big USO shows, we did catch a few of the lesser lights, ranging from good to hideous. Every comedian made some remark about one of our popular breakfasts, dried beef on toast which was known as "shit on a shingle." This was grist for their mills and became old hat to us in a hurry because we had to eat it. It was okay for us to joke about our grub but not for outsiders to do so.

Most of the time, the performers asked for volunteers from the audience as a method of creating interest. On one occasion, a nice looking young lady asked for a volunteer and my good friends forced me up on stage. I was led to the dressing room and told that I was to go on stage on cue and go up to the young lady and give her a kiss. She was not quite as pretty close up, but far more than adequate and American at that. I worked up enough nerve to go over and give her a big kiss, smack on the lips. She looked at me, my face about six inches from hers, with eyes as big as saucers and stammered that I wasn't supposed to kiss her until she was on stage. I replied that I was aware of that, but I had to get in some practice. Everyone laughed and the performance was a great success. The wolf whistles and catcalls from jealous compatriots attending my big moment was music to my ears.

For the first and only time in my illustrious career in the 511th Squadron, I made the log. Sam Weinberg, squadron clerk and author of all written squadron communications, put this in his report to Tactical Air Command:

> Corporal John B. Henkels 3rd, pinch-hitting in a USO show at the field was termed a wolf in a sheep's clothing after his performance opposite a very charming actress.

I wonder what he would have written if he had seen my practice performance.

Fame is fleeting and it was not long before it wore off and I was just another armorer once again. I don't know what I liked best, the short period of fame or kissing the girl. Unfortunately, I can barely remember either one right now. *Sic transit gloria mundo.*

In April, the final promotions came out and I was left waiting at the church once more. I had really expected to make it this time and a lot of my friends were rooting for me. My only consolation was that my Hispanic friend, Gerald Mackey, did make it and he was so thrilled that it took much of the edge off my own disappointment. I realized that my last chance of making sergeant was gone. I piously consoled myself with the thought that I'd rather deserve something and not get it than get something I didn't deserve.

Some evenings, the intelligence department would show us pictures taken from the gun cameras of our planes. Most of them showed steam coming from stricken locomotives, trucks catching fire, etc. Once in a while, a pilot took pictures of the plane in front dropping bombs. The explosions looked like some of the antics in a Sylvester Stallone "Rambo" film.

As I have mentioned, we became relatively immune to plane crashes and pilots being killed. We had one terrible exception to this in England. All three squadrons were assigned to knock out an important bridge in occupied France. Three quarters of the planes were loaded with two five-hundred-pound bombs and the rest were assigned to fly cover for them. Since the bridge was some distance inside France, each plane carried extra fuel in two-hundred and fifty gallon belly tanks. The entire group took off early in the morning.

A plane from another squadron didn't make it and crashed into a house at the end of the runway. Miraculously, neither the bombs or the auxiliary tank exploded. There was no fire, and the pilot escaped without a scratch, although the house and plane were completely destroyed.

That afternoon, another mission was scheduled since the bridge had been untouched in the morning raid. The same pilot was again assigned to carry bombs and a belly tank. We could tell almost immediately that he was not going to make it. This time, however, there was a tremendous explosion when he hit a different house and both plane and house disappeared in a huge, orange ball of flame. A tiny English fire truck hastened to the scene with totally inadequate equipment. Many of the enlisted men also approached the blazing plane and house for a closer view. Just as the fire truck arrived on the scene, the second bomb went off with a roar and a tremendous flash, wiping out the entire fire crew and many of the curious GIs as well. This was the blackest day for the 405th Group. Every squadron lost somebody in the second explosion.

We later heard that the pilot was in a sweat after his morning crash. Evidently, his CO was afraid he might lose his nerve permanently if he didn't go up again immediately. I guess this was logical but it might have been better to let him fly cover where he would not have to carry bombs. This demonstrated one of the tough life-and-death decisions a squadron commander had to make.

The P-47 took off under full throttle and ninety-nine percent of the time, all went well. However, there were times when the engines didn't give full power under full throttle and the pilot had to make a split-second decision on whether to continue his takeoff or abort the mission. Most of the time, it was readily apparent that the plane was not generating full power and a quick-witted flyer was able to abort in time. Not all were that gifted and there were several houses at the end of the runway that were destroyed when the planes crashed into them. We were fortunate that only one of them exploded.

When we crossed the channel, we had a grass strip out in the boonies, so it was no longer as critical when a plane lost power. There was lots of bare field for the pilot to land in. The plane might be destroyed but the pilot usually survived.

All our missions involved knocking out bridges and bombing marshaling yards and other transportation facilities in order to isolate the invasion area from the rest of France. After dropping bombs, the pilots were free to shoot up " targets of opportunity." Just about anything that moved qualified as fair game for our zealous pilots. The havoc they wrought was unbelievable. Nothing was safe. Livestock, trucks, locomotives, horse-drawn vehicles were all considered fair game. In at least one case, an engineer on a locomotive stopped his engine, got out, and waved the pilots on. Many other groups did as ours did. It was a wonder that the Germans had any vehicles or locomotives left by the time we crossed the channel. Since we flew two missions a day, weather permitting, all road and rail systems of central France were in shambles.

A few of the more important bridges were protected by anti-aircraft guns. The Germans were good shots since they got a lot of practice and our planes were vulnerable when in their dive. Had they been the Douglases of Tampa, they would have been slaughtered, but the speed and ruggedness of the P-47 made things tough for the German gunners. Occasionally we did lose a pilot, and that sobered us up a bit. On rare occasions, we encountered German fighters and some lively action would ensue. It was the ambition of every pilot to become an ace by shooting down five enemy planes but none of ours even came close since our exposure to German aircraft was minimal.

The Luftwaffe used virtually all its strength to combat the heavy bombers of the Eighth Air Force who were pummeling the Fatherland. Although the B-17 bombers used by the Eighth Air Force were heavily armed, they were no match for German fighters so they had to be escorted to and from their targets. While the P-51 Mustang got the major credit for the success of this escort system, P-47s also were important. They were probably the ruggedest plane that the Allies had, and any Luftwaffe pilot who tried to outdive them was a dead duck. At first, the German pilots were able to turn inside them and escape but with the advent of our new paddle props, this advantage was denied them. Thus, the P-47 was an unsung hero in the final destruction of the German Air Force.

After we had been in England a short time, Herr Hitler came up with another of his surprises, the so-called buzz bomb. These unmanned and ungainly monsters consisted of a primitive jet engine and a winged warhead of about seven hundred pounds of TNT. We saw them every once in a while, sputtering along about three hundred fifty miles per hour on their way to London Town. When the engine conked out, it was Katie bar the door. They plunged to earth and went off with a tremendous bang. We didn't mind the ones we could see, but the Germans were unkind enough to send them at night and some others came directly overhead. A seven hundred pound warhead propelled by a sputtery jet engine was a spooky intruder to our sleep.

During the day, it was fun to watch these junkers sputtering on their way to eventual destruction. We saw many of them conk out in the distance and plunge out of sight. Shortly thereafter, we heard the explosion. Watching them at a distance made us forget how lethal they were. As soon as we took them for granted, one would go overhead or one we did not see would go off in our area. On one occasion, one conked out in our vicinity and hit about a mile from us. The ensuing explosion was very impressive. The thing that really bugged us about them was their unreliability. We knew that London was their target, but a sizable percentage conked out long before they reached their objective. It was the random nature of their flight that gave us the creeps. They were a weapon addressed "To whom it may concern" and this could well be us.

We never took them too seriously as a weapon that could turn the tide of the war, but evidently some of the big brass did. In his book, *Crusade in Europe*, General Eisenhower says that if the Germans had launched them six months earlier, they would have upset the Allied invasion plans (page 260).

Finally, the RAF realized that they had to do something to counteract these brutes which caused a lot of damage in southeastern England and in London, and were affecting the morale of the invading forces who feared for the safety of their loved ones at home. They organized several squadrons of fighters to shoot them down. This was not easy, as they moved very rapidly and were a small target. The RAF then devised a method by which a fighter plane would catch up to one of them, put its wing under the wing of the buzz bomb and then try to flip it over. When this succeeded, the gyroscopes on the bomb went out of sync and it plunged to the ground. Of course, the pilot had to pick the right spot because the plunging bomb would damage whatever it hit on the ground. Both methods were moderately successful but the buzz bomb menace was not completely eliminated until the launching pads in Holland and Belgium were overrun by Allied ground forces. These bombs and the possibility of being shelled by German artillery when we first set up camp in Normandy were the only real exposures we had to enemy action.

Our first group of 47s had a sectionalized canopy which was in line with the fuselage, so they had a blind spot directly behind the pilot. The Germans were quick to take advantage of this weakness on the few times they attacked. These planes also had standard propellers. As our old ships were replaced, sometimes due to old age but more frequently to enemy action, we were given a new model with a raised teardrop canopy of Plexiglas which was not only more streamlined but which gave the pilot much better visibility aft. They were also equipped with a radical new paddle-blade prop. This was much shorter and wider than our old props and was almost as wide at the end as it was in the middle. This new prop decreased our turning ratio and took that advantage away from our opponents. They were no longer able to turn inside as they had been in the past. I think that the new type prop had less area than the older version, which reduced air resistance. They looked like hell, but they sure got the job done. "Nuff said."

Chapter Eleven

Going to War

A Time for War
—Ecclesiastes chapter three verse eight

In England, we were attached to the Ninth Air Force. All our missions were flown to prepare for the coming invasion of Festung Europa by isolating the Cherbourg Peninsula. We knocked out dozens of bridges, shot up scores of locomotives, and thousands of vehicles. We also hit railroad marshaling yards but this only inconvenienced the Germans since they were experts at repairing them with French slave labor. Our guys were so zealous that anything on wheels was in imminent danger of getting shot up.

Each of us armorers was assigned to a particular plane. Mine was officially designated as K4-M. The K4 was our squadron code name and the "M" was its designation in the squadron.

Each plane had its own pilot who flew the majority of his missions in it. Occasionally, we had a different pilot but that was the exception rather than the rule. My pilot was a Creole from Monroe, Louisiana, Mike Varino by name. He was short and dark with bright blue eyes and a ready smile, and was probably the best shot in the squadron.

When I first met him, he was busily waxing our plane. After I introduced myself, I started to help him and asked how much speed he would gain as a result of all this hard work. My enthusiasm dampened considerably when he told me that it might add as much as five miles per hour. I had good reason to regret all this effort for another more cogent reason—it made the wing as slick as hell. I took some hideous spills on them before I found out how to walk on them safely.

Mike had a good sense of humor as I found out early in the game. Somehow the wretch found out that after takeoff, I took a siesta, leaning against a little pill box adjacent to our hardstand. I faced the runway so I could see the planes as they landed and thus be prepared to jump on mine as soon as it parked. One afternoon, instead of peeling off and heading toward the runway as was customary, he broke formation and buzzed my little pill box, barreling along at some three-fifty miles per hour. I was enjoying a delightful dream when a faint hum woke me up. I looked up and saw an enormous radial engine coming at me with the speed of light. He came so close that he had to make a slight bank to avoid hitting the pill box. As soon as he passed, he pulled up sharply and rejoined the landing pattern. The tremendous roar of the engine as the plane whizzed by knocked every vestige of sleep from me. For a few seconds, I was petrified. He had come so close that I could smell the engine exhaust.

He taxied to our hard stand and parked the plane. He hopped out of the plane, gave me a big grin, and asked me how I liked his little buzz job. By this time I had regained my composure so I grinned back and complimented him on his fine flying. To avoid any repetition of this nonsense, I moved my resting place ninety degrees around the building where I could still watch the planes land but was safe from any future scurrilous attempts to interfere with my siestas.

Each squadron consisted of four flights which were the basic units of a fighter squadron. They were designated "A," "B," "C," and "D." As I have mentioned previously, mine was "C" flight. Four planes from each flight usually flew on each mission and pilots paired up as assigned at the preflight briefing. On a bombing mission, the squadrons acted in concert. They all attacked the same target. After dropping their bombs, each flight went its own way, attacking targets of opportunity.

The P-47 was powered by a large radial air-cooled engine, the Pratt and Whitney R-2800. This was the largest radial engine in the world at this time. I think that the "2800" stood for horsepower although they were rated officially at two thousand horses. When an extra burst of speed was necessary, pilots could inject water into the engine which gave it extra power. Since this put a strain on the engine, pilots used it only in emergency situations.

We encountered many problems with our P-47s, since it is impossible for the manufacturers to anticipate everything. Many of these didn't surface until a piece of equipment had been flown in combat for weeks or even months More about this later. As Von Moltke was fond of saying, "No battle plan survives contact with the enemy." We armorers had to change our bomb racks when the new type which came with the planes failed to release properly. We were faced with the problems of bombs hanging up for a split second and others that failed to release until the plane hit the runway after returning from their mission. This was particularly true on the few missions when we used armorer-piercing bombs which were narrower the our general purpose bombs.

At first, when this occurred, the pilot was supposed to bail out and abandon the plane, but this was only possible over the British Channel and the odds on a pilot surviving in the cold water of the channel were prohibitively low. Thus, the brass decided that the risk of the bomb exploding as it skipped down the runway was preferable to the almost certain loss of both pilot and plane if he bailed out over the channel.

The original racks that came with the plane were supposed to be an improvement over the ones we had used in Walterboro. They were easier to load and arm, but they malfunctioned on many occasions and bombs failed to release. When a bomb failed to drop, the pilot put their arming toggle on "safe" and then landed, hoping for the best. Most of the times, it fell off the plane on contact with the runway and its momentum made it bounce head over heels down the runway for hundreds of yards before coming to a stop.

As luck would have it, my hard stand was just opposite the place on the runway where the planes first made contact with the ground, so the bombs dropped off just in front of me. At first, I hid behind my little pill box but as time went on and none of them exploded, I took things in stride and watched them bounce along the ground after they fell off.

A squadron from a nearby group had a hanging bomb explode when it fell off on landing and the ensuing explosion killed the pilot and some nearby ground personnel. Nobody could account for this tragedy, but it is possible that the pilot forgot to put it on "safe" before he landed. This was the only incident of its kind that I am aware of, but there were probably more since hanging bombs was a widespread problem in the Air Force.

We decided to go back to our original racks to avoid this hazardous situation. The improvement was immediate. However, we never eliminated this problem completely. It was not until long after the war when I first read the history of our group that I realized that the problem of hanging bombs was far more serious than I had imagined. We were not aware of those that hung up for a second or two when released over the target area. We had no way of knowing this unless the pilots told us. Some of them forgot and others didn't realize it as the bomb sometimes fell off in flight without their knowledge. When a bomb hung up, the pilot was forbidden to strafe for obvious reasons. On occasion, some didn't realize that they hadn't released and strafed. When this happened and the bomb dropped off during his strafing run, both pilot and plane went up in smoke.

I was either lucky or skilled, since I never had a bomb hang up. Some of the other armorers had no problems either. Unfortunately, no study was made to correlate hang ups by plane and by pilot. Had this been done, we might have found out and eliminated the cause. Hang-ups were tragic in more ways than one. First, we lost some good pilots, and second, they had enough on their minds while on a mission without worrying whether or not their bombs might hang up.

When we had completed all our preliminaries and the pilots had worked off their accumulated rust in flights around our immediate area, the 511th was ready for combat. The Big Day finally arrived, and our pilots took off for a fighter sweep over a quiet region of western France. On a sweep, fighters fly over an area to make certain that no enemy aircraft are there. We ground crew were as green as the pilots and we were almost as excited as they were. We were in a dither until we heard engines in the distance and the first plane made its appearance. No planes were lost, but they had encountered some antiaircraft fire. One plane actually had a small hole in the vertical stabilizer! One of the flyers came up with what became a classic. Quoth he, "That's the worst flak I have ever flown through!" Little did he know what was in store for him.

We discussed this mission in our tent that night and came to the conclusion that bored German ack-ack gunners, watching our planes passing high overhead, woke up long enough to loft a few shells at our planes so that they could tell the Fuhrer that they had taken some action against those nasty interlopers on their turf. After firing a round or two, they probably continued their interrupted nap. They were also unaware of what awaited them.

Tactically, a fighter sweep is a complete waste of time and talent since the German Luftwaffe was not about to challenge them. However, in this case, it accomplished its goal because our guys experienced enemy fire without being endangered. As they flew deeper into Occupied France, they learned the importance of accurate navigation and how to spot good targets quickly and accurately.

After several fighter sweeps, they flew a strafing run over France and had a ball shooting up all kinds of German equipment. Their targets of choice were steam locomotives, since steam poured out of them in a very satisfactory manner. Trucks sometimes caught fire and some even exploded, but locomotives were not only their favorite target but probably their most important one as well.

A week after this series of strafing missions, we flew our first bombing mission. Our target was an important bridge over a large river. I think it was at Mantes Gassicourt. After the bombing, they were to strafe military targets in that area. Our guys interpreted "military" rather loosely as anything on wheels. The mission was a success, the bridge was destroyed, and a large quantity of trucks were shot up. For the next two months, we flew two missions a day, knocking out bridges, bombing marshaling yards, and shooting up all kinds of German equipment. We were gradually putting a stranglehold around the invasion area. Once the landing in France had been made, it would be difficult for the Germans to bring up reinforcements since all bridges and other strategic points were destroyed. The success of the invasion was a strong vindication of our activities.

As armorers, it was our job to load bombs, to maintain and load eight machine guns, and to make certain that the gunsight inside the cockpit functioned well. The latter job was our easiest, as all we had to do was replace a defective bulb once in a while. In order to load our guns, we had to mount the wing, open a square panel in the top of it, and put in four hundred rounds of caliber-fifty ammo per gun. The panel was part of the wing and was held on with dzus fasteners which were very reliable and could be released with a single twist of a screwdriver.

Inside the wings were little bins, perhaps eight inches square, which held the ammo. We had to take some care in placing it so that it moved smoothly from bins to gun without a hitch when the guns were fired. After placing ammo in the wing compartments, we fed it into the gun and then charged it so that all the pilot had to do was turn on his gunswitch and pull the trigger on his stick.

Every night we discharged the guns to avoid putting undue strain on the firing pin spring. As time went on, we were forced to leave them hot at nights since an emergency mission might be called and we would not have time to open the wing and charge them. This worked out well, since our fear of spring exhaustion was exaggerated. We never experienced a single case of it in the entire war.

These guns gave the P-47 terrific fire power. Each gun could spout out between four and five hundred rounds per minute. Thus a plane only carried enough ammo for a minute of nonstop firing. However, this was more than enough if a pilot used it judiciously. He only fired his guns in short bursts. This not only saved ammo but it gave the barrels a chance to cool between firings.

Our ammo was lethal. Each bullet had an outer copper jacket with a little thermite powder inside the front tip and a core of armor-piercing steel. On hitting the target, the copper jacket adhered to it while the thermite ignited, heating the target and taking some of the temper out of it. Then the hard core of steel penetrated it. All this occurred in nanoseconds. It was excellent for targets such as locomotives, trucks, armored vehicles, other planes, and some light tanks. Also, the thermite sometimes acted as an incendiary when it hit a combustible target. Although it could not penetrate the armor of heavy tanks, they still ran for cover at our approach.

Originally, every tenth and the last ten rounds were tracer bullets. These were hollow copper-jacketed slugs filled with a combustible compound that burned with a red flame, very similar to the road flares of today. Following tracers theoretically helped the pilot's aim. There were two problems with this theory. The first was that tracers burned unevenly and then flew off at oddangles, and the second was that the pilot might be distracted by watching them in flight and thus not look through his gunsight.

Most pilots disliked them. Captain Sams had all of his removed and replaced with standard ammo. He felt that tracers were a waste and used up space that could be filled with "good" ammo. He said, and I quote," When my f——— don't shoot, I'm out of bullets." You can't beat that for common sense.

It was not too long before all the others followed suit. Our ordinance department spent several weeks taking out all tracers from our existing supply of ammo and then eliminating them completely. Nobody knew what happened to the excess tracers and nobody cared.

I was surprised, while attending a recent reunion of our group held in Seattle a year or so ago, that many of the pilots who also attended told me that they were disappointed when their tracers were removed. Previous to this, I had always thought that their removal had been universally approved.

Friend Sams had another virtue. He liked his armorer and insisted on his being promoted to sergeant. What he wanted, he got and his armorer was promoted forthwith. No other pilot in our squadron ever attempted to have one of his ground crew promoted throughout the entire war. This was too bad, since we had a few openings because our boss was often skimpy about filling them.

Every evening when K4-M came in from its last flight, I checked the guns and occasionally put some oil on them when they appeared to be dry. However, after a plane had completed a hundred hours of combat flying, we took it out of service and gave it a rigid inspection against a checklist. While the mechanics worked on the engine, I removed and stripped down the machine guns. I noticed that the oil on them was quite dirty, probably because of residual powder particles.

On my first inspection, I did what the herd did; I soaked all the parts in 100-octane gas and swabbed out the barrels with it as well in order to get rid of the dirty oil. This was a disaster. The 100 octane removed the ingrained oil from the guns and they rusted like hell even after I had reoiled them. Luckily, I had charged them right after I reassembled them and had reoiled them as well or they would have frozen so tightly that I would never have been able to do so. When I looked down the barrels, I got a real scare. They were deeply pitted and appeared to me to be ruined. I asked Mike if he would fire a few rounds on his next mission whether he had a target or not. I hoped that firing them would clear up the barrels. When he returned, all the pits were gone and the barrels were bright and clean. The guns were freed up and in much better shape. The heat generated when the guns were fired enabled some of the oil to penetrate once again and I was off the hook. From then on, all I did was remove them, wipe off the old oil and reoil them and replace them. This method took less energy and did a better job. Plain wiping was in, gasoline baths were out!

Preparation for a bombing mission took the efforts of all. Five-hundred pound GP (general purpose) bombs came with two thick cardboard bands around the loading lugs. We removed them and attached a large steel fin to the top of the bomb by means of a threaded ring. These fins kept the bomb from tumbling in flight and made certain that it would hit the target point first. Then we hooked two lifting bars to the bomb lugs and lifted it onto a hydraulic dolly. We pulled the dolly under the wing and below the bomb rack and then jacked up the bomb until we could hook the lugs onto the rack. We loaded the other wing in the same fashion. Then we went to the next plane and followed the same procedure until all planes in our flight were loaded.

When all planes were loaded, each of us returned to our own plane and tightened up the four holding bolts on each wing so that each bomb not only faced directly forward but was snug so that it wouldn't move in flight. After this we fused the bombs so they would detonate on the target.

Once in a while, we had to load a bomb on the belly. This was more difficult because the belly rack was lower than wing racks and the clearance from the ground was less. We mostly used the belly rack either to hold an auxiliary gas tank or to carry a two-hundred-fifty gallon napalm bomb. It was a bit of a trick to fasten the arming wire on the belly rack, but I got the hang of it early in the game so I usually attached all the arming wires for our flight.

If a mission were scrubbed, we always removed the bomb load unless we got instructions to the contrary. We *never* left them on overnight. We never knew from one mission to the next what our bomb load might be. If we left bombs on at night, the mission for the next morning might require a completely different type of bomb and crucial time would be lost while we were changing. The Japanese found this out to their sorrow at the Battle of Midway when their bombers were caught on carrier decks while trying to change from bombs to torpedoes.

Targets and bombing techniques varied, so we had to use different types of bombs. Our standard was the five-hundred-pound GP. The 47 carried one under each wing. They were cylindrical in shape and tapered at both ends to streamline them. They consisted of a steel outer shell and were filled with TNT or some other stable explosive. They required a more sensitive explosive (fuse) to set them off.

Both the nose and tail of a GP bomb had little threaded cylindrical recesses in them about four or five inches deep and perhaps two inches in diameter. We screwed fuses into them to detonate the TNT when the bomb hit the target. Nose fuses projected about an inch from the surface of the bomb, while the tail fuse protruded out well over a foot.

Fuses had little propellers and a rigid piece which projected out from the main body. A cotter key connecting the prop and the rigid piece prevented the propeller from turning. These fuses were preset and we couldn't change them in the field. If a mission was changed from a dive-bombing mission to a skip bombing, we had to change fuses. For dive bombing, we used an instantaneous fuse, and for skip bombing, we used a forty-five second delay so that the plane could escape the blast after dropping its bombs.

After the bombs were loaded and the fuses were in place, we removed the cotter key and replaced it with an arming wire which had a ring in the center. We threaded the wire through the hole in the little prop and through the stationary part as well, and then put a fahnstock clip at the end of the wire to prevent it from pulling through the prop. We placed the ring of the arming wire in the arming hook on the bomb rack. The same procedure applied to both types of fuses.

The pilot had the option of dropping his bombs armed, so that they would explode, or safe so that they would not. To arm his bombs, he pulled a little toggle switch in the cockpit. This prevented the arming wire from pulling free from the rack when the bomb fell,. As it fell the prop was free to turn and finally it unscrewed and flew off, exposing the firing pin of the bomb. When the bomb hit, the firing pin was driven into a very sensitive explosive, such as mercury fulminate, which detonated. Since this detonation was not strong enough to set off the mass of TNT, a booster charge was placed just above the mercury. When the mercury detonated, it set off the booster charge which in turn set off the main explosive.

The fuse at the top of the bomb, surrounded by the fins, was over a foot long as mentioned earlier. This distance was necessary in order to drive a striker forward by inertia when the bomb hit. The striker set off the mercury fulminate and the same chain reaction occurred.

If, for some reason, the pilot wished to jettison his bombs without their going off, he set his toggle on "safe" when he pulled the release. Then the arming wire went with the bomb, preventing the little props from rotating and then flying off.

This Rube Goldberg arrangement was far from perfect. Chemicals have a mind of their own and sometimes refused to cooperate and blow up. TNT was very bad in this respect. Some bombs didn't explode when they were supposed to, and others did the opposite. In his book, *The History of the U.S. Air Forces*, David Anderson graphically states just how serious this situation was. I quote him: "Perhaps as many as twelve percent of the bombs never detonated, a chronic problem that plagued both the USAAF and the RAF."

This averaged out to one out of eight bombers going through hell just to drop duds. Twelve percent is an appalling statistic, and I wonder why nothing was done about it. Was it because we dropped so many bombs that one out of eight being duds was of small consequence? I imagine our squadron's percentage was the same, which was very discouraging when one considered the danger that our flyers underwent to drop them.

I imagine the Germans had similar trouble, since on my visit to London, I saw holes in the ground from which duds had been removed. The most noteworthy of these being the big one in St. Paul's Cathedral. I heard that some of the German fuses consisted of a strong acid that was supposed to eat its way through a metal barrier and then set off the bomb. These must have been particularly spooky for the bomb disposal crews.

I often wonder how many unexploded bombs still remain undetected in Germany and other areas of occupied Europe. I know that the British are still finding some German duds and we dropped many more bombs on Europe than the Germans did on Britain. Duds were difficult to detect, since they plowed some ten feet into the ground and the hole they made was about eighteen inches in diameter. These small holes were quickly filled in by the weather. With our record of twelve percent duds, it is almost certain that a lot of them remain to be discovered.

In addition to our bread-and-butter five-hundred pound GPs, we had thousand pounders which were identical with the GPs except for weight. Then we had such exotics as white phosphorus, napalm, fragmentation bombs, or "frag bombs" as we called them. Occasionally, we loaded armor-piercing bombs when we were attacking concrete pillboxes or very sturdy bridges. They were similar to our GPs except they were narrower, had a thicker steel jacket and had a sharp point on the nose which enabled them to penetrate the target before exploding.

We used several methods to drop bombs, each of which required a different type of fuse. For wide areas such as marshaling yards, pilots dropped their bombs from level flight and we used instantaneous fuses. When required to knock out a bridge, they dive-bombed in order to be as accurate as possible in hitting such a small target. After bomb release, they sped away rapidly so that once again instantaneous fuses sufficed.

However, if the target was a fortification having an impervious roof or a cave-like structure, pilots came in very low and horizontal so that they could skip their bombs into the structure. The plane was directly over the target when the bomb hit, so we had to use delayed fuses to avoid our plane being caught in the ensuing explosion.

After dropping their bombs, the pilots put their racks on "safe" so that the arming wire dropped off. This prevented it from flailing around and perhaps getting caught in one of the control surfaces.

The meanest substance in our formidable arsenal was napalm, a jelly-like substance made from gasoline, powdered aluminum, and a rubber-based gelatinous substance. This goo was poured into a two-hundred-fifty gallon belly tank. We loaded it on the belly rack, tightened the stabilizing bolts so it wouldn't wobble in flight, and fused it so it would ignite on contact with the ground. Since it had no stabilizing fins, it tumbled as it fell and ruptured as soon as it hit the target. The gunk exploded with a spectacular blaze. It not only burned fiercely but consumed much of the surrounding oxygen, and many of its victims died by asphyxiation. Its worse characteristic was that it clung to whatever it hit. If it happened to splash on an individual or a tank, there was no possible way to remove it.

Napalm was not suited for knocking out bridges, so we didn't use it while stationed in England. It was very effective against forts, pill boxes, and heavily armored vehicles which were impervious to our caliber-fifty ammo. Thus, we used lots of it to help the Third Army take the city of Metz which was surrounded by many underground forts.

White phosphorus bombs weighed one hundred pounds and were so small that we had to make special adjustments to the racks on the few occasions we had to load them, since our racks were designed for the five-hundred-pound GPs. While we did put fuses on them, they exploded spontaneously when exposed to air. The purpose of the fuse was to make certain that the bomb case ruptured and exposed the white phosphorus to oxygen. They exploded with a spectacular flash and emitted a dense cloud of white smoke. They inflicted horrible, deep wounds on their victims. Once ablaze the only way to extinguish them was to deprive them of oxygen.

I think that these bombs were the forerunners of napalm and that the latter really replaced them. This led me to believe that we dropped them more or less to get rid of them. While white phosphorus bombs did remove oxygen from the air, they were small, didn't cling to fortifications as napalm did, and didn't burn nearly as long or as hot.

Next on our list of treasures were frag bombs. They were twenty-five pound beauties made up of high explosive surrounded by a helix made up of brittle steel that appeared like a tightly coiled spring. They came in clusters of twelve. The container was so designed that it broke in midair and scattered the bombs over a wide area. They came with fuses similar to the ones we used on the other bombs. Each bomb had its own little prop and its own cotter key which we removed before takeoff. We always retained these cotter keys until we knew for certain that the bombs had been dropped. Occasionally, the planes didn't drop them and if they landed with the canister still attached, it was vital that all of them be replaced. These fuses were designed to set the bombs off on contact with the ground. Since they each had fins, they struck the ground vertically and scattered razor sharp bits of steel in all directions. Some even came with springs attached so that they sprang six feet in the air and then exploded. We never used these in our outfit, but many others did. The regular ones were very effective against troop concentrations or tightly-packed truck convoys. They were also effective against enemy soldiers sheltered by forests and the like. The Germans were skilled in concealment, so it was anybody's guess just how effective they were when dropped on forested areas. They certainly worked well in the routs of the German armies in Normandy and at the conclusion of the Battle of the Bulge. We were fortunate that none of these bomb clusters ever hung up.

Our last type were leaflet bombs, commonly known as "bullshit bombs." Leaflets were put in a large canister with a small charge of black powder in the bottom. When dropped, the powder went off and scattered the leaflets on all directions. The pilots hated them because they had to risk their lives to drop toilet paper on a formidable adversary. They were a real nuisance to load, since we had to put wood slats between the bomb and the stabilizing lugs to prevent them from wobbling in flight. One of our guys understood German and he read the contents of one of the leaflets to us. We chuckled at the idea that any of our tough opponents would be swayed by these blandishments. What a relief they must have been to the haggard German soldiers who dreaded the sight of our fighters when toilet paper dropped into their laps instead of death-dealing bombs.

A typical day in England consisted of a morning mission with a take-off between seven and nine o'clock. We usually loaded two five-hundred-pound GP bombs since our targets were bridges, etc. When the planes returned, we reloaded the guns and then put on two more GP's. The afternoon flight usually took off before two P.M. because all planes had to be home well before nightfall.

If a bomb hung up and fell off on the runway during landings, it was the unpleasant job of the ordinance department to defuse it. The head of the department, Tech Sergeant Feuer, felt that it was his duty to do the honors in this respect. While in England, he must have defused about twenty-five bombs. None of us felt that this was particularly heroic until we heard a explosion at a nearby airbase, the result of a bomb falling off a landing plane and exploding. Feuer was awarded the Soldier's Medal for his efforts which he really deserved.

All missions from England were over Occupied France and initially were close to the west coast. As time went on and all nearby targets were destroyed, we had to range further afield. This meant that we had to use auxiliary gas tanks which we armorers hung on the belly rack. The mechanics then made the necessary connections to the fuel system. They used a glass tube for this purpose which broke when the tank was released. When the pilots used all the gas in the tank, it was jettisoned. It was also jettisoned if the Luftwaffe appeared, since this gas not only slowed the plane and interfered with its flight characteristics but also because it became a torch when hit. For safety's sake, it was never used on takeoff, but the pilots switched it on as soon as they could once they were airborne.

Our complete load of two five-hundred pounders and thirty-two hundred rounds of caliber-fifty ammo per plane added some thirteen hundred pounds weight to each plane and increased the takeoff distance. Our runway at Christchurch was sufficient for this load, but things got a little squeaky when we added a belly tank or loaded thousand pounders instead of our usual five hundreds.

Correct fusing was a matter of life and death. We had one case when a plane was not fused correctly. This occurred when a level flight was scheduled and bombs were fused accordingly. The flight was delayed and one of the armorers in our flight asked to go to lunch. He was granted permission and took off to eat. The flight was delayed and then was changed to a skip bombing mission. The rest of us changed fuses to forty-five second delay, but we forgot about the other plane until after it took off. When the armorer involved returned and found out what had occurred, he quickly notified his flight chief who in turn notified headquarters. The pilot was told of the situation and dropped his bombs from a safe altitude. At first there was talk about busting the poor armorer but the pilot would have none of it. He was grateful that the armorer had acted as he did. This was really our fault. It was our obligation to change fuses for him while he was at lunch. It was a lesson cheaply learned. From then on, we made certain that this did not happen again.

Before we changed our faulty bomb racks, we had the misfortune to lose Captain Joe Marr, the most respected pilot in our squadron. According to his companions, he skip bombed a small fort. One of his bombs hung up for an instance then fell off and exploded as he pulled out of his run. Fortress and plane both disappeared in a huge ball of orange fire. We felt that we had lost an old and valued friend and an excellent pilot. Whenever we lost a flyer, we realized our own mortality and just how tenuous our hold on life could be. Death came with the territory and all our pilots knew it.

Our main purpose was to furnish ground support for the armies who were to invade the continent after they crossed the channel. The P-47 was ideal for this purpose. It had lots of firepower and was fast and rugged. While a specialized plane such as the German Stuka or the Douglas Dauntless were better dive bombers, they were virtually helpless against enemy fighters. The P-47 was a very good dive bomber and could hold its own with any fighter plane the Axis could put in the air as well. This was especially true when we got the newer model with the teardrop canopy and the paddle prop.

I sat in the cockpits of both the German Stuka and the Me109 fighter after the war. They were comfortable and the sticks handled very well. The pilot in these planes did not sit upright in the cockpit but put his feet almost straight forward, with his knees slightly bent so the cockpit was more compact than those on our ships. I was surprised that this position was quite comfortable for the short time I spent in the cockpit, but I imagine it would have taken our pilots some time to be comfortable in this position on long flights.

The real virtue of the P-47 was its ability to take terrific punishment and still bring its pilot back in one piece. All these virtues added up to its being the finest fighter in the war in my opinion. The P-51 Mustang may have been a slightly better pursuit ship, but it was not designed for ground support; the '47 did both superbly.

The Germans were strong on ground support aircraft and this support was an important reason for their early success in the war, but they neglected to design or use any strategic bombers, which was an important reason for their defeat in the Battle of Britain. Charles De Gaulle mentions this ground support capability when he stated in his memoirs:

"In March 1935, Goering announced that the Reich was providing itself with a powerful air force and that it would include, besides many interceptors, numerous bombers and *a strong force of divebombers... the German armored mass, supported by the airforce could quickly demolish our defenses and produce among our population a panic from which it would not recover.*"

This is exactly what happened in 1940.

Since we seldom flew escort and then only for medium bombers such as the B-26, the only bombers attached to the Ninth Air Force, we had few chances for aerial combat. As previously mentioned, it was every pilot's dream to become an ace by shooting down five enemy planes. None of our pilots even approached this number, although some of those in one of the other squadrons who had done some combat flying in another area may have attained five kills.

Each squadron was physically separated from the others in order to minimize the risk of damage due to enemy action. However, many of our missions were flown as a group, that is, all three squadrons would attack the same target. This represented a formidable amount of firepower, some forty-eight planes, each with eight machine guns.

War was an expensive operation and we lost quite a few planes. Most were to anti-aircraft fire but pilot error and equipment failure also took their toll. We had our share of runaway props where the propeller control failed and it kept turning faster and faster until it either flew off or the engine froze. In either case, the pilot had to make an emergency landing or bail out.

In Normandy some German Me109s jumped our guys and shot down three of them, our worst day in the entire war. It was a grim reminder to us that the Luftwaffe, for all its troubles, could not be taken for granted.

While any type of combat flying was not for the fainthearted, I think that flying ground support was probably the most dangerous.

Chapter Twelve
Personnel

Give me some men who are stout-hearted men.
—Victor Herbert

We were part of the 405th Fighter Group which consisted of three squadrons, the 509th, the 510th, and ours, the 511th. Our group in turn was attached to the 22nd Tactical Air Command which was higher up the chain of command than I could comprehend.

The commander of a group was always a pilot and all three squadron commanders were as well. Squadron commanders were usually majors, although we once had a light colonel for our boss. Group had its own administrative staff, as did each squadron. Group had no planes of its own since the only pilot was the commander. When he wished to fly on a mission, he chose one of the squadrons and they furnished him a plane.

Group commander appeared to me to be selected for his administrative and strategic abilities rather than for his skill as a pilot. The squadron commanders were always good flyers and leaders. From what I observed, the group commander flew less than the standard pilot while the squadron commanders usually flew the same amount. All pilots were required to fly at least four hours per month to qualify for flight pay, which was in addition to their base pay.

When the group commander chose to fly, he had to break up a combination of flyers who flew together on many missions. His experience made up for his lack of familiarity with his wingman. He also flew the same plane in each squadron which aided in discounting his unfamiliarity with the flight habits of the other pilots. I didn't know how often the group commander flew with the other squadrons but he never seemed to fly much with our squadron and he never flew in my plane. Being human, they probably favored a particular squadron and flight.

The chief responsibility of the group commander was administrative and tactical, that is, making sure that the squadrons were doing their job. They were veterans with lots of experience, and perhaps combat flying had lost much of its appeal to them.

As mentioned, squadrons were physically isolated from each other for reasons of military safety, even though we used the same runway and flew missions together. We enlisted men had very little contact with our peers of the other squadrons. We did use each others' transportation to and from town, and once in a blue moon we might watch a big USO show together.

Prior to a mission, each squadron had a briefing to discuss the aims of the mission and the duties of each pilot. Although each flight had a permanent leader, other pilots were often selected as squadron or flight leaders for individual missions, so most of them had the opportunity to lead the entire squadron. This developed a sense of responsibility in the individual pilot and prepared them to take over in case of emergency.

Since all missions were flown over enemy territory and the pilots broke off into flights of four after releasing their bombs to hunt up "targets of opportunity", they had lots of opportunity to gather valuable information about enemy troop displacements, etc. They were debriefed after every mission and any information of value was passed on to the proper department for evaluation.

Our squadron was similar to any other fighting unit in the army. It consisted of two entities, line personnel who did the fighting, and the staff who performed all the support functions. We had about fifty officers, most of whom were pilots and some two hundred and fifty enlisted men. Pilots, mechanics, armorers, and radio technicians were line personnel.

All other elements were staff. They existed to keep us going. This group consisted of squadron administration, the supply department, ordinance, communications, medical services, and the mess department. Line folk worked directly on the planes while the staff members remained in camp.

Our three hundred men, including pilots, enabled us to put sixteen planes in the air at one time. This amounted to about eighteen men per plane. We only got planes off the ground; they still had no objectives. Selecting targets was the function of Tactical Air Command with the assistance of infantry observers from the army we supported. When these personnel are added to our squadron, the number needed to support a single plane rose to over thirty. In other words, it took a lot of people to make a single mission possible.

One characteristic of the air force was the stratification of personnel by craft. Although I had many friends who were not armorers, I spent most of my leisure time with my fellow armorers. This was true of each craft. Of course I was close to the crew chief and his assistant on K4-M while we were on the line, but after hours, they went their way and I went mine. This was only natural. Members of each craft had something in common which others did not share. Much of our off-duty conversation concerned our work, which was Greek to outsiders. Hence, it was difficult to make friends in other departments.

At first I thought that this insular behavior was strictly military, but when I returned to college, I found that the student body at Haverford College was split into two groups which were the so-called "athletes", who were good time Charlies, and the "grinds" who allegedly spent all their time in class or in the library. I had friends in both groups, but this was more the exception than the rule. There was a strict line between officers and enlisted men. The army was much like TV's *Upstairs, Downstairs* in this respect. We all accepted this division without a second thought.

As a Catholic, I met others from different departments. They in turn introduced to me their friends. Although we were only about twenty percent or less of the outfit, every department had at least one Catholic, so meeting them at Mass gave me an entree to every department in the squadron. I enjoyed meeting different people, particularly those from different backgrounds than mine.

I had few contacts who were not line personnel. One was a switchboard operator, John J. Higgins. He filled me in on some of the inside dope that was not confidential but was still not for publication. I also got to know Sam Weinberg, our company clerk since he took care of the duty roster and my name appeared on it all too often.

I had friends who were static chasers, mechanics, and a couple in the ordinance department. After the planes took off, I used to wander around and talk to guys from the other flights and from the other crafts, but I never left the line except for meals or at the end of the day, because I had to be available in case of an emergency. In the evenings, I spent my time reading, playing penny ante poker, or shooting the breeze in our tent with my tentmates.

We lived in a relaxed atmosphere. We had no dress code other than all our clothes had to be GI. I got a Cleveland Indians baseball cap from my father and put it on and started out toward the line. Our administration officer saw me and said it looked great on me, but I couldn't wear it except in the enlisted man's day room. I tried wearing it then but got so many comments that I put it away. Some of the guys grew beards, and many of them were dressed in rags—GI rags, that is. It never occurred to any of us to shine our shoes and no one ever inspected our tent or our equipment. However, we lived in such close quarters that we kept our individual areas neat out of respect for our tentmates.

One of the beauties of the air force was its informality. We didn't march, had no retreat in the evenings, nor any of the other bits and pieces that other branches of the army had to put up with. Our job was to keep our planes in good condition so our pilots could do their job. That was what our existence was all about. We had neither the time nor the patience for chicken shit drills which would just have interfered with our duties.

Enlisted personnel had some social contact on the line with the pilots who flew their plane but virtually none with any ground officers except in the line of duty. Our ordinance officer played volleyball with us in Tampa, but that was the extent of any joint social activities until after that war.

Many of us thought that most of the department heads were unnecessary. There was a lot of truth to the story about a veteran colonel discussing the setting of a fifty-six foot flagpole. When the colonel asked the young officer how he would go about it, the correct answer was "I'd ask a sergeant to do it." The armament department was commanded by a First Lieutenant and there is no question in my mind that things went better when he didn't interfere.

We also had a master sergeant, a tech sergeant, and four staff sergeants, each of whom was in charge of one of our four flights. Those of us in charge of planes were either buck sergeants or corporals. Our Browning machine guns were virtually trouble -free and we knew our jobs, so we seldom sought or required outside assistance.

On the rare occasions when something stumped one of us, we first asked our flight chief and if he couldn't help, we sought help from either our master sergeant or his assistant. It didn't take us long to realize that Tech Sergeant Lake was the guy with all the answers. Lake was a real whiz, who despite his outward taciturn and seemingly caustic attitude was not only a nice guy but extremely competent and dedicated as well. He was never stumped and was a godsend to me on at least one occasion.

After my original K4-M was replaced, I couldn't get the guns on the right wing to fire. All of us in our flight were stumped so I sent out an SOS for Lake. He ambled over from his tent to my hardstand. I had quite logically confined my investigations to the wing itself. Not so Lake. He went straight to the cockpit and almost immediately put his finger on the problem which he left for me to correct. I was impressed with his ability to find the trouble so quickly and told him so. In his usual self-deprecating manner, he told me that he had just read about the possibility of this particular problem occurring in an army manual only the previous day. It was typical of his thoroughness and dedication that he poured over the slue of technical literature that proliferated about anything mechanical in the army. Most of these rags were poorly written and incomprehensible to the ordinary mortal and frequently thrown away unread. Not Lake. Nothing escaped his eagle eye and thus it was to him we turned when we were stumped. This was the only time during the entire war that I was unable to solve my own problems. However, it was a nice feeling to know that I had someone of Lake's stature to bail me out if I ever got stuck.

We never contacted our department officer since he was of little help and we liked to let sleeping dogs lie. What he didn't know wouldn't hurt him, and more importantly, wouldn't hurt us. He made only one trip to my plane during the entire war. This occurred when Captain Sams flew my plane and had to abort his mission due to engine trouble. Although I am not certain, I thought that there was a strict law that all bombs jettisoned for any reason had to be dropped "safe."

On his way back, Sams evidently decided to "bomb" the Atlantic Ocean with the two five-hundred pounders he was toting. Instead of putting them on "safe" when he jettisoned them, he evidently decided to see what kind of a splash they would make when they exploded in the water. We could hear the sound of the explosion before his plane came into view. I was already aware that he was aborting his mission, so when I heard the explosions, I wanted to put on an asbestos suit. For some reason, after he landed, he claimed that he had put his racks on "safe."

I was tempted to ask him if he had sunk a sub but I'm glad I didn't because all kinds of hell quickly broke loose. Out came the overhead, including our worthy lieutenant, scratching their heads on why the bombs had exploded when put on "safe." Of course they came up with zero because in my humble opinion, they missed the obvious—Sams was a devil-may-care pilot and it should have been apparent to all that he had wanted either to kill some fish or see what exploding five hundred pound bombs did to innocent ocean water. Our lieutenant had to do something, so he ordered me to clean my already immaculate bomb racks and give him a written report when I had done so. When he exited from my hardstand, it was aloha to him for the balance of the war.

Personally, I couldn't see any harm in bombing the ocean if a guy wanted to and I would have done it myself; but I would have jettisoned them farther out to sea where no one would have been the wiser.

In England, we lived in six man pyramidal tents. Since they were roughly fifteen by fifteen, we had a cot on either side of the entrance, one on each side and two in the back. We had a small wood-burning stove in the center with a stove pipe that stuck out the top of the center of the tent. This gave us little room to move around.

We lived with the same people for months at a time which required lots of give and take. My tentmates were Bob Loitz, a great big hombre from Akron, Ohio; Harvey Hallenbeck from Harrisburg, Pennsylvania; Leonard Hitchman from Seattle, Washington; Tom Harrison from Indianapolis, Indiana; and Ernie White, from Los Angeles. We were a diverse lot from diverse areas and backgrounds, and perhaps for this reason we got along very well.

Bob Loitz excelled in hyperbole, a common failing or virtue (?) in the army where it is impossible for anyone to verify another's story. He was a nice guy, nonetheless and I, for one, enjoyed his stories. He was in his mid-twenties but we calculated that he had crowded over twice that much time on his various and sundry adventures.

He could play rough and had some of the characteristics of a bully.

The first week in our tent, he started pounding me on the shoulder. He had a heavy hand and I realized that this could go on forever if I didn't take some action.

After he had hit me for the umpteenth time, I told him sharply to knock it off or I'd punch him out. I was taking a helluva chance, but a one-time thrashing was better than getting "playful" belts on the shoulder ad infinitum. Luckily, he regarded the idea of my punching him out as too ludicrous to take seriously although he was unsure as to whether I would try or not. He couldn't ignore my threat without losing face so he gave me one more stiff one on the shoulder to prove that he was unafraid. I was aware of his intention and let it pass. From then on, we had no troubles and like D'Mico of New Cumberland fame, he was a big guy and therefore a good person to know.

About ten years after the war, I was passing through Akron and decided to give Bob a call. I intended to hoist a few with him, perhaps have dinner and spend the night there. We met in a nice hotel lobby, proceeded to the bar and had a drink and he tried to sell me an insurance policy. There are not many people I dislike more than insurance salesmen so I told him that I had an early appointment in Cleveland next morning. I shook his hand and departed forthwith. We never met again.

Harvey Hallenbeck and I played ping pong at the USO in Walterboro where we lived in the barracks and I enjoyed his company. However, when we lived six in a small tent, it was a different matter. Some faults are easy to overlook while others grate on us. Harvey did this to me and I am certain that this was reciprocated to a certain extent but not near enough to upset the harmony of our tent. He was the consummate army politician and one of the two of us young people to make staff sergeant. He was very thin, almost emaciated-looking, and a bit of a hypochondriac which I think he played to the hilt. For this reason, he was taken from the line and placed in armament headquarters where he used his considerable skill as a politician to make staff sergeant. At this stage in my life, I was a naive purist and very critical of what was colloquially known as "brown-nosers"—those who butter up the power to get ahead. I believed that all promotions should have been made on merit alone so I never took into consideration the fact that without a little hype, no one would know whether you were doing a good job or not. Harvey was light years ahead of me in knowing the facts of life. As I look back over the years, I think that while Harvey may have overdone his hype, I certainly didn't do enough of it and sins of commission are not only much better than those of omission but are also more successful.

Harvey was well educated and a good conversationalist, so I enjoyed the rare moments when we pulled guard duty together. At the end of the war while we awaited transportation home, we buried any differences we might have had and played a lot of bridge together.

Ernie White was an authentic character with a dash of Jewish dry wit. He was a laid-back sleepy sort with a unique way of screwing things up. We had an oilburner in our tent which operated on hundred octane gas. All we had to do was turn on the gas supply, toss in a match, and our tent heated up in jiffy. White was usually the last one up, so this chore was performed by others.

After weeks of flawless performance, Ernie lit it one morning and the damn thing started to spout flames five feet into the air. We were lucky to turn it off before our tent burned down. After things settled down, some one else lit it—no trouble. We never knew what White had done but once burnt, twice smart. We never let him light it again.

He was a nice guy nonetheless and all of us liked him. He could be very funny on occasion. One time a bunch of the boys were discussing the cleanliness or lack thereof of French tarts, and one of them remarked that they used a cold water douche and "a cold water douche don't amount to a piss." Ernie's comment was, "It does if you drink it." The other guy just raised his voice to heaven.

Ernie didn't lack for courage. It was his ship that took off with the wrong fuses and he acted promptly and courageously in telling the proper people which probably saved the pilot's life. As I said before, this whole incident was not his fault.

Ernie made a sloth look like Jessie Owens, which drove us nuts at times, but he was a warmhearted harmless soul so we accepted him as he was. I think he bothered Tom Harrison more than the rest of us because Tom was very gung-ho.

Tom Harrison was tall and handsome and he knew it. He was also a first-rate armorer with lots of original ideas. Tom kept to himself most of the time, but several times a week, he and Bob Loitz exchanged fantasies. When they were at it, nothing suffered but the truth. Hitch and I spent many a pleasant hour listening to them trying to outadventure each other. It was too bad that no Chaucer or Homer was there to chronicalize what could well have been The Great American Epics.

When Tom arrived at Tampa and we had nothing to do, he made himself scarce. We never knew where he was, where he went or what he did— if anything. We thought that he was a gold brick first class. In South Carolina, when we got our P-47s, he worked on his own plane and kept to himself. In short, he was a hard guy to get to know and I never knew him until we got to Normandy as I shall relate. He was the most relaxed guy in our tent—I never saw him lose his cool the whole time we shared the same tent.

When we arrived in England, Tom made his move. All our bomb releases were just toggle switches on the floor of the cockpit and it was difficult for the pilots to pull them and keep their eyes on their targets at the same time. Tom came up with a lever type of release which solved this problem beautifully. Our whole squadron followed suit in short order, and a nagging problem was solved. He also designed the hundred octane heater for our tent, which worked perfectly and which went a long way to make our dull French winter tolerable. His invention was foolproof, except when White tried to ignite it. He was a great problem solver and therefore much respected by the enlisted brass of our department. Since he got along with them so well and could talk their language, he spent much of his time with them. I always found the lesser lights who were more my age to be more simpatico than these older guys, but to each his own.

Tom also thought that he was God's gift to women and I could not prove otherwise. Every time we had an occasion to meet women, Tom always came away with the cream of the crop. This was particularly true in France and in Switzerland where his type of looks and personality were particularly appreciated.

I didn't know Tom very well until the Battle of Falaise, which I will go into later. Our squadron had flown about a dozen missions one day and my plane was on all of them. They landed about ten o'clock at night after the last one and I had to prepare it for the morning. I think that Tom's plane had been hit on an early mission and was disabled. He voluntarily came over at ten and helped me clean, oil, and reload my guns for the next day. We worked together from about ten P.M. until about midnight. During this time, we chatted about personal things and I got to know a little about him for the first time. However, he never got that confidential with me again.

In my life, I have met six men who were kindred spirits and lifetime friends. One of these was Leonard Hitchman, tentmate extraordinaire from Seattle. Although we went through armament school at the same time, we didn't meet until we arrived at Tampa and were assigned to the same flight. Here we quickly realized that we were kindred spirits. We took almost weekly trips together to Clearwater on our day off and enjoyed swimming in the warm waters of the Gulf of Mexico. In South Carolina, we went to town together and made some trips to Charleston as well.

However, it was when we went overseas that we really hit our stride together. We spent our free time in England visiting some of the historic sites in London. He was more reserved than I and served as a welcome leavening to my exuberance. Coming from the Northwest, he was an avid outdoorsman and thus didn't have the cultural background that I had, so we enjoyed going to places like Brussels, Paris, and London and a host of others together. This was, of course, our first trip to Europe, but I had some idea of the historic and cultural background of many of the places we visited and I filled him in on what I knew. There was much that I didn't know and we had lots of fun learning together. Our big adventure was our attempt to hitchhike to Cologne, several days after its capture by the First Army. More on that later.

Whenever either of us had a hundred-hour inspection, the other would jump in and help. He was more conscientious than I and so he worked longer than I. When I realized how reliable our Browning machine guns were, I decided that some work I had been doing was unnecessary, so I discontinued it. Hitch continued and his dedication paid off when he was promoted to buck sergeant.

After we were discharged, we have gotten together every four or five years and reminisce on the fact, "that times were tough in the ETO." One of the beauties of our relationship is that our wives get along very well also.

There were a host of others whom I knew and liked. Francis Murphy from Highland Falls, New York, was one. He was the only mechanic with whom I was close. He was a lot of fun to kid around with and we shared a cup of spirits at the EM club on occasion. As mentioned already, John J. Higgins, switchboard operator who had previously been a fireman in New Britain, Connecticut, was also a good pal. "Hig," as we called him, was an emaciated-looking individual who was a real leader and became manager of the best softball team in our group. Working on the switchboard gave him access to all kinds of secret but unclassified information which he passed on to his friends. He was very religious and visited the local parish priests whenever we made a move. Sometimes he took me along to meet them after he had made the initial contact. I remember two of these meetings well, one at Picauville in Normandy and the other at Ghenk in Belgium.

Gerald Mackey, from Santa Maria in California, was another "C" flight armorer and good friend. He was the first Hispanic I had ever met and we hit it off immediately. We roamed around together on the line at Drew Field at Tampa, blowing on pitot tubes and creating all kinds of mischief. He was my accomplice in trying to coax four hundred miles an hour out of a standing Douglas dive bomber. We were good friends since we enjoyed life and liked to clown around. He was the first Hispanic with whom I was ever close since they were virtually unknown in Philly at this time. We went to town occasionally in the States but not overseas, where he started courting the gals.

Carl Hadra, from somewhere in Texas and an armorer from a different flight was another good friend. Carl was blind in one eye and I never could figure out how he got in the army. I think that he enlisted early in the war when the army was not so selective. He did a good job on the line and was fun to play penny-ante poker with. He, Harvey Hallenbeck, a gent named Brumlevy, and I played bridge together when the war was over and we had lots of free time, cooling our heels in various transfer camps. His lively comments on anything and everything kept the rest of us from becoming too serious.

We had an eccentric by the name of Raymond from some hamlet in New Jersey. We called him "Bugs" because of his protruding eyes. He was one of our more conscientious armorers who disarmed his guns every night. We all did this at first but a hurry-mission one morning caught us flatfooted with our guns unloaded. The mission scheduled for the day had to be put on hold until we all completed loading them. This took at least a half an hour and some of the pilots were very unhappy and we all got a nifty ass chewing from the squadron commander. I decided that this would never happen again to me and from then on, I left my guns cocked overnight so my only worry was loading and fusing bombs.

Raymond, however, persisted in unloading his so he could check firing pin release in the morning. This operation consisted of cocking the guns and then pulling the trigger on the stick in the cockpit and then checking each gun to see if the firing pin was visible, i.e. if it had released.

One morning, he cocked the guns in the right wing which faced in my direction, performed his check and then proceeded to load the guns. I saw him disappear over the fuselage to the other wing. I presumed that he was loading them also. To my horror, he went into the cockpit to check the release on the left wing, completely forgetting he had already loaded the right one. The peace and tranquillity of the line was interrupted by the staccato sound of four caliber fifties spewing slugs into the air. Naturally he froze so at least fifty rounds from each gun flew into space. This woke up everybody within a quarter of a mile in every direction from his plane and afforded some welcome excitement on an otherwise placid morning. Of course, it brought out the brass who had nothing better to do and they swarmed around poor Raymond and his plane like so many angry hornets.

K-4M, Thunderbird #One in Normandy. Next day a German 40mm shell hit it in the tail section and it barely limped home. It was replaced by a newer model P-47 with paddle prop.

Luckily the nose of the 47 sticks up in the air so no damage. The folks in a glider factory just across the runway were understandably upset as the bullets whizzed overhead. Bugs shot off so much ammo that it had to be replaced. Since this was not an easy job, and speed was essential, as the pilots were on their way to the planes, Hitch and I pitched in to help him. From that moment on, he joined the club of those who left their guns cocked overnight.

As I understand it, Bugs stayed in the Army after the war and flew small planes such as the Piper Cub which was used as a spotter plane by the infantry.

It was in St. Dizier that the greatest character of the 511th joined us. One evening, Sgt. Sibley caught me and introduced me to an unfamiliar gent who turned out to be a newly arrived armorer; a burly lad named Miller. I was heading to the movies and invited him to join me. The show happened to be an undistinguished western in which Walter Brennan played a prominent part as the star's sidekick. In this masterpiece, Brennan always referred to his companion as "Bub."

After the show, I took Miller to the em club to introduce him to his fellow armorers. Since I had forgotten his first name, I introduced him as "Bub." I couldn't have done anything that would have pleased him more, and I became his friend for life. The name stuck, and I don't think anyone ever did learn his first name.

Bub was an expert checker player, easily beating the best we had. He took on eight at one time and thrashed them all. He stood in the middle of a circle of checker boards and turned from one to another and then made a move. He turned to the next board and did the same. In a few minutes, all eight of his opponents were beaten. Every time a new guy joined the outfit, his first duty was to take on Bub in checkers. Bub never lost.

I watched him wield his magic for a week or so and thought I had checkers figured out. I sought out a mechanic from Arkansas who was pretty good and challenged him. I won the first three of four games, and then he looked at me and said, "I know how you play. You won't win again." Sad but true, he took me every game from then on. He never told me 'till then that he had learned the game at a country store back in Arkansas, where the old folks played on cracker barrels. When he told me this, I grinned at him and said that he had cheated because he hadn't told me he was a pro. We both laughed. I shook his hand and bought him a beer.

Bub was, at best, a mediocre armorer who never had his own plane. This suited him to a tee since this gave him lots of opportunity to utilize his numerous talents as a businessman. He bought all our surplus cigarettes and other salable items and sold them to outsiders. We all knew that he was cleaning up this way, but none of us had any desire to join him. I have no idea how much he made, but I am certain that it was a bundle.

Every smoker sold cigarettes to civilians on occasion, when we were short, because they were more liquid than the script we had been issued as money. While this script was supposed to be completely liquid, it didn't appeal to the natives since it was completely different from the money already in circulation. So cigarettes became the universal medium of exchange. All we got for ours was perhaps a bottle of champagne, a small bottle of perfume, or a meal — never anything of consequence. We exchanged butts as a matter of convenience and not to get money to send home.

Bub was different. He jumped from one currency to another in a flash and somehow managed to exchange local money for U.S. bucks and send it home. This was not easy since the censors checked any amount of currency sent home with a person's pay to prevent black market operations. Bub was evidently far too smart for any censor. It was obvious that none of the brass in our squadron ever had an inkling of his activities.

His most daring exploit occurred when we were stationed near Hasselt, Belgium and had just received orders to move to Kitzingen, Germany. Bub must have had a large inventory of cigarettes which he couldn't move without detection. Also, there was no market for them in Germany since our no fraternization policy was strictly enforced. He faced not only a severe financial loss but a possible embarrassing inspection as well. Bub's answer was to go to the motor pool about midnight, "borrow" a jeep, load his wares on it, speed off to his contact in Brussels, make his deal, and then return before dawn. In retrospect, I am certain that there was some collaboration from someone in the motor pool because there were too many checks and counter checks for someone to take out a jeep without authority from squadron headquarters.

For some unknown reason, Bub liked me and always filled me in on his capers. He took some fearful risks, but I think he enjoyed them as part of the game.

In St. Dizier, France, I won a week's furlough in France. He asked me if I would sell it to him. At first I was inclined to accept, but then I realized that money could be gained at any time. Furloughs were a once in a lifetime opportunity, so I turned him down. Then he asked me if I would go to Paris, meet a contact he had there, and change a large illegal bill for him. He would give me half the proceeds. This was not for me, so he gave it to a cook who was going on furlough at the same time. Cookie agreed to exchange his bill. But on his return, he stated that he had taken it to the contact, given it to him, but then lost his nerve and ran without waiting for his money. There was no question in my mind that Cookie had appropriated all the swag, and I though Bub would be furious at this double cross. However, he mentioned his belief in Cookie's duplicity with no trace of rancor at all. Evidently he just reasoned that you win some and you lose some, and losing was just as much a part of the game as winning.

He was cold-blooded by nature and hated St. Dizier's miserable weather, so he wore his overcoat at times when the rest of us were comfortable in light jackets. He assured me that this was true even when he enjoyed the favors of St. Dizier's most desirable queens. Since he was on the plump side, this operation must have made an interesting sight.

Of course there were others in the outfit with whom I came in contact. Chief of these was Major John Eikenberry, for whom I had a great deal of respect. He and First Sergeant Sibley worked very well together. Several years ago, I obtained John's address in Pasadena, California. I contacted him and invited both him and his wife to have lunch with my wife and me. The lunch was a great success, and we had a fine time discussing personnel and our individual adventures while in Europe. I mentioned the supply clerk. But before I went any further, Ike mentioned that he was a good man. I put any opinions I had on the back burner. I could see how a man could easily appear as a good man to the executive officer of the squadron but as a pain in the ass to a flunky on the line. Beauty is the result of whose ox is gored. I also didn't mention our department officer since I am certain that Ike had no knowledge or interest in what took place on the line. The four of us were having such a good time that I didn't want to stir things up by mentioning picayune things that took place fifty years ago and probably meant little then and nothing now.

My wife got along so well with June Eikenberry, who was a charming soft-spoken woman, and John and I were old acquaintances, so during our visits, we have discussed the various personnel and rehashed our comings and goings. Despite the fact that he was top dog, and I was way down the ladder, it was surprisingly personal. I had trouble with two people and got along well with the rest. He mentioned a few that he wished he could have replaced.

The 511th had very competent em department heads. First Sergeant Sibley, the noncom in charge of all administration, had one of the toughest and most critical jobs in the outfit. The buck stopped with him. He had to pacify everybody and referee the jurisdictional disputes that arose between strong-minded department heads. He acted as a lightening rod, and by staying cool under all types of trying circumstances, he did a great job keeping us enlisted men on an even keel. He let all his department heads do their thing with a minimum of interference, and most importantly, he was an excellent contact between the officers and the ems.

Sibley liked to patrol the area occasionally, and I always ducked him because I was afraid that he might have some extracurricular activities such as KP on his mind. Despite my efforts in this regard, he caught me three times, and each one resulted in a good deal — one was a nifty jeep trip to Czechoslovakia.

154

Troy Robinson, whom I have mentioned previously, was an excellent cook and a good guy to pull KP for — if you had to pull KP. It was always an ordeal, but Troy was not a make-work chef as many others were. Most of them felt that it was their sacred duty to get the full measure of devotion out of the forced laborers who were assigned to his domain. We were lucky that this was not Troy's way. If he had no work for you, you could relax but couldn't leave the premises.

Our squadron was divided socially into four groups. The first were the pilots who put their lives on the line every time they took off. They were young, gung-ho, and liked to do their own thing without any restraints. Since they had so much responsibility and pressure, and had so little in common with the rest of us, they tended to associate with their fellow pilots. They loved to fly but were always aware that each mission could very well be their last. Our obligation was to make their job as easy and safe as possible. We took this responsibility very seriously.

Their only extraneous duty was an occasional night as Officer of the Day, i.e., taking charge of the guards. Since an individual pilot pulled OOD every six weeks or so, it was more of an inconvenience than a problem to them. I think that their constant preoccupation with flying gave them an unconscious feeling that any other duty was superfluous, and so they took their OOD duties rather lightly.

The second group were the ground officers. They consisted of Major Eikenberry, our executive officer, Captain Piland, his assistant, all department heads, the squadron doctor, and our Protestant chaplain.

Captain Baxter, squadron doctor, did a good job. He had been a pediatrician in civilian life but took to army life like a duck takes to water. He did keep banker's hours which was inconvenient for those of us who worked on the line. If one of us got really sick, he remained in camp until the doctor showed up. Those who were just uncomfortable loaded their ships for the morning mission and then reported to the medical tent. Most of those who were incapacitated were victims of vd, and the good doctor was not very sympathetic. He gave them a lecture and then usually let his medics give the necessary shots. This was fine since they got a lot of practice and were much better at it than the doc. I was fortunate. I only got sick once; another attack of nasal pharyngitis. He did his best to relieve me of my discomfort, but, like handling a common cold, all I could do was let it run its course.

Both our medics were excellent. They knew their jobs and performed them with the skill and compassion. I liked them both personally since they were literate and interesting conversationalists. I visited them on occasion after hours and got a kick out of the casual way they would leave their seats, load up a needle, tell the patient to drop his pants, stab him expertly in the rear end, and wipe off the wound without missing a word of the conversation.

One was an alcoholic — going on monumental benders about once every six weeks. After tying one on, he was terrified of falling out of bed, although he occupied the bottom bunk positioned a foot and a half from terra firma. He slept on the floor, naked as a jay bird in both winter and summer. Either he was immune to pneumonia, or the booze protected him because he never got sick. Nobody wanted to get a shot from him the day after he went on one of those benders. His hands shook like a leaf, and his breath was like that of a vulture. He seldom had anything to do. We all waited for his complete recovery. The first time this occurred, after I had joined the squadron, was in Tampa. I had just had my twentieth birthday a month or so previously and was not prepared to see a bare behind sticking out into space between my bunk and his. In the army, if it can happen, it will happen. The bizarre is an everyday occurrence.

Below the ground officers were the upper three graders., the staff, tech, and master sergeants. They were the backbone of the squadron. They were the enlisted department heads, the flight leaders, mechanic crew chiefs, the chief cook, our first sergeant, and the supply sergeant. Every enlisted man's goal was to make on of these grades, but we newcomers had very little chance since these positions were filled before we came on board. A few of my classmates at Buckley Field formed new outfits and were able to be tops. However, they had to train linger and missed out on a lot of overseas activity. Some never left the states at all.

Our upper graders were a close-knit group and were fine people. With very few exceptions, they were very competent. It still amazes me how a bunch of civilians, with so little experience, were able to perform all the highly technical operations necessary to keep our planes airworthy.

When our first batch of P-47s landed in England, our pilots detected something amiss with the water injection system in the engines. The engines of the P-47 were fitted with a system that allowed the pilot to inject water into the engine in such a way as to give it an extra burst of power for a short time. Every engine had to be checked, adjusted, and then rechecked to make certain that the system worked as specified. To check out the engine, the plane had to be in line of flight. This necessitated the construction of a ramp so that the tail of the plane could be raised. It was tied down securely, and then the engine was run at full speed, and the injection system checked. The engine was killed, the necessary adjustments made, and then it was rechecked. As I recall, the only thing that the mechanics had to go on was a small Air Force manual, written in obscure Armyese. The procedure was too complicated for the individual crew chiefs, so the department heads helped them out. Within two weeks, every engine was checked and ready to go. I have always thought that this was one of the greatest accomplishments made by our

156

ground crews during the entire war.

I invented a funny little wrench which solved an irritating problem for the mechanics, so I became a good friend of our mechanic flight chief. We used to talk together, on occasion, when the planes were aloft which is unusual in the class-conscience Army.

We armorers got along very well with our crew chiefs. After our initial clash back in Tampa, when we were scrimmaging some of our new tools on the antiques that masqueraded as warplanes, we had no problems. By the time we reached Walterboro, they realized how important our job was. After all there was little sense in getting a fighter plane to the scene of the crime if it had no bombs to drop or ammo to shoot up enemy equipment.

The fourth group were buck sergeants, corporals, and any men of lower rank who were last to join the outfit. If something scruffy had to be done — KP, guard duty, shoveling and hauling coke, just name it, — we were elected to do it. We were neither surprised nor resentful. We knew our fate from the moment we joined the outfit. A camaraderie existed among us. We stuck together, bent the rules when we could, and made out very well. We got enough to eat, were reasonably warm, and did our jobs with a minimum of interference.

The armed forces had many faults, but as a leavener of different ethnic backgrounds and religions, it was hard to beat. None of us were untouched by the fact that we had to work with people of different ethnic backgrounds and different religions; people who came from different parts of the country. We were all the better for the experience. We worked so closely together and were so dependent on each other that we had to ignore these differences in order to perform our jobs. The Army, however unintentional, proved that different types of people could work together in a common cause. Everybody was expected to do their share, and all responded accordingly.

The Army also afforded me my first exposure to Hispanics. Most of the many Californians in our outfit were Hispanic. They didn't consider themselves as "minorities" and neither did we. They were a little darker skinned than the rest of us, and most were Catholics, but that was all. They did their job as well as anyone else and were treated the same. No one thought otherwise. We lived in a simpler age and didn't take umbrage at every little offensive innuendo. We lived in an age when "A man's a man for a' that," to quote Bobby Burns.

Everyone took some good-natured kidding about his home state, his religion, or his ethnic background. No offense was meant or taken. All this went with the territory.

Some of our Hispanics were outstanding. Manuel Macedo, from some small burgh in California, was the best aircraft mechanic I ever met. He worked out all the technical problems we encountered adjusting the water injection system. The Pratt and Whitney engines on our 47s were not state of the art and the most powerful ever built until that time, but Macedo was never stumped. I hate to think how our outfit would have made out without him.

It was always tough to get an appointment with our squadron barber, Corporal Rosendo Rosales, but I still remember the relief I felt as great rolls of hair were sheared off my scalp. I think his regular job was chasing static which occupied him almost full time. Fortunately, he did manage to fit in some time to barber for the outfit. There may have been better barbers in the army, but he was more than adequate and was always near at hand when the mop on top was so long and thick that I couldn't stand it. Not only that, but his price was right. He took whatever was offered, which was usually fifty cents. I gave him a buck one time, and he told me it was too much. I replied that he could give me credit for my next haircut.

Heating our tents was a real problem. We scrounged for wood to heat them in England and ended up burning the fiberboard that came in our ammo boxes. This burned with a hot flame but didn't last long. Every night I wrapped my blanket around me but still was cold. I noticed that the others didn't suffer as I did. Suddenly I realized that they put as much insulation underneath themselves as they did on top. The cot was so thin that it was virtually useless for insulation. From then on, I emptied my barracks bag of all my clothing onto my cot and then used the blanket as a top cover. Things improved considerable. I was embarrassed that it took me so long to figure this out.

Fuel was even scarcer in France. At first we used the fiber board again and stoked the fire high just before we retired. This was a disaster because the fire soon went out, and the change from very hot to very cold was miserable. Finally Major Eikenberry got some coke for us. This didn't burn very hot, but it did last a long time, so we were not too cold.

The best thing about the coke was getting on the detail to pick it up. This involved a drive to Metz and back which used up almost the entire day. Most of our extracurricular work was a chore, but the coke run was fun. It broke up our routine and gave us a bird' eye view of the surrounding area.

Once we arrived at the coke plant, we shoveled it into burlap bags and loaded them onto our trucks. We took a break for lunch and then headed back. At camp, we dumped it onto a big pile near the supply tent where the supply sergeant could keep an eye on it. He watched like a hawk, so there was little chance to pilfer any.

In the middle of the winter, Tom Harrison came up with his hundred octane burner and we were set. We kept it on low during the night, so that we slept well, and then a volunteer got up about ten minutes before the rest of us and turned it up. When the rest of us got up, the tent was warm as toast. After we left for breakfast, we shut it off until evening. We were particularly grateful to have it on the many cold rainy days during the winter when our planes were weathered in. We were sure to have lots of company.

On one occasion, in the middle of November, the coke detail returned with wild stories about a Luftwaffe raid on a P-47 base adjacent to the coke plant. They reported that many planes and fuel trucks were blazing away all over the base. I was skeptical, but on the following week, I went on the detail and saw a whole bunch of tail sections of P-47s piled up in a corner of the base where they had been bulldozed a short time prior to our visit. I noticed several grotesque looking fuel trucks, minus tires, all over the field. There was no doubt that the Germans had conducted a very successful raid just prior to our arrival. Our guys were lucky that they had not arrived any sooner, or they might have become statistics as well. Our European Army newspaper, *Stars and Stripes*, noted that on this particular day, the Germans had lost ninety to our "less than ten." Who was kidding whom?

By this time, none of us placed any credence in Air Force statistics. We applied the old adage that "figures don't lie but liars figure." We had a cynical laugh or two at the numbers spouted forth by public relations. However, these hyperbolic figures really annoyed me. I considered all this crap a type of condescension on the part of the responsible party. Our pilots were doing a magnificent job, and the truth was impressive enough. They didn't need to have their results embellished by some public relations fat cat who had nothing better to do than use a multiplication table. Many claims were so preposterous that soon all claims were taken with a grain of salt. This was a grave injustice to those who were doing a thankless job and risking their lives to do so.

The absurdity of many claims were legendary. I imagine it compared with the Viet Nam body count. The enormous scope of the titanic air battles over Germany, on many of our bomber raids, made it difficult, if not impossible, to come up with accurate figures of German losses. In his book, *History of the U.S. Air Force*, David A. Anderson mentions on page 84, "the claims of German aircraft destroyed were consistently exaggerated."

Our B-17s flew in tight formation, so a German interceptor could easily have a dozen guns trained on it simultaneously, and each would claim the kill. Thus a single Kraut shot down could be counted as a dozen. This part was understandable, but no effort was made to ascertain the actual numbers shot down. At the same time, our losses were minimized. For example, on the day our guys saw the burning planes near Metz, *Stars and Stripes* pegged our losses at less than ten and the Germans at ninety-five. Either our counts were exaggerated, or the Germans were past masters at resurrecting downed planes and pilots. On my trip to Metz the following week, I had counted at least ten tail sections in one pile. What a way to run a railroad!

Chapter Thirteen
The Invasion of Normandy

France is invaded
—Napoleon Bonaparte

On the evening of June 5th, 1944, a tremendous armada of every type of bombers in the Allied arsenal passed over us, heading southeast on its way to Occupied France. We had become accustomed to large numbers of British Lancaster heavy bombers flying over us in the twilight on their way to bomb the Fatherland, but they had flown almost directly east. This number of aircraft exceeded anything we had ever seen before and their direction was different. Literally thousands of them flew over in an endless stream. Just before darkness, a whole flotilla of C-47s towing large gliders also flew over. We knew that the invasion of Festung Europa was imminent and we also knew that the focal point was Normandy.

All night long the drone of aircraft flying southeast went on, and we slept fitfully. Some of the more energetic types stayed up all night, looking skyward. I retired about midnight because I thought that next day would be a busy one. This was not the case. Much to our disappointment, we didn't get into action until June tenth. The only fighters we saw in the air were twin-tailed P-38s, which were not our best fighters and were not well-suited for ground support. We were nonplused. We were close to the scene of the action and had a superb plane for ground support but were not called to action. We were all dressed up with no place to go. Later on, we were told that our planes resembled the

The author in front of the Catholic church in Picauville which was the nearest French town to our airstrip in Normandy.

Staff sergeants, Mitchell (in the cockpit) and Warren Estes on the wing and the author on the ground examine the new model P-47 which has just come in. Note bubble canopy.

German Focke Wulfe 190 and the P-51 resembled the Me 109. This was not true if you were an air force type but it certainly did apply to the nervous and trigger-happy anti-aircraft batteries seeing action for the first time.

In the latter part of the war when they should have known better, some of these nutty jerks shot at us. Several of our planes were shot down and one pilot was killed by "friendly fire." One of our more outspoken pilots quipped, "If the sons of bitches shoot at you, they ain't friendly." Sad but true.

However, at this time it was understandable. The brass evidently felt that our ground forces would have enough trouble with the German Luftwaffe while climbing the steep hill at Omaha Beach without having to distinguish between their planes and ours. The only plane the Germans had that was similar to the P-38 was the Me110, a second rate plane and no match for any of our fighters. Ground support was not important at the early stages of the invasion so the P-38 was more than adequate for whatever fighter cover was necessary. Retaining the P-47 and P-51 made it easy for the invading troops—any low-flying plane that was not a P-38 was a bandit.

The author with four friends near our airstrip at Picauville in Normandy just prior to our big breakthrough.

Len Hitchman, Ernie White and the author, left to right, performing a hundred hour inspection on the guns in White's plane. The mechanic on top is removing cowling to check on the engine.

By June 10, the invasion forces were firmly established on the Normandy beachhead, so we began to fly again. However, for the first time since we had begun combat flying, our guys were restricted to patrolling the immediate front instead of ranging far afield hunting targets of opportunity as they were accustomed to. It was virtually impossible to determine how effective our bombing was, but we thought it was not so hot. German defenders were hidden in hedgerows of osage orange and other thicket-type trees, so good targets were scarce. We managed to shoot up some German vehicles whose drivers were imprudent enough to be abroad in daylight, but for the most part, all their vehicles were well camouflaged and hidden in the numerous copses of trees. This proved to be the most frustrating part of the war for our gladiators. They were chaffing at the bit for some stuff to shoot at. Little did they know that it would not be long before they would have all the targets their little hearts could desire.

A week or so after the landing, we started to get antsy. We longed to be in France, close to the action instead of sending our planes across the channel several times a day. However, before the main body of our squadron could move, a skeleton force, the first echelon, would have to go and make the necessary preparations for the rest of the squadron. Of course, everyone wanted to go first, but unfortunately I didn't make it. My good friend, Len Hitchman, shook my hand, gave me a V for Victory salute, and departed. Normally the rest of us would follow in less than a week, but this was impossible since our advance was much slower than anticipated due to strong German resistance. Our airfield at Picauville was still within range of German artillery so the airstrip couldn't be used.

By now, the beachheads were firmly established and the Germans had lost whatever opportunity they might have had to dislodge us. We were flying at least two missions per day from our Christchurch base.

Those of us left behind now had to service two planes per person and this really kept us hopping. When we rejoined the others, we made much of the fact that we had been overworked but it really wasn't too bad. Loading and fusing bombs was relatively easy, but we did have some problems loading sixteen machine guns apiece after each mission. We were lucky that our pilots were unable to seek targets farther afield or it might well have been a mite sticky keeping up.

The invasion changed other things for us. We packed up all our equipment so we would be able to move at a moment's notice. We also posted extra guards around the airplanes to protect them from a possible commando attack by the Germans. Two weeks after the invasion, we were put on alert and all days off were canceled. We moved to an embarkation camp near Southampton where all tents and paths were under trees.

Since we had nothing else to do, we played softball. We soon wore base paths in the open, at home plate and at the pitcher's mound in an otherwise meticulously camouflaged area. Any German pilot passing overhead with any knowledge whatsoever of American customs would immediately recognize these paths for what they were. However, none flew over and the few buzz bombs that did on their way to London Town didn't care one way or the other. Occasionally, one of these beauties would conk out near us, and we all hit the dirt. Fortunately, the Germans had a preoccupation with hitting London, so although several came close, this was by accident and not by design and we were never hit. They did make an impressive bang when they exploded, and we were not sorry that none came any closer than they did.

The author leaning on the wing of K4-M during a break in the action.
St. Dizier, October 1944.

Chapter Fourteen
Crossing the Channel

To War and Arms I Fly
—Richard Lovelace

After a week or so at our Southampton POE, we got the good word that it was time to go to France. A whole fleet of lorries roared into our campsite one evening. We hastily loaded all our gear except our packs and carbines on the first bunch, boarded the others, and it was off to France via Southampton.

The organized confusion at the port had to be seen to be believed. The piers were jammed with ships of all sizes and descriptions; some were loading; others were departing, loaded to the gills with all types of martial equipment. The docks were the same. All kinds of vehicles, armored and otherwise, hundreds of pieces of artillery, and supplies of all sorts were piled up on every pier. Thousands of soldiers lined up on *terra firma*, just inland from the piers, where they patiently awaited orders to load up for the trip to France. We joined them and our little group was quickly swallowed up by the mass of humanity waiting for passage. We wondered aloud how those in charge could possibly find us in that ocean of humanity.

After about an hour or so, our officers called us and we picked up our packs and marched along a battered pier toward one of the smaller ships. This time, our ship was no *Mauritania*. It was an ancient and decrepit New Zealand ship that had somehow managed to survive the German submarine war. We rushed up the gangplank and hopped on board.

Once on deck, we were met by an Anzac sailor with an accent that sounded almost like a foreign language. He led us into the bowels of the ship and down to a dirty room, which evidently had made many crossings since its last cleaning. When we asked if we got something to eat, he replied that we would but that most Yanks didn't like their food. Shades of my first morning on the *Mauritania*!

We settled down as best we could and waited patiently for the promised grub. When it finally came, I realized sadly that the Anzac was dead right. It looked hideous. All I took was some innocuous-looking cheese. The thought of getting the GI's on the beach deadened any hunger pangs I had.

It took almost two hours to load up, so after choking down my ration of cheese, I caught a little shuteye because I knew that we had a big day coming up and I wanted to wake up early to be on deck for the unloading process. I must have dozed off quickly because when I awoke, we were underway. I spread out my jacket and other things I took from my pack and fell asleep again. Much to my gratification, I got a lot more sleep than I had expected.

I woke up at the crack of dawn next morning and tried to go up on deck. One look at all the junk they had there convinced me that this was impossible. Just as I started down the steps, the mast of another ship started to cross our bow. Our skipper turned hard to starboard, and we just missed a nifty collision. This convinced me that we must be part of a large armada, or the ships would not have been so close.

About an hour later, we heard the rattle of chains as our anchor was dropped and the ship halted. We got the good word to grab our gear and head for the deck. Here we were herded toward a gangplank and descended into some waiting LCAs, each of which held about twenty persons. We were told to hurry it up, as the ship had to return to Southampton ASAP for another load of men and equipment. We were the first to leave, and after us there were still hundreds of soldiers and scads of equipment that had to be unloaded before they could return to Southhampton. It was no wonder that the ship was so dirty, it never rested long enough to get a good cleaning. It was bad enough for us and we hated to think of what the passengers next month would have put up with.

Personnel were first off, and I got on the first LCA, which headed for the beach as soon as it was loaded. The trip to shore took perhaps a half hour through choppy seas and finally hit close to the beach. We jumped out into about eighteen inches of cold water and waded ashore, toting duffel bags, packs, a carbine, and our helmets. Our helmsman, a friendly coast guarder, told us that our landing place was Omaha Beach, which meant nothing to us then except we did think it a strange name for a French beach. Subsequently it became very important to us because Omaha Beach was THE invasion beach and lots of prestige was connected with landing there.

Since I was one of the first to land, I had some time to wander around while I awaited the others. The beach was heavily patrolled by no-nonsense MPs, but they had more on their minds than being concerned about a single GI roaming the beach. I wanted to look at some burned out vehicles but they were a tad too far away. The only thing that prevented me from walking to them was the very real fear of being separated from the others and left behind. I looked toward the sea and saw a whole bunch of wrecked freighters which acted as a breakwater. I think that most were sunk intentionally, but some were mortally wounded and placed there. I realized then that invasions are expensive!

As soon as we were all ashore, we headed up a steep hill. The climb on loose sand was easier than I had expected, so we soon reached the top. Here we boarded a bunch of six-by-sixes and headed inland. For the first time in four months, we drove on the right side of the road, a pleasant change. While going up the hill and just beyond, we saw bunches of burned out tanks and other vehicles from both sides, mute testimony to how expensive the conquest of the beach had been.

We went through the little French towns of Carentan, St. Mere-Eglise, and finally ended up beside an inconspicuous grass strip near the town of Picauville. Here we caught up with the first echelon, selected partners, and set up our pup tents which served as our abodes while we remained in Normandy. We were still too close to the front lines for our airplanes to land safely so we had some time to ourselves. We were close enough to hear the enemy guns and soon were able to distinguish the big guns from the small fry. The first echelon had a great time swapping butts for eggs, wine, and Normandy hard cider. I joined them and ate my first fresh eggs since leaving the States.

The retreating Germans had abandoned lots of equipment, and we had fun going through some of it. Among the treasures we found were some beautiful twenty millimeter antiaircraft shells which we took apart and scraped out the explosive. The booster charge was a small metal cylinder threaded into the nose of the projectile which refused all our attempts to remove. I finally got the bright idea that if the projectile rotated clockwise after being fired, the booster required a left hand thread so that the torque given to it going through the barrel would not unscrew it. This solved the mystery and soon all the boosters were removed. Many of the guys brought theirs to me to unscrew. At first, I thought that this was an acknowledgment of my genius but I subsequently found out that this particular booster was very sensitive and the varmints were afraid that theirs might explode. Once I realized this, I refused to do any more.

We also found some orange cardboard cones with a drawstring sticking out of the top. None of us had the nerve to pull the drawstring until a big tall guy named Brumlevy decided to take a chance. We all got into our slit trenches while he gave the cord a yank and started to run for cover. He slipped and fell flat on his face. We all started to laugh instead of ducking. Luckily for all of us, it just gave off a cloud of orange smoke. Within minutes, everybody who could find one was pulling the drawstring and our part of the camp was covered by an orange cloud.

On Sunday mornings, some trucks drove us into Picauville for Sunday Mass. The kids sang the Gregorian Chant as well as I have ever heard it. Their singing reminded me of Holy Week back home where young men studying for the priesthood sang it. Later on, a Catholic chaplain visited us every Sunday and we had Mass out in the apple orchards which by then were leafed out. This beautiful setting gave us a chance to forget about the war for an hour or so. I have never seen a setting so perfect for a religious service than the apple orchards of Normandy and I will always have a fond memory of the Masses I attended there. Many of the Protestants attended services as well in this same setting, and I think that the attendance was better than in England. There is a lot of truth in the saying that there are no atheists in foxholes—or beside a airstrip.

In the evenings, we went to the various farm houses and swapped cigarettes for eggs and an organic solvent distilled from apples which went by the name of Calvados. This was guaranteed to put hair on our chests, take it off our heads, and put fire in our stomachs. Drinking this stuff renewed my confidence in GI dentistry, since it never did a thing to my many fillings. We never entered any of the houses since they looked unsanitary to us, but we did drink calvados from dirty glasses without a second thought. GIs are consistent when it came to booze—there is no such thing as an unsanitary sip.

We had time to host some of the local children who were properly awed by us and very polite as well. We enjoyed giving them some of Troy Robinson's leftovers, which he made sure were something they would like. One nice kid of perhaps fifteen insisted on my meeting his family. One of my friends, who had a camera, came along and took a picture of the five of us, one GI, two boys, a cute little girl, and a cow.

At long last, our idyllic existence came to an end. The Germans gave up sufficient ground so that our planes were able to land and it was back to the war for the 511th and what a war it was! The enemy was so close that we were able to fly a minimum of four missions per day. On just about every flight, the pilots used up all their ammo, so we really had to hop when they returned so that we wouldn't slow them down. We could all feel in our bones that big doings were in the offing.

Chapter Fifteen
Normandy to St. Dizier

To War and Arms I Fly
—Richard Lovelace

The Germans, excellent defensive fighters as they were, found Normandy an ideal place for their specialty. The numerous thick hedgerows of osage orange and other thick-growing trees served as great cover for machine guns nests, bazookas, and antitank guns. Moving them back was tough, costly, and slow, and the German defense, as always, was skillful and tough. As time passed, they became more confident in their ability to contain the Allies. However, they were in for a shock.

The frustrated Allies finally decided on a massive all-out bombing of German positions using every available plane. Over one thousand aircraft ranging from heavy bombers to fighter-bombers attacked St. Lo, their defensive anchor, and other strong points en mass. We watched in awe as this huge armada flew overhead hour after hour. Even where we were, some fifteen miles from the front, we could feel the earth shudder and shake from continuous explosions. The German defenders were reduced to quivering jelly and the Allied infantry and tanks stormed through their shattered defenses.

Following this massive breakthrough, the Allied armies separated and our group was assigned to the newly formed Third Army, commanded by General George Patton. I was dismayed to hear this. I recalled that in Sicily, Patton had slapped some shell-shocked soldiers in the face. For action, he was sacked and retired from public view. We all thought that he had been permanently canned. His appointment as head of the Third Army came as an unpleasant surprise.

His fit of anger in Sicily didn't endear him to me, nor did his habit of wearing two pearl-handled pistols around his waist. This seemed like kid stuff to me. The fact that he was called "Old Blood and Guts" was another thing that turned me off. As time went on, however, we realized that he knew his job and how to get things done. He always appreciated the support we gave him. He was an ardent believer in the usefulness of air power and he used it skillfully. This, of course, made us firm believers in him and his ability to get the job done. I think that his biggest virtue as a soldier was his desire to attack and finish the war as quickly as possible and with as few casualties as possible. He liked to keep the enemy on the run and off balance. In the long run, he had many more plusses than minuses, so I guess that the "ayes" have it BUT please, *don't bring him home for dinner!*

He had a few other things going for him. He was never hesitant about giving credit where it was due. He and his people continually told us what a fine job we were doing and how much he appreciated our efforts. Above all, his liaison officers were real professionals. They didn't ask for the impossible and were grateful for what they got. He was also far and away the most offensive-minded general we had.

In his book, *War as I Knew It*, he stated that when he first encountered the XIX Tactical Air Command of which our group was a small part, "It was love at first sight" (page 96). I have to admit that the feeling soon became mutual. We felt that he would exploit every weakness in the enemy defense and we knew that our efforts would not be wasted. His first assignment was the liberation of Brittany, so all of our missions were directed to that area. He advanced rapidly and scattered the demoralized Nazis like chaff. However, once our planes took off, we had no idea which direction they were headed, so I had the impression they were flying east to round up the remnants of the German forces who had been routed at St. Lo. I had no idea that he had actually gone west to clear out the Brittany Peninsula of enemy forces.

Our squadron was just a very small part of a huge Allied force and our knowledge of the overall picture was necessarily limited. After the war, I read many books dealing with the entire panorama of the Normandy campaign. One of these was *The Fall of Fortress Europe*, by Albert Seaton. According to Seaton, Hitler had split the responsibility for repelling the invading forces to Generals Rommel and Von Rundtedt who were divided in how to carry this out. Rommel favored stopping the invasion on the beaches, while Von Rundtedt wished to counterattack after the Allies had landed. Rommel's plan was adopted but he was checkmated not only by the terrific bombardment from both sea and air, but more importantly by the fact that the German high command expected that the main Allied thrust would be farther north. Thus the Germans held forces in reserve which could have been used with good effect in Normandy had they been used before the breakthrough.

Therefore, Rommel's plan was never fully implemented. Hitler then tried to implement Von Runstedt's plan and ordered a counterattack by his reserves at almost the same time as we stormed through German lines at St. Lo. By this time it was too late and the entire German general staff, including Rommel and Von Runstedt, opposed any attack because they felt that this would play into the Allies' hands. They suggested forming a line of defense farther east while there was still time. They pointed out to

Hitler that the Allies had complete control of the air and a huge margin of superiority in tanks and artillery and that an armored attack under these conditions was not only bound to fail but would leave the way to the Rhine River completely unguarded. Hitler had a phobia about retreating, so he could not be dissuaded from attacking and told his generals to attack forthwith.

Both Eisenhower and Omar Bradley were in ecstasy. They realized that this was a heaven-sent opportunity to eliminate all enemy resistance in the West. They ordered the First US Army to attack from the north and told Patton to suspend his campaign in Brittany and attack from the south in an effort to encircle the attacking German forces. Both US armies were quick to react.

Patton, with the support of the XIX Air Command, and with his usual dash, attacked the left flank of the attacking forces while the First US Army attacked their right flank. This threatened encirclement broke up the attack and forced the Germans into a disorganized retreat, resulting in a monumental traffic jam. German vehicles were four abreast and stretched out for miles. Every fighter group in Normandy and many of those still in southern England pounded the retreating forces with every weapon at their disposal. British Typhoon fighters, armed with rockets, destroyed the larger tanks, while US 47s shot up the other armored forces with machine gun fire. American, British, and Canadian artillery put in their two cents. The result was a horrendous slaughter of men and equipment unparalleled in war. Two German armies were eliminated as effective fighting forces and virtually all German armored equipment west of the Rhine River was destroyed. There was also hardly any organized German resistance between the Allies and Rhine River, the last natural barrier between the Allies and Berlin.

Patton's attack left his right flank open to a German attack by enemy forces remaining in Brittany and by those occupying southern France. In his book Patton states,

> "One of the most important hazards encountered was that of leaving the right flank of the Third Army completely open from St. Nazaire to a point near Troyes. This decision was based on my belief that the Germans did not have sufficient mobility to strike fast and that the ever-efficient XIX Tactical Air Command would spot any force and hold it down long enough to permit American troops to intervene."

We didn't let him down.

Those of us at Picauville thought the Germans had staked everything on their ability to hold the St. Lo line and had made no provisions for the possibility of an Allied breakthrough. None of us had an inkling that Hitler would be dumb enough to attack. We knew that we had far more men and equipment than he could possible muster and were particularly aware of our preponderance in aircraft. We also knew that we had made shambles of his St. Lo defensive line and that they were withdrawing posthaste. Thus, we were completely ignorant of the German attack.

When our pilots came out to the line, they were all business, and when they returned, we were so busy preparing the planes for the next mission or cleaning our guns for the next day that we never had time to ask them where they had gone of what they had accomplished. I have always been struck by the irony of our being in the thick of things without the slightest idea of what was actually going on. We knew that a major disaster had hit the German forces but we hadn't an inkling of how great a defeat they had actually sustained or how they had sustained it. I think that any of us who served in air force as ground crew members who have subsequently read about the liberation of Europe must feel like the abused husband or wife who is always the last to know. There is an adage that if you wish to learn about something, write a book about it. I can vouch for the authenticity of that!

We were not a part of all this excitement until the afternoon of July twenty-nine. In the early afternoon, our group took off on what we assumed was another routine mission. When our pilots returned, they were really hot to trot. They had located a German armored division near Avaranches and had bombed the first and last vehicles so that the rest were trapped in the middle. They then strafed the rest until their ammo gave out. We reloaded the planes and off they went to continue their destruction of the doomed division. For the rest of the day and well into the evening, it was reload, refuel, and up, up, and away. Our squadron dropped over fifty tons of bombs and expended some six-hundred-thousand rounds of caliber-fifty ammunition on this hapless force. This particular activity was cited in *The History of the U.S. Force*;

> The Ninth Air Force, fully geared to its primary task of ground support, bombed and strafed the retreating Germans. On July 29, they caught a boxed-in German armored force on a road between two small French villages. From mid-afternoon until late in the summer evening, P-47s of the 405th Fighter-Bomber Group systematically smashed the three mile long column. It was devastating, the road was made impassable. The attack destroyed sixty-six tanks, 204 vehicles, and eleven guns, and damaged fifty-six tanks and fifty-five vehicles which were abandoned.

After the twelfth and last mission, we worked well after midnight to prepare for the next day. Tom Harrison came over and pitched in to help me prepare for the next morning. I believe that his ship had been disabled earlier so he was footloose and fancy free. His help was gratefully received and we finished cleaning and reloading my guns in the wee hours and long after most of the others had gone back to their tents.

At midnight, just before we were finished buttoning up for the night and while we were still perched on the wing, a German bomber flew overhead and we expected the worst. Since there was no place to take cover, we looked at each other, shrugged our shoulders, and went on about our business, keeping our fingers crossed.

I imagine that either we were not the target or that its navigation was faulty, because it passed directly overhead and a few minutes later, we heard the crash of its bombs exploding in the distance. Then, back it came, passed over us once more, and soon faded out in the distance.

I never saw a German aircraft in action. To my knowledge, the only one that ever flew over us during the day was an Me 109 in England which gave us a quick buzz and then disappeared without incident. For some reason or other, I was not on the line at the time and so lost out on this epic event. Some enemy bombers did fly over us at night while we were on the continent, particularly while we were in Normandy and there was no mistaking them. Their engines made a very distinctive noise, a kind of a throb as if they were not properly synchronized.

Needless to say, this was our biggest day in the entire war, and our brief stay in Normandy was our most active time in the war as well. It was commonplace for our pilots to fly six or eight missions per day for a space of two weeks, shooting up all kinds of enemy equipment including many types that were horse drawn. When we heard about this, we thought that the Jerries were running short on mechanized equipment, but we later found out that they had been using horses in Russia all along.

The German attack changed the Third Army's emphasis from conquering Brittany to an attempt to encircle both German Armies at Falaise. While the noose was never completely closed, the few escapees had virtually no transport, guns, or armor. The Third Army then raced across France, past Paris, and on to Nancy in eastern France. When he reached that point, Patton had to await supplies before continuing his attack. This slowed down our activity as well. We went back to our accustomed two missions per day just to let the Germans know that we were still around.

With the rout of the German forces in the Falaise Pocket, local targets became a thing of the past. We had to place auxiliary gas tanks on the belly-bomb rack to give the planes sufficient range to keep up with the advancing Third Army. While this was our main thrust, we occasionally flew support for the skeleton forces remaining in Brittany when they got into trouble.

With all the excitement of the pending invasion and of our preparations to go across the channel. I didn't realize that I had reached an important level in my life until we were in Normandy. I suddenly realized that I was now twenty-one years old. While I had actually attained this benchmark in Christchurch while awaiting transportation to France, I never gave it a thought. Shortly after our arrival in Normandy, we got our mail and I received some birthday greetings from home. The boys took me out to celebrate this momentous occasion, and I enjoyed my first sip of hard liquor, a small glass of calvados. I took a small swig at first, since I had seen what it did to some of my playmates. With their help and encouragement, I overdid it and paid the price for my indiscretion with a bit of a skull-cracker the next morning.

At long last, I could join my friends in their various *soirees* into town or to farmhouses depending on our location. Picauville was small, but the few people we met were probably the nicest ones we met in all of France, which was not really saying much. These trips were fun and I was glad I was finally able to go along without drinking coke or some other innocuous brew. I mentioned to "Sheepy" Larson that calvados seemed to me to be a waste of good apples. His reply was that it was better than applesauce. As time went on, I agreed with him.

Shortly after our twelve mission day, I began a three-day tour of KP. While I was on the serving line, my pilot, Mike Varino, passed through and mentioned that his guns were not shooting with the accuracy he had been accustomed to. He was the best shot in the squadron, so I knew that something was amiss and told my boss, Warren Cubit. He assured me that he would take care of it.

To my surprise, he reharmonized (reaimed) the guns. This took all morning, so Mike was grounded until the afternoon mission. At suppertime, he told me that things were no better. I replied that I had one more day in the kitchen and then I would fix them. I got up about an hour early after my tour was over, got eight new barrels, and replaced his old ones which had been worn smooth. Normal barrels have rifling inside, causing the bullets to rotate. This rotation is responsible for their accuracy. When a barrel is worn smooth, the bullets wobble off in any direction and the gun is useless.

Preparing new barrels was a tedious job. They came filled with a substance known as cosmolene, a thick greasy substance that clung to metal—and one's hands—as if its life depended on it. This gunk kept the barrels from rusting but was brutal to remove. It was readily soluble in 100-octane gas, but this removed the thin film of protective oil and they then rusted like crazy. The only way to remove it safely was to run a series of cleaning patches through the barrel until all the cosmolene was removed. This was not an easy job, but I completed it in time for the morning mission.

When Mike came back, I asked him how things went, and he was all smiles and he asked me what magic I had performed that the others hadn't. I replied that it was a trade secret. Had I told him the reason, he would probably have said, "Oh, is that all there was to it?" I felt that it would be better for both of us if he were to think I was a genius. This was not only good for my ego, but gave him confidence in me as well.

To this day, I cannot understand why the others didn't check the barrels before going to all the trouble of reharmonizing them. To me, this was the obvious thing to do. In the first place, it was far easier, and in the second place, Mike had flown twelve missions in one day and therefore had taken about forty-eight hundred shots per gun on this one day alone. That was enough to burn barrels to a crisp. To me, it was just common sense to try the easy way first. The gun mounts on the P-47 were very reliable, and I cannot recall a single instance where reharmonization was necessary.

Several days after this, I opened the wing to reload the guns and noticed that one of them still had many rounds left over while the others were empty. For some reason, it had not fired many rounds. I also noticed that part of the brass cartridge protruded from the chamber, and the cartridge had ruptured, so evidently the head space was not quite right. I checked the barrel to make certain that there was no projectile in it. The rifling in the barrel exerted tremendous resistance to the bullet as it made it rotate, there may not have been enough force to expel it from the barrel. Had the bullet lodged in the barrel, it would have made it unsafe, and I would have had to replace it. This would have resulted in my being asked some embarrassing questions. To my relief, the barrel was clear, so I got an extractor and removed the remains of the ruptured cartridge. I corrected the head space, reloaded, and recharged the guns, and it was off to the wars once again for K4-M Uno with no time lost.

I didn't think that Mike was aware of the problem since seven guns had virtually the same feeling in the cockpit as eight, but I thought it prudent to tell him and reassure him that I had taken care of the situation. This was the only major malfunction I ran into during the entire war but I think that this was more a tribute to the reliability of the Browning machine gun than my ability as an armorer.

About two weeks later, K4-M Numero Uno took a fatal hit in its tail section from a 40mm shell. While it destroyed the supercharger and much of the reinforcing in the tail section, Mike was able to bring it back alive. On landing, he kept the tail in the air as long as he could and when he finally let the tail wheel hit the runway, the whole rear end folded up and the nose faced to the sky. It was junk.

Since he was unable to taxi, he left it on the runway, shut off the engine, climbed out of the cockpit, and sauntered in. I realized that he had been hit so I hurried out to meet him. When I caught sight of him, he was walking in jauntily, his parachute over his shoulder with a big smile on his face. He refused to let me carry his chute as we walked in together.

Next day, I went over to the junk yard to salvage the homemade bomb release I had made so industriously, as well as a few other items which I needed. I arrived just in time to see one the salvage crew take a spectacular spill on the left wing. Evidently it was not his first because he said, "This son of a bitch has the slickest f——— wings in Normandy." To which I added a fervent "Amen."

I had become attached to K4-M, but not enough to regret seeing those slick wings out of my life forever. Luckily for me, when K4-M Numero Dos came on the scene, Mike made no attempt to wax it. If he had, I think I would have given the wings a quick dose of 100-octane when he wasn't looking. Life was too short to risk ending up my army career by taking a big-league spill on a slick wing.

After we had been in Normandy for about three weeks, an RAF Mosquito outfit moved in across the runway from us and used the same runway. None of us had ever seen one of these ships close up, so we crossed the runway while our planes were aloft to look them over and to talk with their crews. Each plane had two huge engines with enough plywood wrapped around them so they could fly. Twenty-millimeter guns jutted out of the fuselage, giving them a real warlike appearance, and strange-looking radar antennae bristled all over them. Since they were faster than any German plane in existence at that time, they flew anywhere with impunity. This particular squadron was used to defend RAF heavy bombers from the German night fighters who were scoring significant successes. Night fighting must have been eerie, since the German planes were covered with lamp black and were invisible. The Germans also used some of their best pilots in fast and maneuverable planes and stayed close to the British heavies so that the gunners on the Skeeters not only had to be quick on the trigger, but had to avoid hitting their own planes as well.

One night about three A.M. or so, we heard a crash and then the crackle of a fire across the runway. One of the Mosquitoes had run up the back of the other and both were blazing fiercely. Soon the fire reached the unused twenty mm ammo which started to explode. Both planes disintegrated completely. Luckily, three of the four men who flew were saved.

When we crossed the runway next day, all that was left of two magnificent aircraft was a small pile of ashes. Even the engines were reduced to powder. As I looked at those pitiful remains, I wondered what percentage of our casualties were caused by reasons other than enemy action. After all, a plane lost was still a plane lost and was one unavailable

176

for action, even though it didn't count as such in public relations stats. Shortly after this disaster, our British friends moved closer to the front, where I suppose they got some new planes. We were not long in following them eastward.

Our stay in Normandy was the high point of our time in the army. The weather was warm and sunny, so we didn't mind sleeping in pup tents. The scenery was beautiful. The apple orchards and grape arbors which surrounded us were in full leaf and the sky was blue during the day and full of stars in the evening. Those of us who were city bred had never seen the heavens so clear.

We got a little time off and the squadron furnished some trucks to take us to Carteret and Barneville where we swam in the ocean, walked the beaches hunting for shells, or just relaxed in the warm sunshine. The water was a mite nippy but really refreshing, since we had little opportunity to shower. On one occasion, I looked into the water while wading at Carteret and saw an artillery shell almost at my feet. It looked to me like a dud 88mm German shell and it brought back some memories of our landing on the beach.

Normandy was as close to the action as we got. After our planes arrived, we were as busy as beavers. Targets were so close that missions were of short duration and there were lots of them. We used every type of bomb in our ample arsenal except napalm and white phosphorus, and scads of machine gun ammunition as well. Our guys shot up everything in sight, so we had to reload the guns completely after every mission.

We also had to change barrels often, since the pilots got excited over all the things they could shoot at and kept their hands on the trigger constantly instead of in short bursts as they were supposed to. Mike was not only a good shot, but he also was good about shooting in short bursts, so my barrel changes were less than some of the others.

The people we met in Normandy were more pleasant than those we met elsewhere in France. The invasion had gone through this area near the landing beaches so rapidly that few of the houses had been damaged. We found that the friendliness of the inhabitants of an area was inversely proportional to the amount of damage we inflicted on them. We noticed that many people didn't appreciate having their houses destroyed even for a good cause. Although most of this damage was caused by the infantry and tank corps as they cleared out snipers or by the retreating Germans who had no compunction in destroying possible strong points as they retired, we took the rap since we were the only ones they could blame. I am just glad we were never stationed at St. Lo!

On one occasion, I had a nasty cold. I helped load and then fused two five-hundred pounders on my ship and then decided to go back to my tent and sack out for a while. For some reason, the takeoff was delayed but I gave it no thought. Ten minutes after takeoff, my boss, Warren Cubit, was at my tent boiling mad. Our original mission had been scratched and we had to load "bullshit" bombs.

These were an ordeal to load at the best of times, so when they arrived at my plane and found no one at home, Warren was justifiably upset. It was not so much my absence that he objected to since there were enough people to do the job, but he was ticked off because I had neglected to tell him. He didn't get mad often but when he did, his face got fiery red. That was his condition when he arrived at my tent. He knew from past experience that I was reliable and that this was an aberration on my part and not my usual *modus operandi* so I was soon forgiven, but to this day, I am mystified as to why I pulled such a dumb stunt without at least telling him.

As mentioned earlier, Patton and his army tore across northern France, smashing what little resistance that the Nazis put up, helped liberate Paris, and finally had to stop at Nancy for lack of supplies. We were ecstatic. There were no forces between him and the Rhine. We had visions of the war being over soon. All we had to do was cross the Rhine and then on to Berlin. At that time, he was far in advance of any of the other Allied armies, and we expected him to receive supplies so he could continue his pursuit of the German remnants.

There is many a slip twixt and cup and the lip. For some reason, Eisenhower decreed that emphasis would be switched to the northern armies, including Montgomery and the British Eighth Army for the impending attacks on Holland and Northern Germany. This policy probably had its inception when Eisenhower was put in command of the entire invasion force. I imagine this was to placate Monty's ego.

At any rate, Patton went off like a land mine. He knew that the Krauts were on the run in his area and that he was in great position to give them a knockout punch. He vented his frustration by taking the fortified city of Metz, which could have easily been bypassed (Basil Liddell-Hart, *The Other Side of the Hill*).

As things turned out, Monty got bogged down and the Germans made their usual remarkable recovery and the war dragged on. All of us military experts felt that this was the price we had to pay to soothe Monty's colossal ego.

Patton hollered that, "My men can eat their belts but my tanks gotta have gas." He also said, "To hell with Hodges (commander of the First U.S. Army) and Monty. We'll win your goddam war if you'll keep the Third Army going." These were our thoughts as well. Patton was no Prince Charming, but he knew how to take advantage of a breakthrough as none of the other generals seemed to.

All of us were upset by this development. All I could think of was

Shakespeare's speech in *Julius Caesar*.

> There is a tide in the affairs of men
> Which taken at the flood, leads on to fortune
> Omitted, all voyage of their life
> Is bound in shallows and in miseries.

We neglected to take this tide and paid dearly for our neglect.

We felt that Patton never again had the all-out support which he enjoyed at our original breakthrough at St. Lo. We learned after the war that many of the newer P-47s were equipped with rockets. Unfortunately, all of them were sent to the squadrons which supported the First and Ninth armies which were to the north of us. Rockets were more accurate than bombs and were more reliable and safer as well. A single rocket could knock out the largest tank, while our caliber-fifties just rattled off them. I have always regretted that we never had the opportunity to work on them and I am even sorrier that our pilots never got to fire them. They would have been a welcome challenge.

In June of 1994, my wife and I watched a TV program, *Fighter Pilot*, the self-told story of a P-47 pilot, Quinton Aanenson of the 366th Fighter Group who went overseas shortly after we did. His group supported the First and Ninth U.S. Armies and saw a lot of action while we were bogged down. The losses of the 366th exceeded ours by a good bit since they were in the thick of the action. We didn't see any real action again until the Battle of the Bulge in late December.

Shortly after Patton's stop in the Nancy area, the brass decided to move us closer to the action. We had to use belly tanks to reach the front, which didn't leave us much time to strafe the enemy and also reduced the number of missions we could fly each day. Accordingly, we packed up our belongings, broke camp, bid Normandy and Picauville a fond farewell, and headed east.

Chapter Sixteen
Winter in St. Dizier

Blow, blow thou Winter Wind.
—William Shakespeare

We left our little airstrip early one morning and headed south. We passed through St. Lo, which was in shambles, and then headed eastward. After a drive of perhaps an hour, we picked up the "Red Ball Highway," which was the main road to the front. It got its name from the conspicuous red circles which served as direction markers. Since it was the only road in relatively decent shape, it was jammed with traffic flowing at top speed in both directions. The drivers of these vehicles floorboarded their rigs and depended on their steering to avoid accidents.

Neither the French nor the Germans had spent a nickel on road repairs from the fall of France until the end of the war, so they were in wretched shape. The Corps of Engineers had done some repair work on the "Red Ball" so it was in better shape than most, but that is only a relative term; it was still no superhighway and was covered with enormous potholes which we hit with enough force to jar every tooth in our heads. GI trucks, known to us as six by sixes since they had five wheels on the ground and a spare tire on each side of the truck, were built for utility and longevity, not for comfort, so we took a fierce pounding every time we hit one of these holes which I think averaged about one per second.

The heart of "C" Flight Armament section. From the left: Sgt. Collins, Sgt. Len Hitchman on top of five hundred pound multipurpose bomb, and Flight Chief Staff Sgt. Warren Cubit. The author is just in front of the bomb.

Every town we passed through which had either a major intersection running through it or a river nearby was heavily damaged and some were in such bad shape that traffic was significantly slowed down as it threaded its way around piles of debris. We saw lots of wrecked German equipment and many American tanks knocked out as well. I remember one American tank in particular because its mortal wound was an 88mm hole right in the front of its turret where the armor was the thickest. Although the Germans were unable to make a major stand, they were very skillful in setting up small but costly ambushes as they retreated.

It was our hope to go through Paris and receive the accolades of the grateful French populace, but somewhere before we reached there, we were shunted off Red Ball onto secondary roads which headed southeast at first and then curved almost due east. This new route took us through Fontainebleau instead of Paris. The ride was beautiful and the picturesque town was unharmed by the war. Few of the towns we passed through on this route were damaged, and the people were correspondingly cordial. This very pleasant and peaceful drive was a welcome respite from the hustle and bustle of the Red Ball Highway.

Missing Paris, which appeared to be a catastrophe at first, turned out to be a blessing in disguise, since I managed to spend lots of time there prior to our departure for home. Had we gone through "Paree", I would have missed Fontainbleau and we would have had our brains pounded to jelly as well. I think that somebody upstairs knew what was good for me.

After about eight hours on the road, we arrived at St. Dizier, a small French town with a deserted German airport nearby, paved runway and all. We quickly set up our tents and other appurtenances and were ready for war once more.

St. Dizier reminded me of a small, dusty west Texas town which had been transferred to France prior to our arrival. Four years of harsh German occupation created results similar to four years of drought. Every time the wind blew, clouds of dust choked us. There were several cathouses where the ladies of the night did for their American clients what they had done for the Germans only a month or so before. Some of the guys who frequented these pleasure houses told me that the girls said the Germans were more polite but the Americans paid better.

St. Dizier was a typical army town. It was too small for the number of soldiers stationed there, so we were bored stiff because there was nothing constructive for us to do off base. I imagine that the German occupation had made them leery of foreign soldiers, and I can't say I blame them. Our morale officer made overtures to them through the city government to set up dances, etc. We did have some, but there were never enough girls to go around so I only stayed for a few minutes. French pulchritude,

Celebrating the opening of the Enlisted mens' day room in St. Dizier. Major John Eikenberry is just to the left of our squadron insignia.

St. Dizier style, was not up to my standards even though they got lower every month as the war progressed.

I am sure that the parents of many of the "nice" families didn't permit their daughters to attend. Evidently they were familiar with the sexual habits of the military. From the limited experience I had at this time, a hostile attitude pervaded toward us over most of the country and that was the chief reason why I waited so long before revisiting France after the war.

Since the town bordered on the Marne River, we went swimming before the weather got too cold. On our day off, some of us outdoor types took hikes along the river and into the countryside. Once in a while, we encountered odd looking vehicles using charcoal as fuel. These were strange-looking rigs with a large, cylindrical charcoal burner projecting from one side. Charcoal-fueled vehicles sound bizarre, but the ingenuity of man is infinite. As I understood, steam made by the burning charcoal passed through it and formed methanol or wood alcohol which was the actual fuel. These ancient relics had three things going for them. They were better than walking, they were so decrepit that the Germans left them alone, and our pilots left them alone because they were so obviously French. At this time, they were a lifesaver for the French who had no way to obtain gasoline except via the black market.

When the weather turned cool in late October, I remained in camp and amused myself by reading and catching up on my correspondence. Normandy had been hectic and conditions there made writing almost impossible. It was a known fact that if you didn't write, no one wrote to you. I knew that those back home became apprehensive when they didn't receive mail from me on a regular basis. The quiet of our new base gave me a good chance to catch up.

We all dreaded the advent of winter and looked forward to a life of unmitigated boredom. The only place we could play cards or chew the fat was in our six-man pyramidal tents. These weren't too bad for sleeping in the early fall but were too cluttered for any outsider to visit.

At this stage, Major Eikenberry and some first-rate scroungers came through with a lot of where with all to build an enlisted men's dayroom. Ike got us a tent, which we insulated, and we built a bar out of some lumber somebody had scraped up from packing cases we received on occasion. We found some beat up furniture that was still usable and even got an old piano. We hooked up some electric lights which worked off the squadron generator. This made reading far more comfortable than it was in our tents. We had a gent who could play popular music by ear, and every evening he sat down and played whatever tunes we requested. Sometimes we had to hum a bar or two, but there were very few he couldn't pick up. We were also lucky enough to have another guy who could play classical music, provided we had the sheet music for him. He played at dinner times on festive occasions such as Christmas and New Year's. This dayroom was a nice place to spend a few hours in the evening before hitting the hay. Either through Eikenberry's intervention or by an out-of-character act of generosity by the supply sergeant, we acquired two wood stoves to heat up the joint. In a word, we never had it so good.

Poker games flourished as of yore. On paydays, there were a bunch of different games as the pros spread out to fleece the small fry. The following week there were about half as many games and during the last week, there was the one big game where the experts had it out with each other. This was the fun game to watch. Some of us small fry steered clear of the biggies and had little games of our own. These were lots of fun since the stakes were high enough to make the game interesting, but not too high for any of us to get hurt.

We acquired a host of paperbacks on virtually any topic under the sun. Beer and wine were available at reasonable prices if we wished to imbibe.

On Sunday morning we had Mass in the dayroom so we no longer had to make the cold trek to the church in town. Mass was scheduled so the maximum number could attend. This was great for the priest and even better for us. Evidently, the Catholic Church bent over backwards in selecting chaplains because all the ones I met were first rate.

We obtained a movie projector and saw some of Hollywood's latest. Ever so often, we got to look at some of the gun camera shots of our pilots in action. Since they showed us only the best, they were spectacular. To our great regret, we never got to see the pictures of our Turkey Shoot at Falaise Gap.

It was at this time that they showed us the "Mickey Mouse" film that started the mad rush to the houses of ill-repute in town. In the fall of 1992, I had lunch with John Eikenberry in Pasadena, California. In the course of our reminiscing, John mentioned that the only time he had any trouble with his superiors was in St. Dizier when he was questioned about a sudden rise in venereal disease in our squadron. The army at this time furnished a little gadget called a "pro kit." It consisted of a little tube of some goo which a guy was supposed to insert into his penis after intercourse to kill any venereal bugs he might have picked up from his lady love. They were far more popular gathering dust than in use. It was Ike's job to see that all guys going into town had one of these things with him, and HQ evidently thought he was remiss in this respect. Ike himself was happily married and didn't indulge in such unseemly activities and had not seen the movie, so he was unaware of its contents. When I told him about it, we both had a big laugh.

We spent more time at St. Dizier than any other place overseas. We were there from late August until the middle of February. Life was a repetition of arising at six, breakfasting, and heading to the line to prepare for our first mission which took off as soon as there was sufficient light for the pilots to see.

Since we had made such a rapid advance against the Germans, our planes had long treks to the front, forcing us to use belly tanks for many missions as we had in Normandy. It was the armorer's job to hang the tank and then the mechanics were responsible for the hookups to the fuel system with breakable glass tubes which readily broke when the tank was jettisoned.

About every ten days or so, this monotony was broken by a crisis at the front, and we had to get up extra early to prepare our planes. This involved loading planes in the dark so that they could take off the instant it was bright enough to see. We complained about the inconvenience, but we really didn't mind. We knew that the dogfaces had it much tougher than we did, and we wanted to make their jobs easier if we could. I think that in the long run, we appreciated the fact that these missions broke up the monotony of our existence.

The weather was raw, so keeping our tent warm was a real problem from the word "go." Tents were okay for Boy Scouts, but they were awful cold during the winter. They trapped in the bitter cold in winter and the stifling heat in the summer. They were always worse than the ambient temperature.

In England, we found that the cold came through the bottom of our cots as well as the top, so we got sheets of corrugated cardboard which we placed on the cot and then put our blankets on top. We slept between the cardboard and the blankets and were thus able to keep warm except on the coldest days. We scrounged up some old wood from packing cases and from the grounds of the old mansion so our tent was warm when we retired. The only problem we faced was getting up and dressing in a cold tent in the mornings.

Loading a 500# bomb K4-M at St. Dizier, France in November of 1944. Author is pumping up bomb with hydraulic jack. Len Hitchman, under the wing, will cock bomb rack when bomb is in place. All bombs were loaded first and crew chiefs of each plane returned to fuse them.

In Normandy, we slept in pup tents, but the weather was almost perfect so we had no problems. St. Dizier was a cat of a different color. As it got colder, sleeping became more and more uncomfortable. Cardboard was not available and the only fuel we had was some fiber boards we took out of empty ammo cans. They burned very hot for a very short time. At first, we put in lots of them at one time just prior to our going to bed. It quickly burned out and the contrast between the original heat and the subsequent cold made it almost impossible to be comfortable. Then we tried to burn a little at a time but once we fell asleep, it quickly burned out since none of us refueled the stove. Once again, we had to get up in the cold.

Squadron headquarters made arrangements to get some coke, and we were issued one bucket per night per tent. This kept our tents above freezing but it did nothing to eliminate our getting up in a cold and damp tent with our canteens frozen solid. Every morning we took turns reminding the rest that there was a war going on and we couldn't expect all the comforts of home. This became less amusing as the winter progressed and the days got shorter and colder. We all tried to steal coke from the pile, but our eagle-eyed supply sergeant made this impossible since he watched the coke pile like a hawk both day and night. This surveillance came to a sudden halt one evening.

A whole bunch of B-26s landed on our airstrip on a foggy evening because theirs had been weathered in. The pilots and other officers paired off with their peers, and the gunners, who were enlisted men, bunked with us. Evidently these guys were accustomed to sleeping in warm barracks, because they began to holler about the cold and told us to get more coke to warm the place up. When we told them that we were allocated one bucket per evening, they were outraged. One of them grabbed the

The author playing the part of the Red Baron in the cockpit of K4-M #2 in late November, 1944, at St. Dizier in eastern France. Note the one-piece bubble canopy behind me.

bucket and said," Where the hell is the f—— coke pile?" He hustled down the way we told him and returned with a full bucket which he dumped on the floor and went back for more. He told us that he'd had words with the supply sergeant but told him to get his f—— ass out of the way or he'd get his butt kicked. The supply sergeant may have been a tightwad, but he was not dumb and not about to tangle with this tough-looking soldier, so he got out of the way. His defense system collapsed. A steady stream of guys beat a path to the coke pile. Every host tent was as warm as toast all night long, and the coke pile was almost eliminated. We were almost in tears when these tough monkeys took off next morning. We didn't find out until later, but when the guys living in tents without any visitors found out what was going on, they got on the bandwagon and loaded up as well.

Our visitors' plane, the B-26, was a controversial medium bomber and as such got a lot of hype from the brass. We read in "Stars and Stripes" that these marvelous machines could fly on one engine, etc., ad nauseam. I recall the fulsome praise the air force had for the P-39, which everybody admired except those who had either to fly them or work on them. I felt that in the case of the B-26, "the gentleman doth protest too much."

The arrival of these guys gave us a great opportunity to find out from the experts just how good or bad these crates were. The enthusiasm of the brass didn't seem to extend down to our guests, who hated them. When I mentioned about their ability to fly on one engine, one of them replied cynically, "With one engine gone, these goddam crates have the glide angle of a brick." Ever since then, whenever the military wheels started to tell us how terrific an item of hardware was, I wondered what was wrong with it. The concept of "truth in advertising," seems alien to the military mentality. I won't dwell on the ethics involved in having some innocents flying one of these turkeys.

The visitation of the B-26 boys had a real permanent benefit. The good supply sergeant never again got a handle on the coke pile. After a feeble attempt to reestablish control, he threw up his hands in disgust. However, the supply of coke was such that we couldn't sustain the warmth we had come to enjoy while our guests were with us. This wouldn't have been so bad, except we had gotten a taste of the good life and we couldn't shake it. It was a case of "how are you going to get them back on the farm after they've seen Paree?" We were so spoiled that something had to be done.

At this juncture, Tom Harrison came up with his one-hundred-octane "oil burner", and our heating problems were over forever. A group of master sergeants in a tent next to ours tried to emulate Tom's masterpiece and ended up burning down their tent. Nobody was hurt and we got a great laugh out of watching them scurry out of their tent and stand around sheepishly while another one was procured for them. Since they were wheels, no inquiry was made and the incident quietly passed into history.

We were still attached to the Third Army, which was at a virtual standstill for lack of adequate supplies. One miserable day when we were not flying, we received an urgent SOS from one of Patton's units. The Germans had made a surprise attack and had broken through the lines. We hastily loaded all our planes, and all three squadrons took off carrying two general purpose bombs per plane and headed into the miserable weather to help break up the German attack. Our squadron got lost, but the other two did a fine job and pummeled the hell out of the poor Krauts, breaking up the attack completely. Group headquarters got a glowing letter of thanks, not only from the unit commander, but from Patton himself. For this bit of derring-do, group was awarded the Presidential Citation. We all received a letter of commendation and a little blue bar with gold trimming which we wore on the right side of our dress uniform. The only thing I didn't like was the kidding we got from some wise guys of the other two squadrons telling us that we should thank them for winning this citation. Sad, but true.

After this incident, we went back to the routine missions we had been flying, weather permitting. As we flew them, I reflected on how frustrating we must have been to the Nazis opposing us. Every time they caught a unit off guard and started to push them around, we came along and pounded them to bits. Man for man, they were professionals and probably better than our infantry who were in only for the duration. There is no question in my mind that it would have been tough for our foot soldiers if we had not been on hand. We also made it extremely difficult for the Germans to bring up reinforcements, as we roamed, completely unopposed, far behind their lines, shooting up locomotives, trucks, and armored vehicles. One P-47 from another group, shot up Rommel's staff car, wounding him severely. Thus, their most reliable general was out of circulation for a long period.

We dropped numerous frag bombs, white phosphorus and our 500-pound GPs as well. I guess the frags were very effective, but I think that the white phosphorus bombs were really too small to be effective. They did make a spectacular explosion, though.

One of my responsibilities was to load and unload film from the gun camera which took pictures of all the gunnery. These films were analyzed by intelligence and then returned to the individual squadrons. The pilots had their own projector and watched themselves in action. Some pretty hot rivalries developed between various flights and some individual pilots as well. It takes a large ego to make a good pilot, as I soon found out.

On one occasion, during our stay at St. Dizier, Varino had a day off and another pilot flew my plane. After he had landed, he didn't take the customary jeep ride back to the debriefing tent. I was at a loss to figure out why he hung around. It was at least a half mile to the tent and it was cold and raw. Finally, he drew me aside and asked if I could destroy the gun film. This was strictly taboo, and I piously reminded him of this. I asked why he wanted it destroyed. After some hesitation, he confessed that he and his wingman had seen a whole bunch of German fighters on the ground, just waiting to be plastered. Greed got the best of them and they decided to hog the whole mess for themselves. Back and forth they went, shooting up a storm.

After their third pass, they realized that none of them had caught fire. One more pass revealed the ugly truth. Their acres of diamonds were made out of paste. All the German planes were made out of cardboard, and the other pilots had realized that and had not been tempted. The dilemma faced by these two birds was twofold: first, they had been fooled, and second, they had been too greedy to cut in their fellow pilots on this lovely nest egg. Guys like Sams and some of the others could be pretty acerbic and ironic after they had hoisted a few, and the others dreaded to be the butt of their sarcasm.

I didn't think that his feelings were worth my deliberately violating my responsibility. After all, it was his problem, not mine, so I told him nothing doing. As per standard operating procedure, I turned the film over to the proper authorities. However, I think he got someone else to short circuit it for him, because the film was never shown and I never heard about his being roasted by his peers. Ultimately, the story leaked out as it was bound to, but by that time, the sting was out of it. I don't know whether the officers got to see it, but we never did. This was too bad because we would have enjoyed watching those poor paper airplanes catching hell.

Probably the funniest thing about this whole affair was the fact that every enlisted man knew all about it before he had reached the debriefing tent. I guess his wingman either 'fessed up" or thought it too funny to suppress, and the gossip line took it from there.

We liked and respected our pilots, who had a tough and thankless job. None of them had enlisted to fly cover for the infantry, yet all accepted their lot in life without complaint and did their jobs well. The Sir Galahads of the air force were in the Eighth Air Force, doing combat with German interceptors who were trying to kill the Flying Fortresses bombing the Homeland. We mourned the pilots we lost, but this didn't prevent us from enjoying the occasional embarrassment of one of the more cocky ones when he pulled a blooper.

Of course, it was the burning ambition of all pilots to engage in aerial combat and knock down a few enemy planes, but the wary Luftwaffe carefully husbanded its resources, and our guys had little opportunity to check out the German pilots.

However, October 13th, 1944, was a glorious exception to the above. For the second time since we had crossed the channel, the Germans made an appearance in force, and some lively dogfights ensued. Five Me 109s and some FW 190s came out of the clouds and attacked our squadron. Our pilots shot down five and hit five others without loss. Varino was one of the lucky ones to score a kill, the only one he was destined to get in over one hundred missions. He was all smiles when he landed and told us about it. Another victory was scored by Lt. Loesch, who was our youngest pilot. He told his ground crew that he saw a 109 coming right in front of him, so he fired his guns and the 109 pilot flew right into his line of fire and exploded. His enthusiasm was so infectious that the whole squadron rejoiced with him in his moment of triumph.

This fracas partially made up for our first major encounter with the German Air Force which took place in Normandy and was a disaster. Our boys were caught asleep at the switch. A whole flock of German fighters came out of the clouds and swooped down on our planes. One of ours quickly exploded and crashed. In the ensuing fight, three more were shot down while we allegedly got four of theirs, although no one actually saw them crash. The German planes made their first pass before our people realized who they were. We heard that our guys thought that the enemy was a flight of P-47s from another group until it was too late.

Back to the nitty-gritty. Washing clothes began as a big problem at St. Dizier. The only provision the army made for laundry, was to furnish us with "GI soap." This caustic product reminded me of the brown soap we used as kids to dry out poison ivy. We had no problem in England or Normandy. In England we had decent facilities for laundry and in Normandy we had too many other things to worry about without thinking about something as prosaic as being a mite ripe or a bit greasy. Since we were all in the same boat, our various aromas cancelled out.

St. Dizier was different. For the first time since leaving England, we had some time on our hands to write home and to do our laundry. Most of us devoted at least part of our day off to wash our clothes. At first, we washed them in the Marne River where we must have looked like some of Van Gogh's peasants as we scrubbed and rinsed our garments on the river bank.

When winter set in, laundry became a real problem. At first, we boiled our clothes in soapy water and then rinsed them out in hot water which we made by using crankcase oil as fuel. However, the supply of oil was limited and it took forever for things to dry, and more often than not, it was so cold that everything froze before it had a chance to dry out. This got to be a real hassle, and laundry became an all-day chore.

Once again, Yankee ingenuity came to the rescue. We started to soak our clothes in 100-octane gas. This was fabulous. We could do our entire laundry in a half-hour, so it was no longer necessary to take the whole day to complete the job. No matter what we had to clean: dirty socks, greasy fatigues, sweaty underwear, you name it, it all turned out clean as a whistle after a 100-octane treatment. Everything dried out in a jiffy and left no residual odor. All we had to do was bring our laundry to the line, flag down the gas truck, get the driver to fill up a bucket with gas, dump in our clothes, stir them around a bit, throw out the gas, hang the clothes up to dry, and presto! Clean clothes! By lunch time at the latest, things were dry and ready to wear.

We felt a little guilty about wasting gas, but not guilty enough to stop. When Harrison installed our gas burner, we tried to bring our used gas in from the line, but it evaporated so quickly that we were unable to salvage much of it. Of course it was ruined as aviation fuel, but it was still good for our gas burner. We salved our consciences by attempting to save it, but that was about as far as we went.

Ernie White and a few other more conscientious types continued to boil their laundry. This involved putting up with lots of guff from the supply sergeant for wasting such "vital" supplies such as water and soap. Nobody said a thing about using precious gasoline, though. *Viva la Armee!*

The weather became more unpleasant as winter progressed. All flying ceased on rainy days as we didn't have suitable equipment for take-offs and landings when the weather was inclement, and even if we had, our pilots were unable to locate and hit their targets at the front. Some guys slept late when the weather was bad, but most of us got up and breakfasted as usual, and then either played cards or caught up on our reading. Because our tents were uncomfortable on rainy days, we ran our 100-octane burner just high enough to keep our tent dry and take the bite off the cold. I don't know what the other tents did, but they survived, so they must have devised some method to beat the weather. We all sympathized with the infantry, who had to live outside in such lousy weather.

Not having to report to the line or anywhere else in inclement weather created one of the major mysteries of our squadron which remains unsolved to this very day. An armorer from another flight slept late one rainy morning and woke up minutes before the chow line closed. He raced down to the chow line just before it closed and filled up his mess kit with goodies. Then he returned to his tent exhausted by all this effort. He placed his mess kit under his bunk and went to sleep. Come lunch time, he awoke and started to the chow line, but then realized his mess kit, was still full with his breakfast. He sat down and consumed his cold breakfast, cleaned his mess kit and filled it up with lunch. When he returned to his tent, he was not hungry, so once again, he put it under his cot. At suppertime he ate his cold lunch and got some dinner, but he was too full of cold lunch to eat.

The next day was clear as a bell, so back to the line we trudged completely mystified with an important question unanswered. Did this guy ever catch up on his meals, and if so, how? Come on, Sherlock, tell us what happened.

Crew chief Joe Thomas, Pilot Larry Kuhl and armorer Len Hitchman.
Picture was taken in St. Dizier in the Fall of 1944. Note the loaded and fused
500# GP bomb and protruding machine guns on left wing.

Chapter Seventeen
Visiting Xanadu

Paris is well worth a Mass
—Henry of Navarre

Early in November of '44, while we were still languishing in St. Dizier, all the names of the enlisted personnel who were interested in going on a furlough were put in a hat. I put mine in as a matter of habit, but I didn't give myself a chance of winning. To my gratification and astonishment, I was one of the four to hit the jackpot and won seven days in France. However, we winners quickly discovered that the large print giveth but the small print taketh away. The large print said seven days off, the small print said we could go anywhere in France except Paris. We were given a cock and bull story about the city facilities being overtaxed by all the brass who resided there, and we were cautioned that our furloughs would be revoked if we were caught there. Of course, telling a GI on furlough in France not to go to Paris is like taking kids to the beach and telling them not to go in the water.

One of the big differences between Europe and the United States is that the culture of many European countries is concentrated in the capital, where in the U.S. there are many different cultural centers. There is no city in France remotely comparable to Paris. This is true of London in England, Madrid in Spain, and many other European countries as well. Here in the U.S. there are many cities with distinctive and interesting cultures—New York, Chicago, San Francisco, and Boston—to name just a few. If we were awarded a furlough in the U.S. and forbidden to enter any of the above, there would be plenty of alternates. We were not aware of this at the time, but our sixth sense told us that Paris was the place to go.

Three of us decided to go together and headed for Rheims and its cathedral. We hitched a ride and arrived at Rheims in the late morning. We spent the rest of the day finding lodgings and sight-seeing. The big attraction for me was the Gothic cathedral, but there were a host of other things to see as well, so our time was well spent.

We found a small clean hotel near the cathedral with little difficulty and retired for the evening. We fought off a couple of zealous hookers who kept knocking at our door for an hour or more and then settled down for a nice snooze which was interrupted by the cathedral bells counting out the hours.

We had been prudent enough to bring along some grub which we had "borrowed" from the mess hall when our good buddy, Troy Robinson, conveniently looked the other way. After finishing this largesse, we fell back on some K-rations we brought with us for emergency purposes. They were pure ambrosia when we got hungry, and the alternate was some under-cooked goat meat or perhaps a slab of horse meat but they are not meant for long-time consumption since they are highly concentrated and raise hob with one's regularity. They did save our lives while we were in Rheims, but we realized that we had to find a better source of nourishment before long. Breakfasts were no problem, as eggs, toast, and ersatz coffee were not hard to come by, but lunch and dinner soon became a problem.

Not being able to eat decently in Rheims was a harbinger of things to come. Getting food was only part of the problem, not knowing what we got on the few occasions we did was also a major concern. The French had not yet recovered from the occupation and decent food was scarce. I am sure that they gave us the best that they had, but what WAS their best?

We felt that one day was sufficient for seeing Rheims, so we were faced with the dilemma of where to go. We were certain the rest of France would be no different from Rheims as far as getting decent meals was concerned, as the Jerries had been inconsiderate enough as to take a lot of the good eats and drinks with them as they retreated to the Fatherland.

After some thought, perhaps a second or two, we decided to head for Paris and take our chances. Paris was IT, so we traipsed down to the railroad depot to catch a train to *Gay Paree*. As saviors of France, we were able to ride the trains *gratis*. We checked with an English-speaking railroad man before boarding the train in order to ascertain how long the trip would be. He replied that on a good day, it would take about ten hours. We thought that perhaps he had misunderstood the question. No train in the world, even in war-ravaged France could possibly be that slow.

We boarded ancient coaches, complete with hard wooden seats, and settled back for a luxurious trip to Paris. Our confidence in a rapid trip increased as we started out at a rapid clip, zipping along at about thirty-five miles per hour. We felt sorry for the ignoramus back at the depot who didn't know how quickly his trains really went.

Then our bubble burst. About fifteen miles out of Rheims, we were shunted to a siding where we cooled our heels for about an hour. We were puzzled by the delay, but stayed put rather than doing something foolish like pulling the pin and trying to walk to Paris.

Finally we got underway once more and went another twenty miles before we were once again shunted to a siding. I looked out the window and spotted an ancient locomotive shifting ancient box cars around. It took me a few minutes to put two and two together and realize that it was our engine, which had been uncoupled from our train, that was shifting these freight cars around. I am not a genius by any matter or means, but it didn't take much brainpower to figure out that this was going to be a *long* ride after all, and that the ten hours we had been quoted might just be a mite optimistic and so it turned out. We stopped at every painted post between Rheims and Paris and some that weren't painted. The engine was uncoupled and it did its thing in the yard and then hooked on and took us to the next stop where it did the same thing.

At first we were irritated, but after a few stops we realized that we couldn't do anything about it, so we got out of the car at each stop, bought a bottle of wine, walked around, and enjoyed the scenery. We amused ourselves betting on how long the engine would be at each location. One of my companions said that only in France could you get a free train ride and still get gypped.

Another pal tried to stick the blame for the long train ride on me. He claimed that if our zealous pilots hadn't shot up so many locomotives with the guns I had mothered with such loving care, we would not have been in this sad predicament. I pointed out, a little weakly I admit, that if we hadn't made all those fascinating stops, he would have missed a lot of interesting scenery. I also told him that if we hadn't shot up their locomotives, the Germans would have hustled them off to the Fatherland and we would have had to walk.

We chuckled sadly as we recalled how much we had enjoyed watching gun camera pictures of the boilers of French locomotives emitting steam from a score of wounds after our pilots had given them the business. Somebody got the last laugh, but it was not us.

We finally arrived at the *Gare du Norde*, where we kept a weather eye for MPs who might apprehend us for trespassing on sacred ground. We inconspicuously attached ourselves to a group of official looking GIs, and boldly walked out of the station, past some MPs, and into town. Here we were lucky enough to find another clean fleabag where we spent the night.

In the morning, we got up early and hunger pangs started to hit us for real. We were starved and didn't know where to get anything to eat. The only decent place was the army transient mess which was close enough for us to spit on, but which might as well have been on the moon as far as we were concerned. We watched enviously as unconcerned GIs showed their papers and went in by the hundreds to eat their fill. Somehow, if we were to avoid starvation, we had to find a way to crash the joint without getting pinched. We feared having our papers being pulled, but we feared being considered failures by our peers at camp if we returned early even more.

The mess hall was surrounded by eagle-eyed MPs who appeared

ready to pounce on us illegals if we gave them half a chance. We were not aware at this time that their real quarry was the thousands of AWOLs who holed up in Paris. If they caught us, well and good, but we were not their target of preference. As I look back, I sometimes wonder what would have happened if we had boldly gone up to the mess hall, showed them our papers, and tried to enter it on our own. I am willing to bet that we could have sweet-talked our way in without difficulty. After all, we were all enlisted men together and we were not sure that they were even aware of the fact that we were *personae non grata*. At this time, we felt it was not worth the risk. We swapped some butts in a French cafe for a skimpy goat dinner at midday which included some marble-sized spuds and a slice of bread, and subsided on that the rest of the day.

The next morning was crisis time. It was either the GI mess or starvation. One guy, bolder or hungrier than the rest, sidled up to a likely candidate and asked him if he would add us to his orders. He shrugged and said that he wasn't paying for it, so why not? That broke the ice. From then on, it was a cinch to find some sympathetic guy with open papers and latch onto him. Our eating problems were over. We even gained so much confidence that we had a long conversation with an MP who had directed traffic on Omaha Beach. We exchanged adventures and when we saw that he was on duty, we didn't even bother finding a patron. As soon as he saw us, he just waved us through. We all knew that at this time the only people who didn't know that they were beaten were the Germans, so discipline was not near as strict as it had been.

Having gotten over this important hurdle, we were able to concentrate on doing our own thing. We kept our noses clean and didn't flaunt ourselves in their faces, and the MPs reciprocated by ignoring us and by not checking our papers. There were scads of AWOL GIs in Paris and these guys were on the lookout for them.

We didn't realize it at first, but we had another thing going for us. There was a proliferation of free French in town who wore our uniforms. When questioned by the MPs they shrugged their shoulders and said, "FFE, *no compre*," and kept on walking. After getting that answer a dozen times, it's a wonder that they ever checked anyone. Fortunately, none of these birds ever tried to crash the mess hall.

The FFE sword had a double edge, however. Every time we asked a "GI" for directions, he turned out to be an FFE who cut us off with the same curt answer. It was irritating to run into guys dressed exactly like us who were so disagreeable and who made no attempt to help or be sociable. If half these birds had been at the front where they belonged, they would have outnumbered the Germans three to one and we GIs could have gone home.

The only memorable Armistice Day in my life I spent in Paris in 1944.

We had just finished our usual hearty breakfast at the transient mess hall when we noticed a large crowd in a festive mood assembling along the Champs-Elysees where a number of barricades had been set up on both sides of the road to keep people off the pavement. This piqued our curiosity, so we went over and joined what soon became a huge crowd.

Although we were about seven rows from the front, we were taller than the majority so we could easily see the street over their heads. We stood there and awaited developments. After a long wait, perhaps a half hour, a procession of limousines headed toward us and the huge crowd started to cheer as they approached. Sitting in one of the open limos, cigar in one hand and making his famous "V for victory" sign with the other was none other than Winston Churchill, accompanied by Charles De Gaulle. Churchill was all smiles and thoroughly enjoying the tremendous reception he was getting from the enthusiastic crowd. De Gaulle was his usual dour-looking self.

The cheerful crowd was in a festive mood, but the irony of their celebrating "Armistice Day" really struck us. Armistice from what? Here we were in France, just liberated from four years of rugged occupation by the Germans, a France still fighting in an even greater war less than thirty years after the termination of the so-called "war to end all wars." As we went our way, we couldn't help thinking about the folly of man and wondering what the prospects for permanent peace would be when our war was over. Of all the hypocritical holidays, Armistice Day has to be the worst.

My tastes differed from my companions, so we usually split up after breakfast, went our separate ways, and then met at the mess hall and ate dinner together. I wanted to visit some of the historic places with which Paris abounds, the cathedrals and the many museums, while the others were more interested in shopping and people watching. They spent much of their time in the center of the city where there was lots of hustle and bustle and first rate shops. On several occasions, as when I went to Notre Dame and the Louvre, they went with me.

The subway system, or "Metro", as it was known, was magnificent and so accurately marked that I had no problem going anyplace in the entire city just by following the excellent directions on the Metro maps which were available for the taking at every stop. Here again, we were heroes and rode for free.

By the time we had completed our holiday, I had seen Rheims and a lot of Paris. Even with the austerity of war, Paris was a great city and I am glad we had the nerve to see it. I took in part of the Louvre, visited Notre Dame and Sacre Coeur cathedrals, and all three of us spent a day in Versailles. Not bad for a week's work.

As spectacular as this furlough had been, something even better was in store for me. About six weeks after this pleasant interlude from wartime drudgery, my name came up for my regular furlough. This time I was fortunate enough to go with some of my good friends. Several of them were interested in doing some important sight-seeing, and I was just the guy to show them the way.

We hitchhiked into Paris on an army six-by-six and set up headquarters at the hotel I had used previously. I knew the ropes, so meals were no problem. Once again we hit the Metro and went all over Paris. Some of it was old hat, but since we had eliminated Rheims, we were able to spend some important time at the Louvre where I had fun "reading" some of the hieroglyphics to an entourage of touring nurses. I am sure that they didn't believe that I was all that erudite, but my "translations" broke the ice and we had a good time with them for the balance of our museum tour. Once outside the museum, we chatted for a while, had our pictures taken together, and parted ways.

While I had a great time with my friends, I think I enjoyed it more on my own, doing my own thing and discovering the town alone. I stood a better chance of getting rolled (this never occurred to me at the time), but then, all life is a gamble. I don't think I would have changed much had I known of the dangers, although I would have been a bit more careful and would have avoided some of the seamier places.

We didn't realize the best thing about these junkets until we were discharged. They didn't count as time off! Thus we had our cake and ate it also. In my case, this amounted to almost three hundred dollars in additional pay at my discharge. Those bucks came in handy when I started back to college and some stiff bills came due.

Chapter Eighteen
The Battle of the Bulge

With Ruin on Ruin, Rout on Rout
—John Milton, *Paradise Lost*

As winter progressed, it became apparent that the Germans, for all their stubbornness, were beaten. They were retiring on both fronts, and their tremendous losses on both fronts had left them with neither the manpower nor the equipment to continue fighting much longer. We were overrunning the Fatherland, and our pilots were raising havoc both on the front and behind their lines. The Russians had conquered East Prussia and were moving into Germany proper. The Nazis had been on the defensive since their disastrous defeat at Avaranches, and we all felt that this would continue until they either saw the light or got rid of Hitler, which amounted to the same thing.

Life had become a dull routine of loading bombs and reloading and maintaining guns. The weather was cold, humid, and windy, making it almost impossible to keep warm. Nobody complained because we knew that many had it much worse. When things really got bad, someone would say, "Times are tough in the ETO," and all present would smile. Our sense of humor carried us through and we joked about adversity. Everybody was careful not to mention that this was only December and we had at least three more months to go before we could expect any improvement in the weather. All this boredom came to a screeching halt at 2 A.M. one morning.

Our supply sergeant came bursting into our tent in a bloody sweat. He woke up Bob Loitz who was nearest the door and told him to grab his gun and report to the line immediately. Bob told him to go to hell, he wasn't on the guard duty roster. The sergeant started to rant and rave, waking up the rest of us in the process. He told us that Nazi paratroopers were in the area and that our planes were in mortal danger.

Something had to be amiss for him to be up at this early hour, and he had never recruited guards before. We got dressed quickly, grabbed our carbines and a fistful of the extra ammo he had brought with him, and headed out to the line. It never occurred to us what a horrible mismatch we and our little pop guns would be against skilled and well-armed German elite troops. I headed to my plane and the others went to theirs. My two crewmates were already there, armed to the teeth with guns that they hadn't shot since our training days. I suddenly realized with a jolt what we would be up against if the Germans were to attack. I kept my feelings to myself, as the others were scared enough as it was.

"It was bitter cold and we were sick at heart." There was a cold mist in the air and visibility was about fifty yards. Nobody knew what was going on or whom we were to report to. I suggested that the three of us spread out, one guy at the tail of the plane and the other two at the end of each wing. In this way, we could see in every direction and were separated from each other as well.

My crew chief, Wasowski, was the only one with a watch, so I asked him for the time. Luckily, we all had been issued flashlights, so he put his arm inside his jacket to hide the light and read his watch. I don't recall just what time it was but it was in the wee hours.

We stood there for over an hour without an inkling of what was going on and getting madder by the minute. We thought that had there been any Krauts in the area, they would have long since made their appearance. The time for a successful surprise had long since passed.

Finally, someone up the line lost patience and let go with a Tommy gun. This was a signal for everyone to blaze away. The noise of carbines and Tommy guns going off was deafening. I decided to get into the act, but just to be on the safe side for the inquiry which was sure to come, I hollered, "Halt" three times and then emptied my magazine into the air. We had lots of extra ammo so some of the guys reloaded and fired again. We all had a rollicking good time and the air was torn to pieces. The din was deafening and the firing must have lasted well over a half hour. The mist in the air kept the fumes from the guns from rising, so we had a neat aroma to go with all the racket. Soon the guys either got tired of shooting or ran out of ammo and the din ceased as abruptly as it had begun. We made ourselves comfortable and waited for our relief.

At close to six A.M., an officer in a jeep came out. He was furious and ordered all of us to report to headquarters on the double. We were as irate as he was and were spoiling for a confrontation. I don't recall which officer it was, but he got up and demanded the names of all those who had fired their guns. I was the first to admit that I had done so and that I had spotted a shadow which didn't respond to my challenge so I fired at it. I didn't tell him that I had fired my entire magazine at it and he didn't ask.

Several others admitted that they had fired also under the same conditions. The fact that some of us had fired legitimately weakened any case the officers might have had against us. I don't think that they believed us, but they could not dispute our answer. Then one officer really did it. He had the temerity to state that they were afraid to come out to the line with all that gunfire going on. That did it! One of the miscreants jumped up and shouted, "In other words, if the Krauts had been attacking us, you would have left us holding the bag?" That stopped them cold and we were dismissed. As it turned out, no Germans had landed within seventy miles of us.

Of all the events of my army career, this was the one that I have thought about the most. I keep wondering just what would have happened had the Germans really hit us. All I have ever read about German paratroopers is that they were really tough hombres and I am not sorry that they dispensed their favors elsewhere. There are many safer and more pleasant ways to prove my valor than taking on some die hard Nazi paratrooper.

Our officers were faced with a situation that was unique and not covered by the book, and it was interesting to see their reaction. I have always thought that whoever was in charge of this fiasco had pushed the panic button. Having an excitable guy like our supply sergeant who knew nothing about guards or guard duty wake us up was their first mistake. He alienated us from the word "go." I imagine that intelligence had passed the word to our communications people that German paratroops had landed behind Allied lines and for us to be on the lookout for them. This did not require our getting up and racing out to the line helter skelter, nor did it mean that we were targets for the enemy. I guess some excitable guy translated this into our being surrounded by heavily armed Krauts who were thirsting for our blood.

None of us had any quarrel with the decision to wake us up and to give us extra ammunition or to our going out the line. What did upset us was the lack of leadership when we reported to the line and the lack of information we got about what was happening. We had no idea of why we were there or what to expect.

It was obvious to me that no one had taken the time to think out defensive priorities. Their first thought was the safety of the airplanes. However, airplanes, as critical and as expensive as they were, could be replaced much easier than our personnel. It took four or five years to train a pilot, perhaps two years to train a mechanic, and a year and a half to replace us armorers. If we lost all our planes, we would have been out of business for two months at the longest. Had we lost our skilled people and particularly our pilots, it would have been bye bye 511th forever.

We should have protected our pilots first and foremost. Any attacking German might have been satisfied making a big fire of our planes and then departing, leaving our pilots alone. We had neither the arms nor the know-how to fight off a determined German attack, since the line was in the open. However, our officers were in tents surrounded by trenches. Since any German assault of necessity had to be hit and run, we might have held off an attack long enough for help to arrive. As I saw it, we should had a skeleton crew on the line to save the planes if possible and to warn those in camp in case of an attack. Our main force should have been set up in camp. This whole affair was an interesting study in military tactics and we had some fun in our tent acting as military experts. Of course, our officers were all civilian soldiers and it was difficult for them to make a decision of this nature and magnitude. They had neither the training nor the experience to cope with such a complex situation. There is no question that they did the best they could.

This incident was our introduction to the Battle of the Bulge. We found out several days afterwards that the Germans had launched a massive surprise attack in the area between the First and Third U.S. Armies. They found a weak spot in our lines and made significant advances in a poorly defended area. Surprise was not their only piece of good luck. The weather was horrible, so our entire air force was grounded.

We heard that an entire division, the 106th, newly arrived in Europe, was wiped out and several others were severely mauled. Newly arrived units were customarily sent to relatively quiet areas in order to get acclimated to combat conditions and then moved up as they gained experience. It was a well-known that casualties are always greater among the greenhorns than among the veterans. In this case, the 106th Division happened to be in the wrong place at the wrong time. There is a sad postscript to this and I was unaware of it at the time, but one of my high school classmates, who had taken his physical at the same time as I did, was a member of the 106th and was killed in the first German attack.

Our intelligence was unaware that the Germans still had reserves to mount an attack of this magnitude. The German advances were spectacular at first, and the inclement weather which grounded our fighter-bombers was a godsend to them.

As we learned more about this assault, we were relieved to find out that their ultimate destination was Antwerp, which was not in our direction. We prayed for good weather so we could help the hard-pressed infantry. We took advantage of every slight break in the weather, which had been miserable since the attack began, to send up such help as we could. We flew in weather that was marginal at the best, because we were able to bomb areas instead of individual targets. The enemy had to concentrate their forces in order to keep their advance going, and it was much easier for us to hit these concentrations than it had been in the past when we had to attack individual vehicles.

About ten days after its initiating this assault, the German attack started to peter out. The Third U. S. Army began to batter their left flank, and the First U.S. Army attacked from the north. They were unable to capture Bastogne, a key road center directly in the path of their objective. This failure threw their timetable off completely. To add fire to fire, the weather broke and all hell broke loose. Hundreds of fighter-bombers started to hit them. When they attempted to retreat, the Allies battered them with artillery. The retreat quickly turned into a rout and it was Avranches and the Falaise Pocket once again.

As the weather improved, we started to fly from can see to can't see just as we had done in Normandy. We bombed and strafed jammed up German tanks and vehicles from dawn to dusk. According to official statistics, our group destroyed over thirty one hundred enemy vehicles. We worked like Trojans to help the Third Army encircle the enemy forces and thus cut off a huge segment of the German forces between us and Berlin. However, this was not to be. Although their losses were catastrophic, the Jerries still managed to withdraw some of their infantry successfully and thus continue the fight.

The two main results from this attack were, first and foremost, a disastrous defeat for the attacking Germans and the complete disruption of the Allies schedule. It could be described as a monumental defeat for the Nazis and a pyrrhic victory for the Allies. Many units had to be either disbanded or replenished, as our casualties were even greater than in Normandy. An ancillary, but very important result was the lessening of German troops on the Eastern Front, which the Russians didn't hesitate to exploit.

The Battle of the Bulge bought a little time for Germany on the Western Front, but in the long run, it shortened the war and assured the world that Berlin would be taken by the Russians. Hitler did no favor to the German people when he ordered this attack.

We in the ground crews realized that this was no ordinary German attack, but we felt that we had far too many horses for them to have any long-range success. The thing that bothered us the most was the beating taken by our infantry and tank corps. With the plethora of targets and many new pilots, we not only had to load many bombs and machine gun ammo, but we had to make numerous barrel changes since these newcomers kept firing continuously until their guns were empty. There is little doubt that our air power was the most vital ingredient in the defeat of the German attack. Once the weather broke, it became a foregone conclusion that the Germans were going to take a real beating.

Although our pilots never saw any planes at this time, the Luftwaffe did make a strong appearance at the start of the attack and shot up quite a few of our fighters on the ground, but when the weather cleared, they either disappeared or were shot down. I think that the Battle of the Bulge marked the virtual death of the once mighty German Luftwaffe.

The Battle of the Bulge was one of the most fascinating battles of World War II. Military writers have had a field day discussing the pros and cons of both German and Allied strategy. Hitler, with his usual optimism, ordered the attack against the advice of all his generals. His aim of retaking Antwerp was both impossible and ridiculous. He had neither sufficient forces nor any air cover to be successful. His farthest advance still left him over sixty miles from his objective.

However, once he gave the order, his generals skillfully implemented his plan. They caught the Allies completely unaware and skillfully exploited this surprise. However, it was just a question of time before the weather cleared and the Allied air forces messed things up. With no air power, Hitler's forces were doomed. The most intriguing thing to me is that he squandered his few reserves against us when it was the Russians who were his most implacable foe and whom he hated.

For our efforts, we were awarded the Battle of the Bulge campaign ribbon to go with the various others we had already acquired. Like all campaign ribbons, it was a brightly colored rectangle which we wore on the left breast of our dress uniforms. A medal went with each ribbon, but one had to write to receive it, and as of yet I have not done so and I probably never will. Taking part in a battle became important when discharge time came around, since each battle one participated in gave him five points, while a month of service counted one. I think we were awarded the Air Battle over Germany, The Invasion of Europe, The Breakthrough at St. Lo, The Battle of the Bulge, and the Victory in Europe ribbons, but I'm not sure. These ribbons came in handy when the war was over and everybody wanted to go home.

By the middle of January or close to it, all the excitement of the Bulge started to die down and we returned to our routine missions of hitting a concentration of troops here, knocking out a strong point there, etc. The U.S. First and Ninth Armies, the Canadian First, and the British Eighth Armies became the glamour outfits of the Western Front. All the real action and excitement took place in their areas. Many of the P-47's supporting them, as mentioned before, were armed with rockets which were deadly against tanks.

As usual, we heard very little about what was going on. We did know that our particular front was static, so there had to be action elsewhere. *Stars and Stripes* published war news, but it was all in the past tense. We had no knowledge of the British failure to capture a bridge across the Rhine River at Nijmegen in Holland. We were thoroughly bored at St. Dizier and longed to get back into some real action.

At long last, in February, we received orders to go to an airfield in Belgium near the town of Hasselt, and for the first time, I was in the first echelon. We spent an afternoon loading up all our paraphernalia on good old six-by-sixes and could hardly wait for the sunrise to be off and running. Even a pouring rain didn't dampen our good humors. Going anyplace, as long as it was away from St. Dizier, was such a blessing that it would have taken a lot more than a little rain to dampen our enthusiasm.

Chapter Nineteen

With the First Echelon to Belgium

The Bravest of these are the Belgians
—Julius Caesar

We made the trip to Belgium in a driving rainstorm, traveling over war-torn roads and through a whole host of ruined towns and cities. We hit so many potholes along the way; it was lucky that we didn't lose every tooth in our heads. Fortunately, our trucks held up beautifully; we had nary a breakdown along the way. This made me a firm believer in the efficacy of GI tires. They may not have ridden smoothly, but we had no flats, which was more important. A flat under those conditions would have been disastrous. Our drivers were super in their navigation and in getting us to our destination even while driving on unmarked roads and in horrible weather.

The only stops we made enroute were to gas up. It was up to us to take care of our bodily needs at the same time. The weather was so cold and rainy that none of us strayed more than a few feet from our vehicles—we couldn't wait to get back on board and under way.

As I recall, we left about six in the morning and arrived at Hasselt about eight or nine P.M., wet, tired, and discouraged. The trip had been only about one hundred and sixty miles as the crow flies but it had been rugged and exhausting. The prospect of making camp at that hour and under those conditions filled us with despair. Fortunately, our leaders found us lodgings in the gymnasium of a local coal mine or high school where it was warm and dry.

The weather next morning was still raw, but the rain had ceased. The owners of the gym fixed us a hearty breakfast, and then we hustled back into our trucks and headed for the airstrip, some twenty miles away. We were gratified to find that our airstrip was very close to camp. We arrived at our new location at about ten o'clock and set to work immediately on setting up camp. We camped in a large grove of second growth trees, some of which had already started to bud. The ground was muddy as all get out, but the digging was easier than we had expected.

We had to work rapidly because the second echelon was due before nightfall and they expected everything to be shipshape upon their arrival. The great night's sleep put us in a fine humor and we really went to work with a will. It was not long before all the tents were up, the latrine holes were dug, potties were set up, and slit trenches dug around each tent. These trenches were necessary to act as gutters to drain off rainwater and keep it from seeping into our tents. They also served as protection against the remote possibility of a German raid and any errant buzz bomb that might intrude on our sleep.

The second echelon arrived on schedule, and all our planes landed at the airstrip shortly thereafter. We flew our first mission from our new location early next morning, having lost only one day of action.

Belgium was paradise compared to St. Dizier. The people were more friendly and there were some nice wine and beer joints where we could spend a pleasant evening off the base. Drinks were good and inexpensive. The local people liked us, and we enjoyed them. Only a few of the bars fronted as cathouses—a pleasant switch from St. Dizier where every bar had its coterie of ladies of the evening. It was fun talking to the rough coal miners who were regulars at all the bars. We learned a bit of the local language, and they picked up even more English from us.

It was in Belgium that I first noticed that Europeans picked up English more rapidly than we did their languages. There were two reasons for this. First, European countries were smaller than the U.S. and people only a short distance away might speak an entirely different language. Therefore learning different languages was a necessity which they accepted without a second thought. We Americans had a certain built-in arrogance about languages. We felt that others should learn English rather than we learn their tongues. This was unfortunate since we had a heaven-sent opportunity to become bilingual and we passed it up. The locals would have been happy to teach us. I must admit that I was as bad as anyone else in this respect.

Belgium had its hookers, but they were a better class—assuming any hookers have class—than those in France, and fewer of our people indulged here than did in France. There was at least one good reason for the better behavior of the GIs in Belgium. The girls were far nicer looking and behaved better. Even though we met girls at bars, many of them were clean-cut and pleasant to talk to, so we enjoyed spending the evenings dancing, sipping wine, and in two language conversations with them. They reminded me of the girls we had met at Ellitche's Gardens back in Denver. Of course, some of the guys went on the prowl and they had no trouble making out, but this is true in any country.

The advent of spring brought warmer and sunnier weather, giving us the opportunity to explore a completely new environment. We were not far from Hasselt, a good sized town, and the city of Liege was only sixty some miles away. Both of these places as well as the countryside afforded us ample opportunity to explore to our hearts' content. The countryside in spring was beautiful, and the percentage of GIs there to enjoy it was much lower than anyplace we had been since leaving England. For some reason, the fewer the GI's in an area, the better they behave and the more fun they have.

U.S soldiers were great, but too many in any given area tended to louse things up. They usually had more money than the locals and spent it recklessly. Where ever they went, prices of wine and beer tended to rise. This was not good for anyone. Higher prices drove the locals away so that many bars became GI hangouts instead of a place where we could mingle with the natives. We went to town to mix with people, not other GI's. We saw enough of each other on the base.

A transient truck driver stopped for a glass of wine at one bar. When he had finished his drink, he asked for the bill. When he found out how little he had to pay, he told the woman owner of the bar that she was a sucker to charge so little when the GI's could afford to pay a lot more. She immediately raised her prices. This upset her regular customers and drove most of the locals away. Even some of the GI's considered her new price schedule highway robbery, so many of them left, as well. I don't know whether her old customers returned after we left but I am sure that a permanent aura of distrust remained there. In the meantime, Prince Charming who started the whole thing departed for the front and never was aware of the trouble he had caused.

Hasselt had a theater which showed American films, complete with Belgian subtitles. For the first time since Normandy, it was possible to enjoy a good time off the base which didn't entail either booze or women. We got a kick out of listening to the soundtrack while the Belgians had to look at the subtitles. Hitch and I liked to take in the early shows, then hit a friendly pub where we mingled with the locals. I can't remember what games they played, but we were often invited to join in them. They accepted us and we reciprocated.

However, the crowning glory of Belgium was the luscious showers we took about twice a week at a local colliery. About twenty of us at a time piled onto GI trucks and hustled over to the nearby coal mine where we enjoyed the most luxurious showers of my military career. The shower heads were about a foot in diameter, so we stood directly under them while water at the exact right temperature cascaded over us. Every tiny port of the heads was open, so the water fell evenly over every part of our anatomy. They were a lovely contrast to the lukewarm showers we had improvised and used for the past year and a half.

In England, Normandy, and St. Dizier, the best we could manage was a bucket of tepid water that dripped through a perforated tin can. My day off in St. Dizier was Sunday, and I spent a good deal of the time working up enough nerve to face the ordeal of taking one of those horrors so

206

I could live with myself and with my tentmates. In the colliery, buckets of lovely water flowed over me, washing away accumulated dirt, sweat, all my cares, and even a sin or two. I had never realized the soothing power of hot water until we hit these showers. Since the area around Hasselt had scads of water and lots of fuel to heat it, we were welcome to use them at any time except during shift changes at the mine when the miners themselves used them. I am sure that Uncle Sam had to pay for this luxury, but it was so delightful that I, for one, would have gladly paid for them myself. As yet, I have not had the opportunity to return to Belgium, but I will always have a soft spot in my heart for anything Belgian because of those fantastic showers.

I also was impressed by how clean and neat Belgium was. The people appeared to have survived the German occupation very well. There was a lot of austerity, but I don't remember seeing much war damage. I imagine that the Germans had retreated through this part of Europe so rapidly that they had no opportunity to set up any points of resistance which always end up in severely damaging a civilian installations. This also prevented them from doing any looting. I am sure that some of the Belgian goodwill was due not only to their liberation, but to the lack of war damage to the area around us as well.

Several of us hitchhiked into Brussels one day. The city had been virtually untouched by war and everything was neat as a pin. We had some fun climbing to the top of a memorial to the Unknown Soldier, from which point we had a super view of the city. There was much to see, so we spent the whole day doing the town. Since I am an architecture buff, particularly where Gothic architecture is concerned, I wanted to see some of the churches and my friends were nice enough to accommodate me. Brussels had no churches that could compete with Notre Dame or the Rheims Cathedral in size, but one cathedral in particular was a little jewel. It lacked gargoyles and size, but it had a glass roof over the altar. When we were there, the sun was shining on the altar, enhancing the beauty of the entire sanctuary. I bought a post card of it, but in the course of time, it has disappeared so I have no idea either of its name or its location in Brussels. I am sure that Brussels has grown and changed with the times but if and when I ever return, hunting up that lovely church will be one of my top priorities. Since some fifty years have passed and my memory has a tendency to play tricks on me these days, I can only hope that I will be able to find it.

There was a tremendous difference between the French and the Belgians. Many Belgians spoke passable English and enjoyed speaking it, while the French expected us to speak French and resented it when we didn't do so. The Belgian cooperation made it easy for us to get directions and we were able to get around easily. The "FFI no compre" be-

Flight Chief Warren Cubit and best friend Len Hitchman near our airstrip at Ghenk, Belgium in February of 1945. Pyramidal tents in the background were our living quarters for over a year. They were more comfortable than they looked.

came an unpleasant memory. The war was grinding down, and the Germans were on the east side of the Rhine with no hope of ever recrossing it, so our security became lax and many of the local kids came out to the base to look around. Troy Robinson saw some of them digging nuggets out of the garbage, so he kept all edibles separate from the garbage and made sure that the kids had access to it. It was odd how much cake and other sweets unaccountably turned up in the stuff Troy saved for them. These kids were nice and polite and thought we were heroes. We enjoyed having them around and took them out to the line and showed them our airplanes.

By the time we reached Belgium, many of our original pilots had completed their tours and returned to the States. The stress of combat had begun to take its toll on these guys who had seen so much action. Few pilots were able to fly more than one hundred missions, considered a "tour," without getting "flak-happy. They became nervous and irritable and their efficiency dropped. This condition was endemic; some pilots could take more than others, but all except a very few got flak-happy sooner or later. This was particularly true of squadron commanders who had the conflicting responsibilities of safeguarding the lives of their pilots and flying successful missions.

Group commanders did not fly as much, since their overall responsibility for administration and the well-being of their squadrons was so great. Since their combat pressure was not as great as that of the ordinary pilot or squadron commander, they lasted longer.

When Mike Varino, the first pilot on my plane, started something he was determined to finish it. For example, on one mission, his tachometer went out so he was unable to determine the rpm of his engine. It was mandatory to abort the mission under these conditions, since his prop could run away and he might not be aware of it. This was the end of the airplane. The pilot had to bale out or make an emergency landing. If this occurred behind enemy lines, the best that he could hope for was become a prisoner of war. There were many occasions when the irate German citizens got to the downed airman before the troops and a severe beating was the result.

At any rate, rather than return, he stayed behind another aircraft and compared the rotation of his prop against the one on the other plane. If his prop seemed to be going slowly counterclockwise, then the other prop was turning faster than his. If his turned clockwise against the other prop, then his was rotating faster. As long as his rotation was close to the other one, he knew by stroboscopic effect that he was okay. At the time, I admired his tenacity, but on further analysis, I think he was foolhardy. One pilot on one mission was not worth the tremendous risk he took. This was not safe and was condemned by regulations. Better to abort than risk losing a virtually priceless pilot and an expensive plane as well. I was sure that as time went on and his nerves started to fray that he would never had done this.

Mike was a fine guy and an excellent pilot, and we missed him when he finally left for home. It was never quite the same after he left since we had worked together for so long. However, all of us on K4-M rejoiced that he left in one piece. Many of his peers were not so lucky. Some of the more daring pilots returned for more after some time back home, but I was glad that he was not one of them. He made a point of calling our parents when he arrived in the States and my folks appreciated his thoughtfulness.

The character of our outfit changed dramatically after our vets had left. While the pilots who flew my plane were assigned to "C" flight, we never again had one who flew K4-M consistently, so we never had the camaraderie which we had built up with Varino.

For a short time, it appeared that a Lt. Taylor might be his permanent replacement. He was an unkempt individual who always had a couple of days' growth on his chin and looked like he slept in his uniform. He was an easygoing type, and we looked forward to his staying with us. He had much in common with Varino. He was a good pilot and an excellent shot. To our disappointment, he only stayed for a week and seldom flew our plane again.

The time taken for a pilot to finish his tour varied with the individual pilot and the type of missions he flew. Some flew more than others for some reason. Our original pilots lasted the longest because they had always flown together and had started off fresh. Evidently, by the time we reached Belgium, no more complete units were being sent to Europe so the only opportunity newcomers had for action was to replace somebody in an active unit. Replacements had little or no combat experience and had to play catch-up in such fundamentals as formation flying. Some had already flown combat before and had either been wounded or sick and were now returning to action. These replacements came from a replacement depot and were usually not as good as our originals. Others came to us straight from the States and were as green as grass. The older pilots shepherded them along as best they could. Not having a steady pilot took away a lot of the interest we had for our jobs, which was unfortunate for all concerned. This instability was probably due to the rapid influx of new pilots, all of whom wanted a crack at the enemy before it was too late. I believe we lost more planes at this time than at any other comparable period. Our new guys lacked skill and experience and they were anxious to get a piece of the action, so they took chances that the old-timers might never have taken. In their haste to make a name for themselves, they forgot that although the Germans were whipped and had no chance of winning the war, their antiaircraft gunners were as sharp as ever. They had learned a lot and only took high percentage shots in order to minimize the risk of lethal retaliation by our flyers. By now, the war assumed the position of a lopsided pro basketball game. Everyone was just running out the clock and anything accomplished from now on only changed the statistics but did nothing to win the war. In basketball, these stats are referred to as "garbage points" and so they were to us.

As the war went on, the German occupied territory shrank and targets were less scattered and there were more of them. This had a negative side. German antiaircraft batteries became concentrated as well. With little fear of any interference from the air, our guys shot up all kinds of German equipment, some of which exploded very satisfactorily. One of our guys saw a German plane and lit after it. It went past him as if he was standing still. I think that this was the first and only jet anyone in our outfit ever saw.

While we were in England, most of our missions consisted of destroying bridges, communication centers, and enemy transport. Enemy opposition was either very light or nil. After we crossed the channel, we flew support missions for the Third Army. This was a different ballgame because many of the installations we attacked were defended by antiaircraft guns. The milk runs were over.

To use their machine guns effectively, our pilots had to fly below one thousand feet, well within the range of even small caliber antiaircraft guns such as the twenty mm guns. Since they had lots of practice, the German flak gunners were very good at their job. Although our planes were fast and were vulnerable for only a short time, we were bound to lose some. According to the figures I have ascertained from looking at the 511th squadron log, we lost twenty-six pilots during the war due to enemy action. We lost others due to accidents such as runaway props, but these did not count as official losses, although they were just as unavailable for action as the other eighteen. For every pilot lost, at least three planes were destroyed. Many of these were lost in harrowing crash landings or bailing out over unknown terrain.

On every mission, pilots had to expect heavy flak, unexpected changes in the weather, the possibility of attack by enemy aircraft, mechanical problems, and last, but far from least, the very real possibility of being shot at by our own trigger-happy anti aircraft.

As previously mentioned, Charles Loesh was killed by our own flak and other planes were damaged. We considered this to be inexcusable. Our P-47 had only a slight resemblance to the German FW-190—both had radial engines—but these planes were not designed for use against ground positions. They were built as fighters to destroy our bombers and were very effective against the B-17's as they bombed German cities. We tangled with them on two occasions, but I never heard of them strafing ground positions during the entire war. We could never understand why our flak gunners didn't take time to make positive identification before shooting. The German air force was so emaciated by the time we had crossed the channel that it was no longer a major threat. A little restraint on the part of the flak gunners would have saved us a lot of misery. Many of our pilots were so upset at the loss of Loesh that they wanted to return to the scene of the crime and dust the guilty gunners with some caliber-fifty lead. Of course, cooler heads prevailed before we did anything that drastic.

Loesh was one of our youngest pilots and a nice guy to boot. He only flew my plane once. When he came out to take off, he introduced himself and asked us if there were any peculiarities he should know about. When he returned, he thanked us for our good work, shook our hands, and took the jeep back to debriefing. Within a month, he was killed.

From the moment they started up their engines until they shut them off, our flyers were under constant strain. Some could take longer than others, but it was just a question of time before even the strongest buckled under the pressure. The human being was not designed for this type of stress.

I was no expert in the field of psychiatry, but it seemed to me that the flyers, who had to face anti-aircraft fire and other types of weaponry which they couldn't often counter suffered the most. Thus our flyers and to a lesser amount, the bomber crews, suffered more than the interceptors who had to face enemy planes. The latter were at least able to shoot back. The man-to-man nature of escort flying stimulated flyers so that they could last longer than ground support pilots. The interceptors had the added advantage of knowing that the enemy planes were far more interested in shooting down the bombers than they were in attacking the escorts.

Years after the war, I read *Horrido*, by Col. Raymond F. Toliver and Trevor J. Constable. It appears that Herman Goering was not as considerate of his pilots as "Hap" Arnold was of ours. Goering made his pilots fly until they were disabled, killed, or fortunate enough to survive. Some of these birds flew over nine hundred missions, alternating between the eastern and western fronts. Many had over a hundred aerial victories. Some were shot down over a dozen times and managed to survive. The authors make no mention of the many who had few or no victories, which must have been a large number since German air losses were huge.

After reading this book, I wonder if Luftwaffe fighter pilots considered themselves as knights errant—if they considered combat just a stimulating, if dangerous, game. I imagine our escort pilots of the Eighth Air Force had a far different view of flying than ours did. All they had to do was worry about the guys flying planes with the black crosses on them, no flak, no fear of our own trigger-happy gunners. In the Ninth Air Force, there were far too many ways to get killed and our fellows were aware of every one of them.

Enough on that depressing subject. Since I was and still am a practicing Roman Catholic, I didn't eat meat on Friday. The Church gave us a dispensation from this discipline while we served in the armed forces, so I usually ate whatever Troy Robinson served. However, on Good Friday, 1945, while we were in Belgium, I decided to abstain from meat for some reason or other, perhaps from Divine Intervention. I found that they were serving roast beef, which made it more difficult to abstain, but a promise made is a debt unpaid, so I persevered. My meal thus consisted of succulent dehydrated potatoes, watery vegetables, and a dessert of canned fruit. I had to yank my tray back quickly to prevent one of the servers from drowning my spuds in gravy. I always had had a thing about GI gravy since a day on KP when I had seen a massive pool of pure grease form on the top of some which had been left to sit for a short time.

As I ate this spartan repast, I was subjected to some good-natured kidding about qualifying for sainthood. I told these wiseacres that I would be happy to intercede for them when I reached Valhalla and they were down in a mass of flames. After dinner, I proceeded to our tent to do some reading before the sun set and it would be time to retire.

In the middle of the night, the whole camp was in an uproar. Evidently the cooks had tried to squeeze an extra day out of the gravy. The rush to the latrines looked like a scene from the Three Stooges. Guys were hitting trees, tripping over tent ropes, and falling into the slit trenches we had dug as protection against the buzz bombs that never came, in their desperate rush for relief. At least three tents collapsed as agonized guys hit the center pole trying to get out. Of course, the latrines were jammed so many sufferers just headed deeper into the woods that surrounded our camp. Many didn't make it, so our pathetic showers had to work overtime and all through the night as well. I am not sure how welcome some of these sufferers were when they went to the collier next day to clean off.

The hideous din woke me up, but it took me a while to realize what was going on since I was unaffected and still half asleep. All five of my tentmates suffered acutely trying desperately to escape the confines of the tent to relieve themselves.

One of the cooks, a portly gent by the name of Johnson, made a dash for the latrine which was already overcrowded and got the verbal beating of his life, barely escaping a physical one as well.

As luck would have it, an early morning mission was scheduled for the next morning so all the ailing had to report to the line by six A.M. Since I was unaffected by this plague, I did most of the work preparing the planes. Somehow, we managed to scrape up enough pilots so the planes took off on time. I would not have been willing to vouch for the accuracy of their bombing, though, but at least all returned unscratched.

Very few ate breakfast next morning, but by noon things were much better and most appetites had returned by dinnertime. Some of the worst cases persisted for several days until the bug finally relented and went elsewhere.

For once in my life, I had the good sense to keep a discreet silence over my success in avoiding the worst case of GIs our outfit had ever experienced. Most of the boys had a good sense of humor but there was nothing funny in what they had gone through.

Author and a flight chief in Belgium, April 1945, holding up a
two hundred fifty pound bomb, the smallest in our arsenal. They were only
dropped in clusters of three per wing.

Holy Saturday follows Good Friday, and many of us looked forward to some kind of religious services to mark Easter. Our squadron chaplain was a Protestant minister who had services every Sunday which we Catholics did not attend. I was surprised at the frequency with which we were able to attend Mass. The Church had bent over backwards to give us hardworking priests who did their best to make certain that as many as possible were able to go to Mass on Sundays. They were particularly diligent about Christmas and Easter. Many Protestants went to Christmas Mass, since we sang many of the old time carols which transcend every individual Christian religion. This particular Easter was no exception, and all who wished to were able to attend Mass. We Catholics were grateful to the Church for making it possible to attend Mass as often as we did.

We knew that the Rhine River was the last natural defensive position between us and Berlin and that the Germans would sacrifice their all to prevent our crossing. We were electrified, therefore, when we heard that a railroad bridge near Remagen had been captured before the Germans could destroy it. We were also nonplused that this tremendous accomplishment was not exploited instantly. We thought that all available forces would concentrate there post haste and drive through the German forces before they could reform. The high command was evidently not flexible enough to change plans in midstream.

Of course we all blamed this on good old Monty, a guy we loved to hate. He was similar to George McClellan in the Civil War. George always downgraded the number of troops he had and magnified those of his opponent, using this as an excuse for doing nothing. Monty had hesitated in Normandy and was hesitating in Northern Holland as well. We could not understand how Ike could put up with him. We could see the end of the war and we wanted to finish it and go home, so it was only natural for us to resent the lack of exploitation of the captured bridge.

I imagine that the capture of this bridge confused the Nazi defense, because shortly thereafter, Uncle George Patton forced his own crossing and he exploited it fully. This in turn forced Monty to get off his rear end and advance against the disorganized German forces. Thereafter, the German defense collapsed and it was just a matter of time until the war would be over. We had a good shot at being the first troops to enter Berlin. However, the powers had already decided that this honor should fall to the Russkies. This turned out to be a break for us in the short run, because fanatical German resistance, mostly SS who had little to lose, inflicted over one hundred thousand casualties on the Russian attackers.

In his book, *Heisenberg's War*, Thomas Powers relates in detail the dangers that Germany's great atomic scientist encountered when he left his lab and attempted to rejoin his family in southern Germany. SS troops were hanging alleged deserters, and Heisenberg narrowly avoided the same fate by giving his last pack of American cigarettes to one of the less fanatical soldiers who questioned the validity of his self-written pass to travel.

On May 4, 1945, the 511th Squadron flew its last combat mission, a bombing raid near Linz, Austria. Among the German equipment destroyed was a host of planes which had been grounded for lack of fuel. On this mission, Lt. Ritland was hit by flak and reported "missing in action." Before we had time to mourn, he returned, none the worse for his experience. Having a pilot killed at this stage would have been tragic since the war was won and our missions at this time did nothing to change the course of things.

On May 7th, some of our planes flew a demonstration flight over German prisoners of war camps so that inmates would be assured that they were not forgotten. On many of these missions late in the war, the pilots took some time to do a little aerial sight-seeing. Some of them flew over to the Alps and others flew over Czechoslovakia. During the course of the war, and according to official records, the 511th Squadron fired 2,444,317 rounds of caliber fifty ammunition and dropped 1,588.63 tons of bombs. How they came up with these figures is a mystery to me, particularly the sixty three hundredths of a ton of bombs. Unfortunately, no one to my knowledge has ever totaled the number of vehicles or locomotives we destroyed. I am certain that these numbers would be very impressive. Perhaps in the future, I will perform this little chore.

Chapter Twenty

In Search of the Lorelei

On the Banks of the (Wabash) Rhine, far Away
—Apologies to Theodore Dresser, composer.

The weather began to improve while we were in Belgium, so the First Army began its spring offense against the German forces remaining on the west side of the Rhine River. First they conquered Aachen, former capital of the Holy Roman Empire under Charlemagne, and then crossed the Ruhr River at Julich leveling in the process. They finally reached the Rhine at Cologne. Hitch and I and a few others had always wanted to see what life was like on the front lines. The capture of Cologne gave us a golden opportunity to satisfy our curiosity. While at the front, we could see for ourselves what life was like for the infantry and the other combat men while we still had a very wide river between us and the enemy. We would be safe from both die-hard German raiders and sniper fire. We wanted to be observers, not heroes. The only thing we had to fear was the German eighty-eight millimeter cannon. This famous gun was accurate enough to kill individual soldiers at long range. We had heard of incidents where soldiers felt that they were far enough from the enemy to be safe when killed by an eighty-eight millimeter shell. We had no intention of exposing ourselves to the enemy should we be fortunate enough to reach the river.

Four days after Cologne had fallen, four of us, Len Hitchman, "Sheepy" Larson, George Johnson, and I decided to set out on our expedition. We had heard that everyone in the combat area had to be armed so we thought it best to carry our little pop guns in case this was true.

First on the agenda was getting to Hasselt where we would be able to hitch rides to the East. Since squadron vehicles made regular runs to Hasselt, our first step was no problem. Our driver gave us suspicious looks as we entered his vehicle armed to the teeth as we were. I don't know whether he expected us to steal his vehicle or not. However, he asked no questions and we volunteered no answers. We didn't know whether our expedition was legal or not and we wanted to avoid the possibility of being forbidden to go. If it was illegal, we could plead innocence and any punishment incurred would be much less than that for deliberate disobedience.

Getting to Hasselt was a cinch. Here we caught a ride in a weapons carrier heading toward the front. Our spirits soared. Getting our first ride had been so easy that we felt it would be a cinch to get to our destination. We soon found that there was many a slip twixt the cup and the lip.

When we reached the mass of rubble which had once been Aachen, our driver turned off the main highway onto a side "street" which consisted of ground-up rubble. The only resemblance it had with a street was the sign designating it as one. Here our driver dumped us off and we were on our own. Being dropped off in the middle of a ruined town was disconcerting, but we found another ride in a jiffy. A guy in a six-by-six heading in the right direction stopped and picked us up. Two of us hopped in the front and I and another jumped in the back. This time we got as far as the town of Julich, when we were informed by our chauffeur that this was as far as he went. His ordinance depot was hidden somewhere in the depths of the rubble of this ruined town.

Aachen had been bad, but in Julich not a single residence remained standing, it was a sea of pulverized rubble. We were unable to trace even the faintest trace of a street and the GI trucks heading toward the front battered their way directly toward their destination, directly over the debris.

When we were left, we felt abandoned, but once again, help appeared almost immediately from nowhere. Even before we had a chance to raise a thumb, a jeep stopped and the driver asked us if we wanted a ride. We needed no second invitation and hopped on board. This time we were encouraged. The jeep had the identification marks of one of the divisions of the First Army. Our driver assured us that they were stationed on the Rhine. He filled us in on life on the front, but after a short ride, he too left us in the middle of nowhere and again far short of our goal. We became victims of Zeno's hypothesis. Our first ride took us halfway, our second took us half of the remainder and the third half of the remainder once more, and so forth and so forth ad infinitum. Every ride took us halfway but just as Zeno predicted, we never reached our goal.

We were surprised and gratified with the ease we had in getting rides. Everybody who saw us picked us up without question. We rode in six-by-sixes, weapon carriers, jeeps, and even on a large gas truck for a short distance. I imagine that the drivers thought that nobody would be nutty enough to head for the front who didn't belong there. We became so confident in our ability to pick up rides that we wasted some valuable time in exploring our environs where we were dropped off.

At one stop, while we were exploring, we discovered a half-exploded five-hundred-pound bomb lying on the ground, dropped by some American plane. Only the tail fuse had detonated so the back part had exploded and the front part, which remained intact, still had lots of TNT remaining in its shell. We were not the first to discover it. Some unfortunate

Corporal George Johnson and Sgt. Len Hitchman by a half-exploded bomb which we encountered near Cologne, Germany in April of 1945.

ordinance guy had to make it safe by removing the front fuse. We could see the recess where it had ben threaded in. As long as this fuse was in place, the bomb always had the potential to explode. This unexploded bomb was an interesting discovery and proved to us how important it was to fuse both fore and aft of every bomb. I was surprised that the tail fuse had proved reliable in this instance. This fuse has a foot-long tube and was activated by inertial force. When the bomb struck the ground, the sudden stop drove the firing pin of the fuse into the detonator. I thought that this made it less reliable then the nose fuse, which is activated by impact with the ground.

After some seven or eight different pickups, we realized that we had misjudged the distance between Hasselt and Cologne by at least twenty miles. It was now two thirty in the afternoon and we still were about six miles short of our objective. We had agreed beforehand to head back at two thirty so we could catch our squadron truck from Leige to our base. However, by this time, my adrenaline was up. I couldn't bear the thought of turning back when one last ride might get us there. I told the rest that I had to take one more crack at it even if I had to go it alone.

After a short council of war, the others reluctantly agreed to give it one more try. We were immediately picked up by a weapons carrier and everything looked rosy. If my memory serves correctly, our driver had on a combat infantry badge. We really felt like "sojers" in the parlance of Bill Mauldin of *Up Front* fame. Just as we began to relax and think about how we would act at the river's edge, our driver informed us that he had to make a right turn and report to his headquarters. That did it. We were now in what had been an affluent suburb of Cologne and were still four miles to the river. If we tried for another ride, we would probably still be short of our goal and we would definitely be AWOL next morning. We unanimously made the decision to turn back. Had our overconfident decisions to wander around at each stop prevent us from reaching the Rhine? At some of our reunions, Hitch and I have discussed the pros and cons of this. We decided that there was no "yes" or "no" to this. The answer to this question will remain a perpetual mystery. We both agreed that these explorations were a great experience and were worth the delays that they caused.

We soon discovered that rides from the front were less frequent than those toward it. It was getting dark. Since the use of headlights that close to the front were strictly forbidden for obvious reasons, only essential traffic was permitted at night. The entire area was a huge hodge podge of jagged rubble interspersed with numerous deep bomb and shell craters which made driving hazardous after dark.

From the outset, we had decided to return to camp via Liege rather than Hasselt. The traffic from Leige to camp was much more reliable, especially late at night. However, it soon became quite evident that we had no hope of catching the last 511th truck. Reluctantly, we started making plans to spend the night in Liege. At this critical point, we got a huge break. The last truck for the 510th squadron was still boarding passengers for our base. We asked the driver for a ride and he told us to hop aboard. We knew that the walk from 510th area to ours was a couple of miles and we would probably miss curfew, but we would still be able to make it to the line next morning. Our driver was evidently aware of our predicament because he was kind enough to take us directly to our area and left us off so that we beat the curfew by a matter of minutes. Our great adventure thus ended on a happy note.

This whole experiment had been lots of fun and we learned much about the destruction inherent in modern war and, by osmosis, a little about life on the front. One of the eerie things was the deathly silence we encountered that stretched over the entire area from Aachen to the front, just west of Cologne proper. At our closest point to the Rhine, we were well within range of German artillery but we never heard a peep from either side of the river. We accomplished an important part of our trip; we learned a lot about combat without taking any risks.

We met all kinds of soldiers, infantry, armored types, etc. and we were welcomed by all of them. All we had to do is tell them we were the Ninth Air Force and the welcome mat was out. We were aware that much of the destruction we saw was caused by Ninth Air Force planes and some of it might have even been caused by the planes we worked on. This realization was food for thought.

When I look back, I think that the Rhine River was just too far for a day's excursion. I also think we would have been flagged down long before we would have been able to put a toe in the river even if we had gotten that far. Any vehicle adventuring within range of an eighty-eight would not have been long for this world. It would have been a great experience to reach the cathedral. It would have made a fine tale to excite our grandchildren as well. We were well satisfied because at least we had given it our best shot and had lots of fun in the bargain.

It was an unforgettable experience, and last but not least, we got some great pictures including some of the aforementioned half-exploded bomb. We had no regrets and we enjoyed impressing or tentmates with combat tales of our great adventure.

Chapter Twenty-One
Problems over Inventory and Censorship

To Beard the Lion in his Den
—Lochinvar, Walter Scott

After the Battle of the Bulge and again in Belgium, I had two major confrontations with the power. The first involved our supply sergeant and the second our section head, Lt. Hodges, who was acting as censor officer at the time.

A week or so after the Bulge, while we were still languishing in St. Dizier, my day of destiny with the supply sergeant finally arrived. Out of the blue, he decided to make an inventory of all the enlisted men's clothing. I think that dividend time was approaching, and as a stockholder of Air Forces, Inc., he wanted to sell us what we were missing and perhaps increase his dividend. The army had definite regulations concerning replacement of equipment and clothing; however, in a war zone, supply sergeants had a wide latitude on how these regulations were administered. The enlisted man was responsible for all missing items. However, worn-out items were replaced without charge. Our supply sergeant was virtually his own boss and had the authority to waive replacement charges if he so desired. Most sergeants in outfits serving overseas were very understanding in this respect. Our supply sergeant was different, always hewing rigidly to the letter of army regulations without regard to any extenuating circumstances.

At the time of the inspection, I was missing my flight jacket, one of the most treasured items we had and therefore the one most stolen. After we left Normandy, the weather had been warm, so I had no reason to look into my duffel bag except to take out my everyday summer clothing. As the weather became colder, I searched for my flight jacket without success. Rather than go through the hassle of having it replaced, I borrowed one from a friend. He had gone to supply to have his old one replaced. When he obtained his new jacket, the supply sergeant forgot to take his old one in exchange. When I heard that he had an extra jacket, I borrowed it. He evidently had a golden tongue when he had his jacket replaced, because the old one looked fine to me. I had no idea when or what had happened to mine. I assumed that either a Frenchman or another GI who thought that they needed it more than I, pilfered it during our trip from Normandy to St. Dizier.

Since our tent was a logical starting point for his inspection, Sarge visited us right after dinner. He made his entrance into our tent sporting his usual tiny cigarette that extended about a tenth of an inch from his mouth. It was so short that I could never figure out why he never burned his lips. When I saw his dour countenance, I had premonitions of trouble.

This was the first clothing inventory we had since Walterboro, so almost everybody had some items missing and welcomed the chance to replace their missing items. We had crossed an ocean, made three major moves, and had crossed the English Channel as well. These moves were made in haste and under conditions where we couldn't maintain complete control of our possessions. We had enough to worry about during a move without concerning ourselves about our personal equipment. Under these conditions, it would have been a miracle not to have lost something.

The French were hard up for money and clothing, and they thought that every American soldier was made of money, so we were considered lawful prey. Some of our own were not above a little larceny if they were in want. I thought that under these conditions, the good sergeant might show some consideration for all the hardships we had undergone and just replace whatever we were missing.

There was another big reason for compassion—waste in the army was endemic at this time. We watched our tools closely since they were difficult to replace and were essential to our work. I never lost an important tool during the entire war. Throughout the entire army, the black market did a thriving business in selling stolen tools, clothes, cigarettes, and gasoline. Few of us had either the time or the desire to engage in the wholesale theft necessary to be successful in this undertaking. One or two in our squadron may have been active, but they sold only cigarettes that were worth their weight in gold. Gasoline was also a hot item, but I have no idea whether any of our motor pool guys were active in this line. Of course all of us swapped an occasional pack of butts for champagne or a bottle of perfume, but this was just on an ad hoc basis.

According to Basil Liddell Hart in his book, *The History of the Second World War*, (page 564) almost fifteen million jerrycans—five-gallon containers used to hold gasoline—out of some seventeen million which had been shipped to France were unaccounted for by December, 1994. It is not hard to imagine that most of these disappeared filled with gasoline. I was shocked on hearing this; evidently the black market was big business during this time.

We were not aware of these gas losses, but we were surrounded by all other kinds of careless waste. Most of our personal losses were tools which came with our kits but which were seldom if ever used and were ulti-mately lost by attrition. Every time we moved, the dishonest person had a great opportunity to steal whatever he was missing or whatever he could sell, since we had little control of our possessions until we reached our destination. There was a lot of theft, both internal and external, when we were en route from one base to another.

What bothered us the most was the sergeant's penny-ante attitude. None of us lost much, but we had to pay while the dishonest got away with murder. There was rampant theft in the army, but it was the honest who were punished.

At any rate, to prepare for this inspection, I took everything out of my barracks bag, checked for missing items, and then put everything back as neatly as possible. If my bag was in disarray, he would have said that it was impossible to keep track of one's clothes in such a disorga-nized bag. When Sarge entered, his assistant came with him, carrying a large paper pad. Sarge asked if any of us were missing any items of cloth-ing. I gave him the benefit of the doubt, hoping that perhaps for once, he might try to be "Mr. Nice Guy." So I answered that I was indeed missing something. In order to safeguard myself in case he was adamant about our paying, I was careful not to mention exactly what I was missing, and this reticence paid off.

His immediate reply was "Statement of charges," not even a com-plete sentence. This was rapidly followed by, "What are you missing?" His answer galled me not only because I would have to pay for a new jacket, but even more because of his arrogant tone. The fact that he gave me no opportunity to explain my losses really frosted me.

My first thought was that two could play this game, so I replied that I was missing a single sock and where could I sign up to have it replaced.

When my answer had a chance to sink in, he grumped, "Okay, Mr. Wiseguy, dump your stuff on your cot and we will see what you are missing."

I replied that I had already done so in searching for my sock but if he wished to check my stuff, he was welcome to do so. He glared at me and then told his assistant to empty my bag on my cot, and the two of them went through everything I owned with a fine-toothed comb, checking each item against his master list. He looked through the pockets of my shirts and pants, looked under and behind my cot and found nothing missing. Concentrating as he did on my bag, he completely forgot to check the items I had on. Because they were so sought after, each flight jacket had an identification number in it. Had he checked the number of the jacket I had on, he could easily have found out that it was not mine.

While they were going through all my things, I kept up a line of chat-ter and asked my tentmates if they had seen any sign of my sock. Since they were not overly fond of the good sergeant and knew what to expect as next in line, they got into the spirit of things. They looked under their cots and gave the sarge "helpful" suggestions on where he should look. One of them even suggested that he look in our little stove that was radiating BTUs like crazy.

The net result was that for all his trouble, he found nothing missing. This puzzled him, so he asked me what I had meant when I said that a sock was missing. I replied that he must have found it in the course of his search when he had scattered my clothes all over my corner of the tent. I told him that I was grateful to him for finding it because he saved me from buying a new pair. I asked him if he would be good enough to put all my stuff back in my barracks bag and leave it just as he had found it. This added a little kerosene to his smoldering fire, and he left our tent in a huff. This little brouhaha had taken so long that he had to quit for the night. Overnight, he must have concluded that he would encounter the same resistance in every other tent and that the aggravation was not worth it. That was the end of our clothing inspection.

This inspection was really a good idea, and I might have paid for my jacket had he not gotten so hard-nosed. We knew that the war was winding down very rapidly, and none of us wanted to pay big bucks for an item that we would soon be turning in. It was difficult to teach an old dog new tricks, especially an army dog. Sarge was just too set in his ways. Had he not been so disagreeable, everybody would have been happy, and many of us would have gotten some items of clothing that we needed. As it was, I was not about to knuckle under to him.

He also made a tactical error in hitting our tent first. We were all a bunch of free-wheelers who loved to twist the lion's tail whenever opportunity knocked. The war was ending and the strict discipline of the past was impossible to maintain. Nobody wanted to pay for something that they would not need for long. Thus, the sergeant's inspection was too little and too late.

This was child's play compared to the confrontation I had several months later in Belgium. This time I crossed swords with my boss officer, Lt. Hodges, who was acting censor officer at the time. As I mentioned earlier, censorship was a sore subject with us. We thought that our confrontation with our officers in England had settled this problem for good, but we were in for an unpleasant surprise.

One day in late March of 1945, less than two months before Germany finally threw in the towel, several of us were relaxing in our tent between missions. We were waiting for Len Hitchman to bring back copies of some pictures he had taken of us in action, loading bombs, working on our guns, etc.

When he finally arrived, *sans* pictures, he was furious. This was unusual since he was one of the milder personalities in our outfit. When we inquired about the pictures, he replied that the Lieutenant had torn them up, negatives and all. We were dumbfounded. Army regulations were quite clear on this matter. We were permitted to take all the pictures we wanted but all pictures of restricted material were placed in the squadron safe until the war was over, at which time they were returned to their owners. We had taken pictures prior to this occasion. They had been put in the squadron safe and the photographer given a receipt for them.

We were upset because both cameras and film were scarce. We were afraid that we might never again have the opportunity to take pictures of our working on our airplanes. We had just resumed flying full-time to support the various Rhine River crossings and the opportunities to take snapshots were nonexistent for the time being.

We couldn't figure out what had gotten into the good lieutenant to pull this crazy stunt. We knew from past experience that he had his moments when he was mighty tough and that he was not a good guy to cross. However, this was the first time he or any other censor had done anything that blatantly illegal. When Hitch asked him why he had torn them up, he made up some half-assed story about the possibility of revealing photos falling into enemy hands which would enable them to find possible weaknesses in the P-47.

At this moment, the Ruhr was virtually surrounded and the entire Wehrmacht was in complete disarray. They didn't have enough troops for defense, much less for an offense. The idea of their capturing our pictures was too ridiculous to contemplate.

At least two months prior to his tearing up our photos, *Stars and Stripes*, the official newspaper of the army in Europe, reported that there had been many Allied sightings of P-47s with German black crosses painted on their fuselages and wings. Some of them had even taken pot shots at our B-17s . Other squadrons had reported seeing them flying around our ground troops, attempting to lure our own 47' into point blank range of their antiaircraft guns. A few of our own pilots had reported seeing a P-47 with German insignia on it as well. Mike Varino said that he and several other pilots had been lured by one of these planes and almost ambushed before they realized their mistake.

In an air war as colossal as WW-2, where thousands of planes of each type were involved, it was inevitable that both sides would find all types of enemy planes virtually intact after their pilots had bailed out and the abandoned plane had bellied in with little damage. These planes were repaired and flown by test pilots in order to ascertain the strong and weak points of each type of aircraft. The British had flown Me109s and other German aircraft as early as the Battle of Britain. We flew and lost far more planes over Germany than they did over Britain so it was a cinch that they had lots of our planes to study.

Also, in his memoirs, General Patton, commander of the Third Army at the time, reported that during the Bulge, which occurred several months prior to the lieutenant's action, that he heard many rumors of captured P-47s strafing some of his units. After a conference with Generals Spaatz and Doolittle of the Air Forces, they agreed that the areas of Patton's X11 and XX corps were temporarily off limits to our P-47s. Thus any Thunderbolt making an appearance there was a bandit and was to be shot down, no ifs, ands, or buts. This alleviated the fears of those two corps and saved our guys from a probable pasting from friendly fire. There was no further trouble, so I suppose that the Germans were smart enough to use these planes only when some of ours were present as well. The lieutenant had to be aware of all this evidence which made his action all that more incomprehensible.

Of course every enlisted person in the whole outfit was outraged when they found out about their pictures. There were lots of discussions, but nobody knew what recourse we had.

Even though I was in these discussions, I was not involved in the beginning because I thought that this problem was just so much water over the dam. I was not in any of them so I felt no concern. The lieutenant and I had never been on the same wavelength for some obscure reason, so I didn't want to antagonize him any further. I was not aware of any reason for his attitude toward me, but the antipathy was there and I was not the only one who noticed it.

Listening to Hitch and the others bewailing their loss finally got to me, and I started building up a head of steam myself. I realized that this was something we should not ignore. Somebody had to make a move, and the more I thought about it, the more it became apparent that that somebody had to be me.

Normally I prefer the direct approach in conflicts with officers. Most of them were reasonable and easy to talk to and my few complaints were very minor. In this case, I thought that it would be suicidal to take this guy on directly, and this approach might not get the job done, either. An officer with a bean up his nose could really make life miserable for an enlisted man who had no redress. I recalled how he wanted to bust our good tentmate, Ernie White, back in Normandy when we failed to change the fuses on his ship while he was at lunch.

I told Hitch that in my opinion, we had to figure out some subtle way to get redress. One of the first suggestions was an anonymous letter to Major Eikenberry. Both of us agreed that we wanted no parts of anything like that.

After some thought, somebody suggested that we go to Major Eikenberry, head of administration for the 511th. We knew that we could get a fair deal with him, but he was too close to the lieutenant. If we did,

226

Hodges would almost certainly find out who the culprit was, and the guy who belled the cat would be in hot water for the rest of his army career. Finally, I suggested that we go as high up the ladder as we could. This meant taking our problem to the group censor officer. He would not be influenced by personalities as our squadron officers might be. It was my thinking that they got their jobs because they had both ability and experience and therefore would be impartial. The only thing we wanted was a fair hearing without the fear of retaliation. This stopped everybody. In the rush of making my views known, I rashly told them that I would do the honors provided someone came with me. Good old faithful Hitch agreed to accompany me.

I knew that I had to move fast before I lost my nerve. We set out immediately. As we neared group, I felt my courage ebbing away, which buttressed my desire to move fast. We went directly to the censor's tent and hastened into it and asked his secretary for an interview. Luckily, he was available, and we were quickly hustled into a major's office where I saluted and then spouted out our tale of woe. He was a cultivated gentleman and didn't look too formidable, so I felt encouraged until he asked for my name, rank, and serial number. All I could think of was that this was the information that prisoners of war must give their captors. Hideous visions of a lifetime of incarceration in Leavenworth or Alcatraz raced through my brain, and Hitch assumed a position almost directly behind me. My heart sank. I never gave a thought to the fact that he might wish to check on the veracity of our story. I am sure that people in his position got a lot of crank complaints and that he had to sift out the wheat from the thistles.

After I gave him my name, I started to shake like a leaf, haunted by the realization that all officers stuck together. I expected to go back to our outfit in chains and delivered to Hodges to be burned at the stake. At this point, I would have cheerfully settled for full time KP instead of the many gruesome alternatives that ran through my mind. After peering at me for an eternity, he said that he would check into our complaint and take whatever action was indicated. With that, we were dismissed.

When we returned to the line, a lot of guys came up and shook my hand, particularly the photographers whose pictures had been destroyed. This did little to allay my fears, particularly when word filtered down that there would be a meeting of all enlisted men in front of our headquarters like RIGHT NOW.

When we were all assembled, out came the censor officer, livid with fury. He stated that some SOB. had turned his ass into group and that when he found out who this son of a bitch was, there would be hell to pay. We were then dismissed and returned to the line. His reaction buttressed my original opinion on the necessity of remaining anonymous.

When I arrived on the line, some of the guys came up and patted me on the back and congratulated me on a job well done. My confidence in Major Loftus, group censor officer, was justified. He must have checked with somebody in our squadron and found out that our allegations were correct, all without revealing our names.

Our adventure was a huge success. Nothing ever happened to me, nor was this incident ever referred to by any of our brass. From that point on, our pictures were returned to us, negatives and all. No more stashing them in the safe! They even gave us the ones that had been stored in the safe since the word "go."

I undertook this mission not so much for the loss of the pictures but because I was indignant about the censor's arbitrary action. Tearing up our pictures was an obvious violation of one of the few rights we had as enlisted men. Somebody had to take action, and I am not sorry that it was I. While I am glad that I remained anonymous, I knew going in that there was a good chance of being detected, but I still felt that it had to be done. I am glad that I persisted. I am even happier that I wasn't detected!

I imagine that Hodges ultimately would have stopped tearing up our pics, but we had no assurance of this. It was likewise quite possible that the destruction could have continued and we would have no proof of what we had done during the war. A picture is worth a thousand words. We would have nothing to refresh our memories as the years went by of what we had done during the war, and, more importantly, who we had done it with. Our army service was an important part of our lives. We had been together for the better part of three years and had been with one another through good times and bad. It would have been a first class tragedy not to have some pictures of each other and of the planes we had worked on.

While enlisted men have a reputation for sticking together, frequently someone will break ranks for reasons of his own, and others will say the wrong thing at the wrong time, but on this occasion, no one broke ranks and I remained anonymous to the end. We had no idea how the other officers felt or even if they were aware of our problem. Since only enlisted men were affected by this type of censorship, I imagine that few of our officers were aware of this incident and I am certain that none of our pilots knew anything about this little *tête-à-tête*.

Major Eikenberry possibly had an inkling of this affair, particularly if he had gotten the call from group. However, as I look back, I think that Major Loftus must have called Hodges direct. It was a cinch that he had to check with somebody on the validity of our complaint. Be that as it may, we solved our problem without a court martial and no one put on permanent KP.

There was a little addendum to this. Almost immediately after all this excitement, an article appeared in *Stars and Stripes* asking for volunteers to serve as paratroopers in our airborne divisions. Most of us armorers were unhappy with our top man and thought that this item offered a good way to get his goat.

A few of the more adventurous individuals volunteered and asked me to do likewise. They were positive that they would be turned down because armorers were in scarce supply. It took at least as long to train a good armorer as a good paratrooper. I declined, because the idea of jumping out of a speeding plane with nothing but a handful of silk between me and eternity seemed to me to be a gross waste of talent. I was also afraid that since I was no friend of our bossman, he might just prevail on the brass to make an exception in my case.

These characters hit the jackpot. Our boss was furious since his was the only department in the whole outfit who had volunteers, a strong indication that something was amiss. He endorsed their request and said that he would be happy to endorse any others who wished to commit suicide.

As they hoped and expected, all volunteers were turned down. They called me chicken for not trying myself, but I was and am a great believer in Murphy's Law—"If it can happen, it will happen." I much preferred to be chicken than to run the possibility of being the squadron's only exception and end up in the obits as the late Corporal Henkels, killed by terror after being pushed out of an airplane.

In later years, long after the war was over, I heard via the grapevine that some of my fellow armorers had the temerity to visit Hodges at his home in Shreveport, Lousiana. They said that they had gotten the royal treatment from him. He took them out to dinner at a top restaurant and then invited them to his home. I guess it was the pressures of war and being in a strange job that made him such a lousy boss.

After hearing this tale, I couldn't help conjecturing on how he would have reacted to the sudden appearance of his favorite armorer. I never got to Shreveport to find out, and I am not certain that I would have made an effort to catch up with him if I had.

In retrospect, I think that Hodges' problems were not all of his own making. It was true that he didn't have an endearing personality. However, when I began to manage people in civilian life, I found that many do a poor job because no one has taken the time to explain to them just what is expected of them. As far as I could determine, all our ground officers, except those in squadron administration, were just tossed into an outfit and put in charge of a department without any instructions whatsoever. Few of them had the slightest idea of what they were supposed to do, and, unfortunately, few made any effort to find out. The fact that they were officers and hence were in a higher caste than their charge, exacerbated the problem. It really was unfortunate that so few made any effort to dig in and learn about their departments. They never could have attained the lore of our sergeants, but they could have been a major asset to the squadron had they been more active. Of course the sergeants always were and always would be, the backbone of the squadron, excluding pilots. This was true of every other army as well. It was the sergeants who had both the smarts and the experience. They are the grist that made the army run.

Chapter Twenty-two

Entering the Reich and Camp at Kitzingen

A Jug of Wine...Were Paradise Enow
—The Rubiyat of Omar Khayam translated by
Edward Fitzgerald

By late April, it was time to move again, this time into the heart of Germany. Early one morning, we loaded onto GI trucks and headed east through miles of destruction which was all that was left of a cultured nation. Never had I seen such utter devastation. The first city, or rather, the remains thereof, was Aachen, which four of us had been through before, whose destruction was therefore no surprise. Some of the rubble had been removed by the citizenry, making it easier to pick our way through than before. I am certain that they did no more than was absolutely necessary because the war was not over and die hard Nazis would be sure to punish any alleged collaborationists for aiding and abetting the enemy by clearing up roads. Next, we picked our way through the small town of Duren, on the banks of the Rur River, perhaps twenty miles east of Aachen. It was so badly battered that no streets were discernible, and we had to beat our way through the low spots in the rubble to continue on.

We crossed the Rhine River at Bonn on a pontoon bridge which had recently been constructed by our engineers. Bonn was in very good shape. For some reason, the Allied bombers had never hit it. This puzzled me, because I was not aware of any other city which they had spared.

After Bonn, we tooled through some picturesque countryside until we reached Franfurt-am-Main which had been bombed extensively. Frankfurt was the largest German town we had ever been through and was almost a ghost town. We saw very few people on the streets but we were very surprised to see how well much of the rubble had been cleared from the main thoroughfares. Debris was neatly piled along the curbs of the main arteries in town, a striking contrast to what we had seen in Aachen.

Once through Frankfurt, we passed through some nice countryside until we came to Wurtzburg. Here the destruction was as widespread as in Aachen. Much of this wholesale and indiscriminate destruction was caused by night-flying British bombers, carrying six ton "blockbuster" bombs. For a fleeting moment, I wondered why the British had squandered so many young lives and lost some thirty-two hundred heavy bombers in destroying targets that had absolutely no military value whatsoever.

Wurtzburg was about ten miles east of our destination, the small town of Kitzingen which had a fine old Luftwaffe air base, complete with barracks and some fine indoor recreational facilities. The Germans had been kind enough to leave things intact, so we slept in beds for the first time since we had left New York.

Our planes landed shortly thereafter on a paved runway and we were soon back in business. I couldn't understand why the runway was in such good shape. We had battered every other one so why not this one as well? I was to get the answer to this question very soon.

On April 29th, we flew our first mission from our German base, a raid on Pilsen in Czechoslavakia, where we destroyed twenty-seven locomotives, some flat cars, and bombed a marshaling yard. Some of our pilots came back via Prague, enjoying a nice view of the city in the process. These last flights were a bit of a lark for our flyers, so they did some sightseeing after dropping their bombs.

By this time, targets were scarce, but we were soon directed to a Luftwaffe air base at Albing where the guys had a ball shooting up a whole bunch of enemy planes which had been grounded for lack of fuel. On the evening of May 2nd, we heard that German Admiral Donitz had taken over the reins of the government of Germany after Hitler's suicide and had sued for peace. At long last, our guns, which had been active since April 11th, 1944, were muted forever on May 5th, 1945.

Lt. Ritland had the dubious destination of being the last pilot shot down in action. He was hit near Linz, Austria by accurate German anti-aircraft fire and disappeared. We thought his loss was tragic and he was sadly mourned, until, like Tom Sawyer, he turned up for his own memorial rites none the worse for the experience. On May 7th, we flew our last mission, a peaceful one, over a German prison of war camp, our flyers waggling their wings to give courage and hope to the inmates. Several of our pilots took this opportunity to fly over the site of our next base, Straubing-am-Danube, which was still further east than Kitzingen.

Since we were still at war when we arrived at Kitzingen and the Allies had a "no fraternization policy," we never left the base, and no enlisted man to my knowledge had any idea of what the town of Kitzingen looked like or even what size it was. I don't think too many of us would have gone there even had we been permitted. An enterprising enlisted man found a huge wine cellar overflowing with all kinds of vintage wine which the Germans had been unable to destroy in their hasty retreat. It contained literally thousands of bottles of first rate German and captured French wines.

In keeping with the best tradition of the military priorities, the Germans had left such unimportant things as equipment behind while appropriating such important things as fine wines, paintings, and such on their retreat from France. We knew that they would be excellent because nobody had better taste for foreign wines than German officers, particularly when they were stealing it from conquered vassals.

As usual, the officers had first choice and we got the leavings, but this cache was so tremendous that it contained enough for all and then some. Beginning with the evening of May 7th, after the last plane had landed, every interested EM lined up at the extensive bar and was given the bottle of his choice. Some guys guzzled theirs in a hurry and went back for seconds. I sat down and nursed mine through the evening. This made me feel good, and I had no skull cracker in the morning. I experimented with both white and black and could never decide which was best. The white was light and tasty, while the red was much drier. I did find out that I liked chardonnay better than any other white. I learned a very important lesson. The more wine I drank, the less I wished to drink. This was in stark contrast to some hard liquors such as gin, where the more I drink, the more I want. Now on the rare occasions when I go to a party that might end up in a drinking orgy, I drink white wine and after perhaps four glasses at the most, I can hardly look at any type of liquor, much less drink it.

There was enough wine on hand for this bottle-a-night routine to last indefinitely, but we became discouraged at the small inroads we made in the supply. The realization that there was more there than we could possibly drink in the foreseeable future took away so much of our zeal, and many of us started to share bottles with others. In doing so, we discovered that it was just as much fun drinking sanely, and we felt much better in the morning. I am certain that we were better off for this knowledge, but I still have fond memories of the bottle-a-day scenario. Everybody should have a chance to be able to go overboard on some vice at least once in their lives.

We had so much time on our hands that my good friend, Hitch, conned his crew chief to let him run up the engine of his P-47. As I watched him in the cockpit, grinning from ear-to-ear as he put his plane through its paces, I decided to ask my crew chief, Wasouski, if I could do the honors with K4-M. He hesitated and then decided to let me try. I had watched him so often that I felt I knew what to do, although contrary to my usual *modus operandi*, I listened carefully to his instructions.

I hopped into the cockpit, put on the brakes, belted myself in, primed the engine, thus putting some raw gas into the cylinders, and then started to wind up the electric starter. When the starter had reached proper speed, I engaged it and the engine started to turn over. I had my right hand on the throttle, prepared to shove it forward as soon as the engine caught, but nothing happened. The starter kept slowly turning the engine, but either it was too early in the morning or it was aware that the war was over and thought, "The hell with this noise, the war is over and I'm too lazy to start."

Finally, I could take it no longer, so I shoved the throttle forward anyhow, which, I might add, is a strict no-no because the unburned gas dripped out of the exhaust, creating a mild fire hazard. When Wasouski saw this, he started climbing up the wing to replace me. By this time, the engine had evidently felt that it had had enough fun at my expense so it started up and ran very nicely. It was all downhill from there. I ran it up to twenty-two hundred rpm and checked the propeller governor. The rpm changed as it should, and then I checked the magnetos which furnish power to the spark plugs. While the engine could operate on one magneto, it had two, which not only made the engine run smoother but made it much safer as well. Each set of magnetos was controlled by a switch in the cockpit. When the engine was turning at twenty-two hundred rpm, I shut off the right bank and observed the drop in rpm which was less than two hundred, which was fine. I then turned the switch back on and waited until the speed rose to twenty-two hundred once more and then I shut off the left bank. Once again the drop in rpm was satisfactory, so I turned the left bank back on.

Having completed checking the prop and mags, I decided to run it for awhile just for fun. Then I noticed Wasouski was waving at me frantically and pointing to the rear of the plane. I decided that perhaps this might be a good time to shut down the engine and find out what was on his mind. I reduced the rpm to about fourteen hundred and put the mixture control on "idle cutoff." The engine stopped but inertia kept the propeller rotating for a short time, exhausting any combustible gasses which otherwise would remain in the cylinders. Wasouski quickly mounted the wing and told me that the engine was in danger of overheating because I had neglected to open the cooling airducts, which are closed at first so that the engine will warm up quickly. This was something nobody had told me, but rather than make a fuss, I got out of the cockpit without a word. Had they told me of this, I am sure that I would have complied.

My experience made the squadron rounds, and our flight chief, Romeo Gulley, decided that only those qualified would run up the engines. I think that he felt that amateurs should not be messing around $200,000 engines because the ultimate responsibility was his. Rumor had it that if a person was responsible for the loss of an expensive piece of

234

equipment, he was promoted to master sergeant, signed up for thirty years, and his pay was garnished until he paid up in full. We never found out whether this was true or not, but none of us wanted to be the one to find out.

I was surprised at how few of the armorers wanted to run up these engines. Luckily, all of us who wished to had done so before Gulley made us cease and desist. My ordeal was not the sole reason for his decision, but it was certainly the icing on the cake. Romeo was a great guy, and our flight was the only one to my knowledge where any armorers were permitted to run up the engines.

A little addendum to the above: I should have expected the engine to react as it did. Air-cooled engines have been my waterloo all my life. Outboard motors that my kids have no trouble with refuse to start for me. Lawnmowers, power saws, all of them evidently see me coming and decide to get balky. I have literally pulled my guts out on these damnable machines to no avail. On the rare occasions when they do start, they quickly flood and then refuse to start. They undoubtedly have a communications network so that any machine I rent is sure to be in on the plot and either refuse to start or quickly stall after they have done so. After many unpleasant experiences with these cursed machines, I have decided to have nothing whatever to do with them. I refuse to accept invitations to go fishing unless I have a strict understanding with my companions that someone else will run the motor.

One afternoon, a day or so after our last flight, we were told to put on our dress uniforms and report to the line. We hadn't done anything that formal since leaving the USA. After much pushing and shoving on various parts of our anatomy which bulged in unusual places, we finally got dressed and reported as ordered. Each squadron lined up about a hun-

The motley crew attempting to fly one of the Stuka dive bombers that surrendered to us in Kitzingen consist of Carl Hadra, pilot, and the author in the rear as gunner.

dred yards from the runway with our ranks parallel to it. Our planes sat across the runway from us, and all guns were unloaded.

We hoped that some brass such as Patton or some other wheel might show up and thank us for our help in winning the war. We were not prepared for the next event. A flight of planes, obviously German, consisting of several Stuka dive bombers and a bunch of Me109's, flew into view, flying directly toward us. They made a sweeping pass, directly overhead and then landed, one after another. I was horrified when they flew over us, fearing that they might be some diehard Nazis who wished to go out in a blaze of glory by dusting us with their guns and christening us with a few bombs. Fortunately, this didn't occur. All planes landed and several of them made pathetic gestures of bravado by attempting to destroy their planes by ground looping them as soon as they hit the ground.

Several of our upper grade enlisted men went across the runway to show them where to park and then escorted them from the field to the officers' dayroom. Shortly after they disappeared, we were dismissed and we wandered across the runway. We not were permitted to climb on the planes since we didn't know whether the guns were still loaded or whether they had been booby trapped.

I, for one, thought that the brass must have been out of their minds not having at least some of our planes in the air. We were sitting ducks, just asking for some gung-ho Nazi to give us the works. As they flew over, I cringed, realizing that there was no escape. The idea of making the headlines of the *New York Times* by getting strafed and killed by a Nazi zealot after the war was over, terrified me. For a short time, I lost a great deal of the respect I had for our leaders. How could they be so dumb? A week or so later, we found out that they were as surprised as we were. These German pilots had been fighting against the Russians and they knew that the Russkies were very tough on the Luftwaffe personnel they captured, so they radioed 19th Tactical Air Command, offering to surrender to them. 19th Tac told them to land at the nearest American air base which happened to be ours. The first our brass knew of this was when the planes flew over.

Evidently our officers and the German pilots spent that evening downing some of our captured wine. It turned out that one of them was Hans Rudel, the greatest Stuka pilot of the war, who had flown an incredible twenty-five hundred missions and had destroyed more than five hundred Russian tanks. It was no wonder that the Russkies wanted him so badly.

Toward the end of the war when the Stuka was not very effective, he began flying Me109's and did very well with them also. We were amazed that anyone was able to fly twenty-five times as many missions as our guys did and never get flaky. We heard via the grapevine that he had challenged our group commander to a one-on-one dogfight using gun cameras, our colonel in a P-47 and Rudel in his one-o-nine. Of course, this was impossible and our boss declined, but I imagine that Herr Rudel would have been a handful for our best.

We never saw our captives after they had disappeared into officer country. We suspected that they were hauled off to some POW camp early next morning. Their arrival added some real excitement to our end of the war celebration and we all wished them well. After we got over our initial fear, we appreciated the fact that they had landed at our base so we could enjoy climbing over the planes they left behind.

Virtually all of the Luftwaffe's best surrendered either to the British or to us. None wanted any parts of the Russians, but by treaty, we were obliged to turn over those who had flown against the Russians. Unfortunately, this included Rudel. Many of them were incarcerated in Russia for years.

On the day after the surrender of the German pilots, security cleared the German planes and we were permitted to climb over them to our hearts' content. We had a ball, climbing into the cockpits and working the sticks back and forth and up and down. We went on a picture-taking orgy, snapping shots of us sitting in the cockpit, pretending to fire the twenty millimeter cannon, etc. Lots of fun was had by all.

The Stukas were the center of attention because they were probably the most famous airplane of the war. They were sinister looking birds with liquid cooled engines and streamlined unretractable landing gear. The Stuka was the only plane with fixed landing that remained in use during the entire war. The engine was far larger than we had thought. It had gained a fearsome reputation in the invasion of France and during the early part of the war against Russia where competition was second rate. It had been a flop during the Battle of Britain because it was asked to do a job it was not designed for. This ancient relic reminded us of the Douglas Dauntless of our Tampa days. Both these "golden oldies" had something in common. They were both obsolete at the beginning of the war, but they got the job done anyhow.

After I had my fill of the Stuka, I got into the cockpit of a 109, which was much smaller than that of the 47. The German pilot sat upright, but he stretched his legs forward and bent his knees slightly upward to reach the rudder controls. This looked very uncomfortable to us, who were used to sitting upright as in a chair in our planes. The longer we stayed in these strange cockpits, the more comfortable they became. Using this type cockpit enabled the Germans to build smaller planes without sacrificing either speed or firepower.

One of my regrets is that I never checked the armament on any of these planes. Long after the war was over, I heard that the 109 had a thirty millimeter gun, far larger than any guns we had except for the thirty-seven millimeter on the P-39. It would have been nice to see what these guns looked like and how they operated.

We had been in Kitzingen less than a fortnight when we were ordered to report to Staubing-am-Danube, about two hundred miles farther east. Most of the guys were disappointed, some had hoped to be sent back to France and from there to the States, and others wanted to remain in Kitzingen until they had finished all the wine. As a bachelor, I had no desire to go home and back to close order drill until I had accumulated enough points to get out. The possibility of new adventure appealed. At this stage of the game, I had no expectations of getting out in less than a year, so the more of Europe I saw during this time, the better.

Once again I was first echelon, and this time we went by air. A fleet of DC 3s or C-47s, as the army designated them, flew in to pick some of us up. Several war weary B-17s also flew in. I was assigned to a B-17 which I helped load.

We also loaded the C-47s which were to lead the way. One of the guys who boarded a C-47 was a baldheaded gent named Chosky, who had acquired the nickname of "Bubble Canopy" for his lack of hair. As he entered his C-47, a wag turned to me and said, "That's the first time I have ever seen a C-47 with a bubble canopy." We all enjoyed a good chuckle.

While helping to load my B-17, I noticed that the bombardier's compartment in the nose of the plane was unoccupied, so I asked the pilot if I could fly in it. He shrugged his shoulders and told me to go to it. Struggling into that cramped space with a chute on was not easy, and I had some misgivings about bailing out in case of trouble, but the view and the excitement made it worth the risk. The C-47s took off and then it was our turn. We roared down the runway and just as we were taking off, I saw an immense pile of concrete rubble piled up at the end of the runway which we cleared by about a hundred feet. This explained why our existing runway was undamaged. It had been heavily damaged and then repaired by the Germans. They had shoved all the debris to the end of the runway and then started from scratch to rebuild it. I guess our advance caught them by surprise, so we were able to capture it intact.

The view from the nose was fantastic. We flew at an altitude of thirty-five hundred feet, which was low enough for me to pick out landmarks with ease and clarity. We had to follow the C-47's which crept along at about a hundred and thirty miles per hour so our flight was leisurely. I had an opportunity to view a German landscape virtually untouched by the war. It looked so neat and peaceful that I almost forgot that I was over a country that had been at war with us only a week or so ago. We passed over Regensburg where we picked up the Danube River. I was disappointed that we were too far south to pass over Nurnberg.

After flying along the Danube for quite a distance, we landed at an old Luftwaffe air base at Straubing which was to be our home for several months. The barracks there were even better than those at Kitzingen. We still had public bathrooms and showers, but we were only four to a room and all the rooms had tile floors which were a cinch to keep clean. However, the icing on the cake were the German POWs who pulled our KP. For the first and only time, with the exception of a very short time in New York, I was free from pots and pans.

The POW's we had were kids who had served in the Wehrmacht for a few months at the very end of the war and had not been brainwashed with Nazi ideology. They were a nice bunch, anxious to oblige and real hard workers. They were so industrious that for the first time since they had been in use, the outsides of many of our pots were sparkling clean. Troy Robinson's first inclination was to be tough on them but in a short time, he treated them well and made sure that they were well-fed. They reported to the mess hall first thing in the morning, before most of us were up, and left after cleaning up the supper mess. I never knew where they came from or where they went. We had little fear of their trying to escape. They had the best jobs in Germany at the time and they knew it. With these kids doing all the work, I looked forward to a pleasant stay in our new home.

Chapter Twenty-three
Straubing - am - Danube

Grim-visaged War hath Smoothed his Wrinkled Front
—William Shakespeare, *Richard the Third*

Our planes arrived shortly after we did. We removed all the ammo from the guns, gave them a light coat of oil, and forgot about them. We had to tidy them up because they were either being given to the French or they were purchasing them. The higher-ups decided at this point that as long as we were getting rid of our planes, we might just as well get rid of the ammo as well. So back to K4-M I went, took off the wing covering, and reloaded the guns with some thirty-two hundred rounds. That was it as far as I was concerned. I had no intention of doing any more work on my guns since I knew that they were in top shape and the Frenchies wouldn't know the difference anyway. I reported to my boss that K4-M was ready for delivery.

As luck would have it, I got stuck for some kind of duty and couldn't report to the line for a day or so. My boss checked my ship and decided to strip down and clean all my guns in 100-octane. He even did the front bushings, something we had never done before. This was murder. Hundred octane removed all the oil that had permeated the metal and the guns rusted like hell. When I returned to the line, I found to my horror that my trusty guns were rusted in solid, just as they had been in England over a year ago. If he had not charged them, i.e. cocked them, they would have been permanently frozen and ruined.

Try as I may, I couldn't budge them. Luckily, a pilot came out to get in his flying time—each pilot must fly a minimum of four hours per month to qualify for extra pay. I begged him to take my plane and squeeze off a few rounds while he was flying around. I hoped that this might loosen them up so I could reoil them. Since pilots liked any opportunity they could get to shoot, he agreed. When he returned, I found out that this firing had indeed loosened up the guns. I quickly dismantled each gun, soaked every part in oil, and then reassembled them. The following day, I checked them again. There were still traces of rust, but things were much improved. I was now able to charge them myself. I took them apart once more, soaked them in oil, and then reassembled them. To be on the safe side, I checked them once again next morning and all systems were go. I

Cpl. Carl Hadra, facing the camera, with help from the author, fixing up the guns on his P-47 prior to its being delivered to the French.

watched my plane with an eagle eye from then on. I didn't want some jerk fouling up my gats again.

What possessed these guys to soak guns in 100-octane will forever be beyond my comprehension. We made this mistake in England when we didn't know any better, but to do so again, over a year later, was about as dumb a stunt as I could imagine. Later, I discovered that some of the others had also done so and had had no chance to rectify the situation. Some Frog armorers were in for a very unpleasant surprise when they opened the wings to work on the guns. At this stage of the game, I was not enamored with the French, but even they didn't deserve this.

The mechanics still had to run up the planes every day to keep them functioning. Normally they did this in the morning, but now that the heat was off, some waited until the afternoon to do so. Thus we had engines roaring away on the line from dawn to dusk which sometimes interfered with my afternoon beauty rest.

Shortly after I had taken care of the crisis with my guns, the Frenchies came and away went all our planes. We watched them disappear with mixed emotions. It is always an emotional experience bidding an old friend good-bye, particularly when you know that the parting is forever. I had a feeling of nostalgia as I watched K4-M head into the distance as it had so many times before, but this time it would not return. Our flying days were over forever, and we were stuck in eastern Germany with no official duties and lots of time on our hands.

Although my plane had departed and my skills were no longer needed by the army, my bond with the Browning caliber-fifty was renewed some forty-seven years later, in 1992. My wife and I and two kids visited a railroad museum in Ogden, Utah, which is forty miles north of Salt Lake City. In addition to railroad mementos, the museum also had an exhibit of Browning weapons since the Browning Company had made so many of the weapons in that area. On display was a heavy machine gun exactly like those I had worked on so many years ago.

As we entered the room, a visitor asked the volunteer curator some questions on how that particular gun operated. The curator replied that this was not his field of expertise. He had no knowledge of how any of the weapons on exhibition operated. I mentioned that I had worked on them during World War II and would be happy to explain how they worked. Evidently he had been asked similar questions in the past and was only too happy for me to explain the operation to him. I proceeded to do so in detail while he took notes for future reference. I guess knowledge of the Browning caliber fifty is similar to riding a bike or learning the responses for the Latin Mass—once learned, they are never forgotten. What goes around, comes around.

At this stage of the game, almost our sole duty was to keep our barracks shipshape. Perhaps once or twice a week, a minor extracurricular duty might lift its ugly head and we tried our best to be absent whenever it did.

We had some wrecked German planes just off the runway which we had fun climbing over until this became old hat. Our big treat was an occasional swim in the Danube when the weather was warm enough. It didn't appear too polluted to us, but who were we to judge? We knew nothing about pollution. It would be thirty years before it became a concern. The swift current made swimming a challenge, and I can vouch for the fact that it was far from any shade of blue.

One day, a couple of our explorers uncovered a small German ammo dump containing lots of small arms ammo and a supply of high quality rifles to go with it. I not only got myself a beautiful Czech rifle with three lions inscribed on the breech but a Czech dress bayonet as well. We took our newfound guns, found an abandoned rifle range, and had a ball blasting away at anything from dawn to dusk. Predictably, tin cans were our favorite target, but we aimed at other things as well. Sometimes it got a little scary because some of the shooters had no idea of any rules of safety. Since the ammo was about six years older than Methuselah, some of the rounds misfired, i.e., they never went off, when struck by the firing pin. This phenomenon is known as a hangfire and is particularly dangerous since the round could explode at any time when the gunner may no longer be aiming at the target. If a hangfire is ejected immediately, it might well explode in the air with disastrous results. We were very lucky that none of our hangfires went off or some serious injuries could have resulted. I was surprised that no one supervised our shooting, but I am not sure that any of the wheels ever knew about it. They took their duties as lightly as we did ours. After a week or so of constant firing, my shoulder got so sore from the recoil that I had to quit. I packed my rifle and mailed it home.

Since a no-fraternization policy with the Germans was in effect, we had no contact with the world around us. This was a lot harder on us than on them, and many of them made derisive gestures to us about it. We were prisoners in a land we had conquered. At this juncture, some of our natural leaders organized softball teams. My old switchboard pal, John Higgins, asked me to play on his team. He felt that I was a fair to middling hitter but a real Zeke Bonura in the field so he stuck me out in right field where he thought I would do the least amount of damage. When my fielding improved, he put me on third base.

There were three really good teams on the base, ours, one from another squadron, the 510th, and a black team who visited our base frequently. The other squadron team had a real fireballer pitcher who struck out more than half of those who batted against him. I enjoyed batting against him since he was the only challenging pitcher on the base. I got a few fluky hits off him, but he was tough, particularly with men on base. Most games were well-played, but everything was low key so games were lots of fun.

The most exciting games involved the 510th Squadron and the blacks. Smoky Joe had to be at his best because the blacks did everything well. He had the Indian sign on one of them. Every time he got two strikes on this poor guy, he came in with a change-up and the batter almost broke his back as he struck out. It got to be so funny after awhile that even the batter himself had to laugh. Finally after perhaps twenty strikeouts, he caught a hold of a change-up and got himself a double. He got a standing ovation from us onlookers.

After winning a big game, Major Eikenberry gave us permission to buy some beer, so we headed for a local brewery and picked up some kegs. When the proprietor asked for payment, we shouted, "Reparations," and took off laughing like hell. The farther away we got, the worse we felt. Reparations were okay but against a little brewer? When we returned the empty kegs a week or so later, we found that the brewer had contacted Major Ike who had taken care of the bill.

One of our pilots decided to organize a hardball team and asked me to join. Not knowing when I was well off, I agreed. While we were at Straubing, the games were low-key and fun. When we moved back to France and were based at Camp Detroit, everything was played to win and it ceased to be fun any longer. Sports to me have always been a source of relaxation and pleasure. As winning became more important, much of the spontaneous fun went out of the game and it became more of a burden than a source of relaxation. Soon we began having daily practices so that I no longer had any time for anything but baseball. The game was running my life.

I have always been glad that I was born before the Little League era with its strict sense of organization and stress on winning. When I was a kid, every Saturday during the spring and summer, my brother and I walked down the street and met with a bunch of the neighboring kids. We spent the entire morning playing pick-up baseball. Today's opponent was often the following week's teammate. We joked with our opponents as much as with our teammates. We played hard and we played to win, but by the time we arrived home for a late lunch, it was easier to remember hitting a homer than whether we had won or lost. This has always been my conception of how sports should be played. I never had a desire to play at Wimbledon, or in the U.S. Open Golf Tournament, or even in the World Series. My idea of Nirvana in sports is acing one of my cronies at the Cottonwood Club here in Salt Lake City.

Finally, I decided to quit. I knew that the manager would be upset, so I never informed him of my decision. I just pulled the pin. That was a major mistake. No matter how he reacted, it was my duty to tell him and take whatever abuse he chose to give me. I had always prided myself on taking the so-called direct approach after making a decision, but I failed to do so in this instance just to avoid a possible unpleasant situation.

After my baseball fiasco, I tried to rejoin John Higgins' team, but hardball had pushed softball off the stage and his team soon broke up. About this time, somebody up the ladder got us a volleyball and net. I took to this like a duck takes to water. It was and still is a game that I enjoy. Of course some players were better than others so if one team began to dominate, we mixed up the talent so all the games were close. I enjoyed this more than any other sport. We had matches in both morning and afternoon, playing both best out of five. It was both exciting and good exercise. So much for my sporting activities.

One afternoon, right after lunch, I was on my way to my room when the sinister sight of our first sergeant loomed up in front of me. It was always best to avoid him when he was on the prowl lest you end up with some detail or other, so I quickly ducked into the head but not before he called out my name. I approached him warily and he asked me if I could drive. I answered in the affirmative, so he told me to pack some clothes toot sweet and make a beeline for the motor pool where a lieutenant whose name I have forgotten needed a driver. This sounded promising, so I raced to my room, threw some clothes together, and hustled out to the motor pool where the lieutenant and another driver were impatiently awaiting me. The other guy started out driving and I soon found out that our objective was Marienbad, a resort in the Carpathian Mountains where bossman had an officer friend.

We had no deadline to return, so the three of us had a great time. It was midsummer and the nights were short and the days were warm. Our

244

Checking over a wounded P-51 at the repair depot in Straubing, Germany are, left to right, Carl Hadra, Bob "Limey" Nash and Ernie White. Plane was too damaged to repair. Usable parts were cannibalized from it.

officer friend had papers which enabled us to stay at any army base in the area and entitled him to all the gas he needed. Marienbad was a very pretty village in the Sudetedland, and the mountains were gorgeous. It seemed to us that the people in that area were unaware that a titanic war had been fought all around them. Like ostriches they must have had their heads in the sand—and for over five years! They were living as they always had lived. We couldn't imagine how the war had passed them by.

Since we were in no hurry to return, we took a couple of side trips, including one to Pilsen in Czechoslovakia, which at that early stage in peace negotiations was in no man's land. We had captured it, but the Russians were to occupy it. We went into a nice-looking pub and traded cigarettes for beer and post cards and then headed back to Straubing.

While in Pilsen, we passed the massive Skoda steelworks which had taken a real pounding. Not a single wisp of smoke rose from the scores of smoke stacks in the mill—an eerie sight if we ever saw one. A steel mill is supposed to spout smoke and steam and sport all kinds of action, but the Skoda Works were completely deserted—no smoke, no steam, no action. I hinted at an excursion to Prague, which was the only town I knew in the entire country, but cooler heads prevailed. The Russkies were already there in force and we would probably have been nailed as spies and incarcerated in some Russian jail. The cordiality of our initial meeting was rapidly wearing off due to Stalin's paranoia.

After about four days, bossman decided it was time to head for the barn. He told me to drive and I enjoyed passing hay and fragrant manure wagons at top speed. The roads had not been repaired since 1939 so they were hideous. In addition to the blind hairpin turns and steep hills, there were any number of teeth-jarring holes in the road. It was West Virginia all over again.

After about four hours, I reached the Danube which could only be crossed via a rickety one-and-a-half car-width pontoon bridge. Two young German girls were crossing in the same direction as we were when I started across. They should have been on the downstream side so that we could pass them safely on the upstream side. Instead, they were walking right down the center.

As I approached to within perhaps fifty feet of them, I gave the horn a gentle beep. One of the girls jumped a mile in the air, lost her balance and fell into the river, where she thrashed around in panic. I jammed on the brakes and the three of us leaped out and grabbed her before the current took her downstream. We yanked her out of the drink and laid her on the bridge where she screamed hysterically. We helped her to the bank and tried to calm her down without success. While the others stayed with her, I returned to the jeep and continued my crossing.

By this time, she was in much better shape, so we left her in her companion's care and to that of some fishermen who were on the scene. As we continued on our way to the base, we wondered why she was not aware of our coming. As soon as we got on the bridge, our motion really exaggerated the normal back and forth motion caused by the strong current. She and her companion must have been in deep conversation not to be aware of our presence on the bridge.

Once we were assured that she was all right, my two companions called me "Killer Henkels," and good-naturedly blamed me for pushing young German girls into the river. This went on until they found someone else to badger. I was relieved that none of my good buddies were around to witness this scene. They were not so forgiving as these two guys were.

About a month or so after the German capitulation, the army established a series of camps in northern France. They were built as staging areas to facilitate sending home many of the unneeded troops. Each of them was named after a large American city, i.e. Camp St. Louis, Camp New York, etc. Every week or so, *Stars and Stripes* published a list of the units which were departing for the States from each camp. This continued for perhaps six weeks while we cooled our heels in Straubing. We felt like General Halftrack in the comic strip *Beetle Bailey*. The Pentagon had forgotten us. We were not really concerned because we had not been overseas as long as many of those units who were headed home. We had plenty to eat, German POW's to do our dirty work, and had no guard duty to pull. We played volleyball, lots of bridge, and always had the Danube to swim in if the weather got too warm. Things could have been lots worse.

We didn't see the thunderheads on the horizon. We finally got orders to report to Camp Detroit, near Laon, in northern France. We were unaware of its existence since it had never been written up in our newspaper. This lack of publicity aroused our curiosity, but we still felt confident that all was well and that we were taking a giant step toward home.

Then an ominous rumor started to make the rounds. Camp Detroit was a staging ground for troops headed for the CBI—The China Burma India Theater of Operations. This was soon confirmed by headquarters.

Many of the guys were horrified, and one even had to be restrained from jumping out a window. However, it sounded pretty exciting to me and a few of the others who were unmarried. A trip around the world, via the Suez Canal with perhaps a stop in India sounded like high adventure to us. A few of us lacked sufficient points, to qualify for discharge, and we thought it would be much more fun and exciting to serve out our time overseas where there was some action rather than back in the States. Most of the others had sufficient points, so they were understandably upset.

However, just after we learned of our new assignment, the Bomb was dropped on Hiroshima and the Japs threw in the towel. Our CBI adventure was out. I was happy to see the war end, but I regretted missing out on a trip around the world. One fellow's mead is another fellow's poison.

Our assignment to Camp Detroit was unchanged, and we soon got our orders to ship out. First Sergeant Sibley and his crew came out with a transportation list which assigned each person to a particular vehicle. I checked the list about five times and Abou Ben Adem's name was conspicuous by its absence. Since confusion reigned supreme while the guys were loading up, I didn't speak up immediately. Being left off the list often had its advantages and I knew that I would not be deserted, so I just bided my time.

Just before departure and after all the trucks were loaded, I dropped my bomb on poor Sergeant Sibley. He was horrified. He checked his list and then smote his forehead, thought for a minute and then told me to remain with the cleanup detail. This crew consisted of a lieutenant and two enlisted men, and I made four. The lieutenant was new to the outfit and the two GI's were strangers to me.

Author stands beside a B-17 heavy bomber at Straubing, Germany. He rode in one similar to this from Kitzingen to Straubing.

The trucks pulled out with a cloud of dust and the four of us were left to close up camp. We closed all the windows, shut off the water and electricity, and then ate a supper that the mess sergeant had prepared for us. We sat around, chewed the fat for a couple of hours, and hit the hay. The bossman said that we had a week to make Camp Detroit and he had no intentions of getting there early. This was fine by us.

Next morning, we had a cold breakfast and then loaded up in our jeep and headed for Heilbron where the lieutenant had an old buddy. We took the Autobahn to Munich, spent a couple of hours looking at a mass of ruins there, and then went to Stuttgart where we did more of the same. All along the Autobahn, the Germans had cut well-camouflaged revetments in the woods to hide their jets which used the road as a runway. Evidently these revetments had not been detected by our reconnaissance planes because the autobahns were unscathed except where the bridges had been knocked out. It was lucky for the Allies that they had knocked out the German refineries, because we counted more than seventy jets in perfect condition which would have created havoc with our heavy bombers.

We arrived in Heilbron in the late afternoon and spent the night there, he with his pal, and us with the enlisted men stationed there. The next day we cruised down the Neckar River Valley, which was as pretty a drive as I have ever taken. After a drive of about sixty miles, we reached the college town of Heidelberg which was untouched by the war. Ancient and picturesque street cars slowly made their way down the streets, stopping at every intersection to load and unload passengers. We drove down the main stem, and I hoped that our bossman would make a little detour into town where we would be able to observe the castle and the university at close range. However, he took our nonfraternization policy strictly, so we went on our way. Unfortunately, he had less nerve than I. The people seemed to be friendly, and who would tell? It was my belief that fraternizing with the enemy at this time was not a capital crime.

From Heidelberg, we went to Saarbrucken after crossing the Rhine River at Mannheim. Saarbrucken was a dirty steel town, so I tried to talk our boss into going to Luxembourg instead, the only country in that area that I had missed. However, he preferred the more direct way which was via Saarbrucken so I missed out. Luxembourg is a missing link to this day.

We made a few more overnight stops at various army camps before we ended up at Camp Detroit. They must have been undistinguished, since I am unable to remember what they were or where they were. The boss's timing in arriving at camp was perfect. Everything was shipshape when we arrived, and I was soon ensconced in a familiar pyramidal tent with familiar and welcome roommates who were jealous as hell and wanted to know how I had pulled off this caper. My answer was that they needed a Roman numeral at the end of their names and to be under the rank of sergeant. I said that the job couldn't afford their high salaries. Everything returned to normal. The hardball games went on as usual, except that there were now many more teams and competition was that much keener.

Those of us who had been with the outfit before leaving the States and who were still corporals had one more sweat. We knew that ratings would soon be frozen and we hoped that our parsimonious boss would give them out while he still was able to. Every other department in the 511th took this opportunity to reward those who had served the outfit so well. Many of our high-point guys had left for home, so we had plenty of openings. Our old-timers had been replaced by a bunch of low-pointers whose outfits had departed for home, leaving them behind. Instead of rewarding those who had been with the outfit from the beginning, our boss decided that this would be unfair to the new arrivals, so he didn't act and, sure enough, ratings were frozen and nobody got them. This was a rotten shame. It would have been far better to give them to the newcomers than let them go by default. His indecision in this was no surprise to us but it was a bitter disappointment nonetheless.

Bridge now became our new craze. Games were going on all day long, from can see to can't see. I spent several hours a day playing, but that was enough. I spent the rest of my time wandering around talking to guys from other outfits. There were many infantry and armored units represented, and I enjoyed talking to them. Some had been in Normandy, so we had something in common. A few others recognized us as the guys who had come to their rescue at times. Many had some real horror stories to tell and some wild adventures as well. Their lives had been exciting, but I was satisfied with mine in the air corps.

I went into Laon once, but I cannot recall what it was like. I can remember a cathedral (which were my specialties) but not much else. I returned to base and never went back. Since the war was over, discipline was minimal, just strong enough to prevent anarchy, so we had more fun on the base than we did in town which had not recovered completely from war damage.

Perhaps two weeks after our arrival, some units started to move out, headed for the States, not the CBI. We got our hopes up that perhaps we might be next, but August passed without a hint of our going. Then September came and went with still no news. All the high-pointers had now departed. Were we slated for the Army of Occupation?

Chapter Twenty-Four
Camp Detroit and Furlough Time

Now was the Autumn of our Discontent
made glorious Summer
—William Shakespeare, *Richard the Third*

We were now a shadow of the past. Our planes were gone, and most of our high pointers had also departed for other climes. We were just a shadow of the first-class fighter squadron we had been only three weeks before. Nobody knew what to do with us remnants. Some of our officers tried to institute close order drill, but after the first day when only about ten percent of the squadron showed up, they gave up. Most of us also missed roll call but the officers knew that this failure was due to laziness, not from anyone flying the coop. We knew that the only sure way to get home was to play ball with the power.

German POW's pulled KP, there was nothing to guard, and no planes to maintain. We had to use our own wits to find something to do. Bridge occupied some of our time and we played volleyball and baseball. I did a lot of reading and also wandered around and talked to people in other outfits, but we still had time to burn.

Out of the blue, five of us decided to go to Paris. We asked for and got three-day passes and headed for Paris which was still off-limits. This time we decided to take the bull by the horns and show the MPs our passes right off the bat. We had no problem. Our Ninth Air Force badges were a red carpet for us. Most MP's were ex-infantry who remembered the many times we had bailed them out. They were still on the lookout for AWOLs but couldn't understand why we were not allowed in town. Once we had assured ourselves of a reliable source of food, we felt free to explore Paris to our hearts' content.

This was the first time I had been in Paris in warm weather. It made all the difference in the world. On our first day, we strolled along the Seine for miles, enjoying the scenery and looking at the tiny kiosks that specialized in old books, maps, prints, and manuscripts. One guy even found an old comic book which he had read many years ago. A bargain hunter could have made it big here, but we had neither the money nor the expertise to take advantage of any possible bargains.

The next day, my friends insisted on going to Pigalle, THE red light district to end all red lights. It was the headquarters in all of France and perhaps the world for kinky sex. It was so bad that we called it "Pig Alley," which was more descriptive than original. We took the Metro, got a table at an outside cafe, and observed the antics of the girls as they tried to lure us into their casbahs. Two of our guys thought that they knew the ropes about sex, but they admitted that they were strictly minor league in Pig Alley. This whole escapade was an eye-opener to us. The climax came when one of the natives approached us and asked us to buy some far-out pictures of himself, herself, or itself in action. That did it. It was *au revoir* to Pig Alley. When we returned to camp, we told all our friends about Pigalle so of course it became a "must see" for all the other groups going to Paris from then on.

After our sojourn in Pigalle, we went to the Eiffel Tower. Once again a guard was there, but we decided to climb it anyway. He glanced at our papers and passed us. I was cocky enough to hand him mine upside down. We were only allowed halfway up since the Signal Corps had preempted the top half, but the view was still spectacular. Since I had already spent fourteen days in Paris prior to this, I qualified as an expert and pointed out many of the famous landmarks to the others. As I look back, I am glad that none of them were able to check my accuracy.

All this took a short time, so we spent the rest of the day at the Louvre which was in much better shape than on my previous visit. Here we took in the big three, "The Mona Lisa," the "Winged Victory of Samothrace," and "Venus de Milo." Then we spent the rest of the day in the antiquities. None of us knew enough about art to think about seeing the impressionists which was a pity.

The next day was Sunday, so I went to Mass at Notre Dame. I left the group after we had arranged a rendezvous point for later on. Two of the others decided to make an investment in Parisian pulchritude while I was gone. Upon my return, they had a gal lined up for me. Before I had a chance to protest, they assured me that this particular girl, who was not bad looking, didn't work on Sunday. They all wanted to catch a movie with their queens and this girl was odd one out so would I please take her to the movies with them? Feeling very adventurous, I agreed. Inside the theater, I daringly tried to put my arm around her and was rebuffed. I felt that I had given it my all and had escaped unscathed.

After the show, we had a sip of wine and then the gals wanted us to take them to dinner. This was where I drew the line. The others wanted out also. None of us had much money and didn't want to waste what little we had on these gals. We were not enamored with the idea of eating horse or goat meat when we could eat civilized food at the GI mess. Here the food was not only better but more plentiful as well, and the price was right. We bid these fair damsels fond *adieu* and headed to the mess hall.

Everyday, we kept losing our high pointers by attrition, and Sam Weinberg, company clerk and head of the duty roster left. These guys were replaced with all kinds of rookies, some of whom were not even in the air force. However, we did gain a dozen or so real green armorers, including a guy from my neighborhood in Philadelphia. It was like old home week as we went over the doings of a list of mutual friends. He had, left for the war long after I had so he was more up to date on the status of friends than I. When we returned to Philly, I went back to college and never saw him again.

The army break off point on points was eighty, and I had seventy-eight, which now made me and the others who had gone overseas together the new group of high pointers. We had too many points to go back on regular duty, but not enough to get out. The army had two options for our squadron, army of occupation, or going home. If we were to become part of the Army of Occupation, our squadron would have had to be almost completely reorganized. We had few pilots, fewer mechanics, half our compliment of armorers, etc., so this option didn't seem likely to me. Rumor had it that the Army of Occupation was to be more a police force than anything else, and we made very poor policemen. Things looked good for a trip back home.

At this time, the Swiss government, which was under a cloud for allegedly helping the Nazis, was anxious to show off their country to us GIs, so they arranged some nifty tours at very attractive rates. I quickly volunteered and managed to scrape up enough money to qualify. A one-time payment included everything except drinks and souvenirs. About six of us went off in the first batch. We rode GI trucks to Basle where the Swiss took over, Major Eikenberry went along and when we arrived at Basle, he jokingly told me to pick up his bag. I grinned at him, pointed to the Swiss sign, and told him, "Thanks but no thanks, you're nothing but another GI here." He smiled back and we both went our separate ways.

When we met in California last year with our wives, I reminded him of this incident which he had completely forgotten. That summer, when he was in Switzerland, he sent me a postcard giving me hell for not being on hand to take care of his luggage. This has been a topic of conversation every time we get together. I am in hopes that he will find some other country to visit in the future.

We had a wonderful time in Helvetia. The people were super and the country was gorgeous. However, that old bugaboo of not being able to ride a bike came home to roost once more. I rented one, gave it a whirl for about an hour, and then gave up in disgust. Although there was plenty to do that didn't require riding a bike, I missed out on seeing some of the beautiful countryside and so returned with the completely erroneous belief that Switzerland was a tinsel country containing nothing but quaint little cities. The lucky ones who made it into the countryside thought it was beautiful.

Our particular tour took us from Basle to Luzerne, where we spent three days. Here a dogface with a combat infantry badge joined the three of us to make a merry foursome. Our little hotel furnished lunch and dinner. At each meal, they placed a bottle of wine at each of six tables. Most of the other people didn't finish their bottles, so our infantry friend and I went around and caged the half-empty bottles, which annoyed our hostess no end. I think that they regarded the unfinished bottles as a windfall since their guests had already paid for it. We also regarded them as such, and we were a mite faster than they were in getting to them. They found out that the toughest thing in the world was to beat a thirsty GI to a bottle of wine.

After our sojourn in Luzerne, we took a lovely train ride through some rugged mountains and arrived at Montreaux, a really pretty town on Lake Geneva. This was my favorite place and I regret we were there for just a short time. It was in Montreaux that I purchased my first ever wristwatch from a very pretty saleslady. I am lucky that she was honest, because I am sure that she could have sold me the Brooklyn Bridge or stock in some nonexistent Swiss gold mine.

After eight short hours there, we departed for Lausaunne, which is also on the lake where we spent the night. The trains in Switzerland were pulled by electric locomotives which made for a smooth and comfortable ride. It was also possible to correct your watch by them. Riding these trains was a welcome change from our rusty-dusty-never-on-time troop trains.

Our last stop was in the village of Olten. On our arrival, I took a stroll by myself and met a nice young lad who had learned English in high school and wished to practice speaking it. We walked around town for an hour or so while he practiced his English and showed me the few items of interest Olten had to offer. He had an excellent command of English, and I was surprised to learn that I was the first person he had ever talked to in English. His syntax was perfect and the only help I could give him was a few additions to his already substantial vocabulary.

He gave me his picture and asked me to be a pen pal. Reluctantly, I agreed. I was not much for writing letters, particularly to someone with whom I would not have much to say. When I got home, I completely forgot about him until I came across his picture about four or five years later, and I thought that was a bit late to start writing. However, other groups of GIs followed us, so I hope that he finally found someone who would be willing to exchange letters with him.

That evening, we spent our last day in Switzerland at a small restaurant in Olten. We met a group of the natives and spent the evening trying to decipher each other's conversation. They spoke no English and couldn't understand my German. Somebody came up with an accordion, and we sang together. We sang some of ours, they sang theirs, and then we sang some together, they in German and we in English. After a while, the difficulty in communications got to us, so after a short hike around town, we retired early.

The next day we were scheduled to catch an early train through Basle to Strasbourg in France where trucks were to pick us up and take us back to camp. Due to some foul-up, our train was late and we got into Strasbourg around nightfall and found out that our trucks were long gone. Another truck was scheduled for the next morning, but in the interim we had to find a place to sleep. The town was as dead as a doornail, so it looked like a night under the stars for the four of us.

At this moment, I got one of my infrequent brainstorms. Why not sneak into the nearby GI motor pool, find an unlocked ambulance, and button down for the night? This idea was received with great enthusiasm. We sneaked into the motor pool, found an open ambulance, and had a great night's sleep.

Next morning we awoke early, folded up the blankets, hopped out of the vehicle, unlocked the doors, and looked for a restaurant. We walked around some of this picturesque town and then came back to catch our ride. When we got back to the motor pool, we saw two GI's arguing about something as they walked into the motor pool. We were amused when they got to our ambulance, still upset with each other. The driver opened his door and hopped in but the other door was locked. Evidently we had forgotten to unlock it when we left earlier in the morning. We think that the guy on the passenger side thought that his companion had locked it on him deliberately, because he was furious. We were curious as to how things turned out for those two guys as they sped away still arguing.

Our ride was later than we had been told originally, so we looked over the town again and were joined by some other GI's who were also awaiting transportation, and some free French types who had just returned from looting part of Germany. They had all kinds of money, jewelry bracelets, etc. I guess they were trying to regain some of what the Germans allegedly had stolen from France. They turned out to be ideal bargaining opponents, with lots of money, little patience, and no sense of value for what they had or for what we wanted to trade. I sold a few trinkets that I had purchased in Switzerland for what my trip had cost and still kept my watch. The other guys did even better because the Frenchies were hot for watches. I reluctantly turned down a handsome profit for a watch I had bought for my father.

I love to bargain and I guess it showed. A guy from the other group of GI's asked me to sell an extra watch for him. When one of the Frenchies inquired about it, I told him that he didn't have enough money to buy it.

He took the bait and pulled out a wad of money that would have choked a horse. I had tentatively reached a price in my own mind, but the sight of all that money changed my mind and I upped my price some twenty-five percent, which he paid without a murmur. It was too bad we didn't have more time and merchandise to sell these birds. We could have made enough to retire.

When we got back to the base, some other guys were just starting out and asked us what they could use to bargain with the Swiss. We told them cigarettes, soap, and other toilet articles. These had worked for us. Evidently these needs no longer existed, because when they returned, they told us that they had been stuck with everything but the cigarettes. They accused us of giving them a bum steer. Our rejoiner was that it was unfortunate that they were poor bargainers. Sympathy is a rare commodity in the army.

In mid-September, our fate was evidently decided. We were informed that we would be leaving post haste to Marseilles, a large port in southern France from whence we would be shipped out, destination unknown. This was a surprise. Virtually all troops who returned to the States left from Le Harve or Southhampton. If we were going home, why were we headed for Marseilles? Perhaps we were going to the CBI after all. This didn't bother me too much, but if I had known what was going to happen in China, I really would have been upset.

President Truman had decided to put all his cards on Chiang Kai-Shek in the latter's struggle against the Chinese commies. The possible use of ground forces depended on how far Truman would go in backing Chiang. Luckily for us, he decided to transport Chiang's forces to Manchuria but not to involve us any farther. The commies blew Chiang's forces out so rapidly that Truman had no chance to change his mind. Had he sent in ground forces in the beginning with a group or two of P-47s for support, they would have been taken by the commies with unpleasant results. I, for one, shudder when I think what might have happened to me if Truman had been just a hair more bellicose. I would probably have ended up working in some communist rice field.

Early in September, our trip to Marseilles became a reality. We loaded what little equipment we had onto forty-and-eight railroad cars. This designation began in World War I and stood for forty men or eight horses. We picked the best-looking cars and settled in. They were so decrepit that our pilots had passed them up on their strafing runs rather than waste good ammo on them. This was another punishment for our efficient destruction of French transportation.

I don't recall how long this trip took, but no train ride in France at this time was fast. We made a few stops during the day to stretch our legs and all of them were in the sticks, never in town.

A year or so after I had returned to the U.S., I took out a map in order to trace our route. Unknown to any of us, we had gone down the Rhone River Valley, through some of the most interesting parts of France. We had gone through Avignon, Lyon, and even the Van Gogh land of Arles. What a sight-seeing tour this would have been if we had a few more days and had gone through these cities during the day. I was not that familiar with French history at that time, but I still would have enjoyed those interesting towns even if I was unaware of their significance.

In Marseilles, we loaded into trucks and headed to a camp up in the hills that surrounded the city. It was now autumn, and we were constantly subjected to the unpleasant and strong winds known as the Sirocco which blew clear across the Mediterranean Sea and which stirred up a red dust that permeated everything. We looked like people from Mars, covered with red dust from morning till night. We were disappointed to learn that it was back to the kitchen, no more German POWs.

Prior to the war, Marseilles had a Barbary Coast second to none, but German thoroughness took care of most of it. They must have lost some soldiers in the city, because they dynamited the entire blocks of the worst areas. Much as the French hated the Boche, they agreed that this was an improvement. The town was still no bed of roses and we were forbidden to enter town alone. There were still a bunch of weirdos who had no loyalty to anyone, French or German. Len Hitchman and I went there several times and I have to admit that it had a certain rough fascination. There were tiny little grog shops all over the place which we peeked into but didn't enter. We bought some souvenirs but never had a sip there as I recollect.

We visited a Catholic shrine, Notre Dame de la Gare, which was a pretty little church on top of a hill which had a tremendous view of the harbor and the Mediterranean Sea. Out in the distance, we could see the little island, Chateau d'If, where Edmond Dantes, the Count of Monte Cristo, was incarcerated for fourteen years. We visited the church and then wandered around the area for several hours, enjoying a rare respite from the Sirocco and the fantastic views.

As mentioned previously, we were now back to doing KP. Three days after pulling a tour, the guy who took over the duty roster after the departure of Sam Weinberg came to our tent and told me that I was on again next morning. I was furious and told him that I would not report until he got his roster in order. He said that he would have to inform the captain of my refusal. I said he could inform Eisenhower as far as I was concerned and I still wouldn't report. He left in a huff.

He returned in about ten minutes, all smiles, with the news that I was to report to the captain immediately. I got up from my cot and trotted down to the orderly tent, where I entered and gave the captain my best salute. Our old officers had long since departed, so this guy was a stranger to me. He looked like a nice guy who was genuinely concerned and wished to get this mess straightened out. He asked me what was the big idea of refusing to report for KP and said that he was able to put me on for the rest of my career.

I replied that I was aware of this and stated that I was willing to do my share, but I would be damned if I would go before the duty roster was adjusted so that it was equitable. I told him I pitied the cook who had me as a full-time KP. I stated that I had been off only for three days, and that was more than my fair share.

The captain looked at the duty clerk and asked him if I had been actually been on three days prior to this, and the answer was yes. He asked for the roster, looked it over, and then said," Sergeant, get this goddam list straightened out; I don't want any more of the goddam wild men coming in here giving me hell."

I pulled no more KP for two weeks, and all duties were assigned fairly. The duty sergeant was new to the job and took the easy way out. If anyone bitched about being assigned he was let off and replaced by a non-bitcher. I must have started out as one of the latter until he overplayed his hand.

At the royal palace in Versailles, France during furlough in November, 1944.
Author is in second row, eighth from the left with hat canted to the right.

In 1993, I wrote to Len Hitchman, told him I was writing this book, and asked him if he remembered anything of interest which I could include. His reply was that the thing that really stuck in his mind was the time I told the duty sergeant to get his goddam roster straightened out.

While all this excitement was going on, Major Eikenberry was trying to persuade the port officials and the wheels to permit us to go home as a unit despite the fact that some of us were lacking a few points. Points were based on the following: total service in months, service overseas, and five points for each battle a soldier participated in. We had participated in five battles, which were The Bombing of Germany, The Invasion, The Breakthrough at Avaranches, The Battle of the Bulge, and the Conquest of Germany.

In the beginning, the powers were adamant. Anyone with less than eighty points stayed. Period. Then, after a short time, they had second thoughts. The vast majority of us would soon have eighty and would then be eligible to leave. How useful would we be in the short time we had left and what could we do in the interim? Ike came back one day in early October with the news that we would not be broken up and that we would be taking the next ship available back home. The idea of actually going home took a while for us to digest.

Chapter Twenty-five
Homeward Ho and Adieu to the Army

For this relief, much thanks
—William Shakespeare, *Hamlet*

It was a relief for us to be assured that our next destination would be the U.S. and not to be part of the Army of Occupation. The thought of going home after almost two years of combat was overwhelming. However, I, for one, would never be completely at ease until the deck of a ship was under my feet. Everybody stayed close to their tents lest they miss the boat. As usual, though, the army bided its time. One week became two and still no ship. We began to wonder. Then bright and early one morning, we were informed to pack up immediately because trucks would pick us up in two hours to take us to the pier. Our ship was in! Packing was no problem, we had been ready for two weeks. We spent our waiting time collecting the home addresses of our friends.

Suddenly, a different meaning of going home struck many of us. We would soon part from our comrades with whom we had gone through so much—training in South Carolina, landing in Normandy, a dull winter at St. Dizier, the Battle of the Bulge, and the final triumph ending the war. Chances were prohibitively high that we would never again see about ninety-five percent of those with whom we had shared so much. Of course, we would be together on the ship but once on shore in the States, we would part forever. I thought, "You can't have it both ways."

Trucks arrived right on schedule. We loaded our gear on some and boarded others. Once loaded, we bid *adieu* to our dusty camp and headed for the harbor. It was ironic that our last glimpse of Europe was the narrow, twisted streets of Marseille where we had stayed a less than month instead of one of our familiar haunts.

When we reached the harbor, we unloaded our gear and formed loose ranks close to the gangplank but far enough away so we didn't impede the boarding process which was already underway. Our ship was a coast guard transport named the *Admiral Capps*. Although I spent ten-plus days on board, I never found out whether the good admiral began his last name with a "C" or a "K." Obviously, this was not high priority with me. My main concerns were that it was seaworthy and was headed in the right direction.

We endured the usual delay in boarding with uncharacteristic patience. From past experience, we knew that with troop ships, it was not only first in, last out, but it was also the sooner the entry, the lower you went.

Finally, our time came and up the gangplank we went. At the top, we were met by a coast guarder who shepherded us to our quarters, which were as crowded and as spartan as we had expected. However, it had been built as a transport, so the ventilation was better than that of the *Mauritania* and was able to accommodate almost as many troops, ten thousand versus twelve thousand. I think that its top speed was close to twenty-two knots while the *Mauritania* could do over thirty. However, twenty-two knots was well over that of the swiftest submarine at that time, which was all that counted. Thank heaven the coast guard was not as traditional as the Royal Navy. We had bare cots to sleep on instead of hammocks. Each of us staked out a cot by placing our sleeping bags and our barracks bags on it.

As soon as I was situated, I hastened up on deck to watch the departure and to make myself scarce in the unlikely event that the army changed its mind about sending me home. I enjoyed watching the orderly confusion of departure. In a surprisingly short time, all lines were aboard and the big ship slowly backed into the channel. As it finally put out to sea, all my doubts dropped from my shoulders like the albatross from the Ancient Mariner.

The harbor of Marseilles was really beautiful. On our port side as we set out was the Chateau D'If of *The Count of Monte Cristo* fame. It was nothing but a small, bleak castle jutting out of the water. On the starboard side, a small group of reef-like rocks rose from the sea and an occasional wave broke over them with a burst of white foam. Several beacons marked those nearest the channel. The Mediterranean Sea was a solid deep blue stretching out in every direction.

As we left port, we made a turn to the west and headed toward the Pillars of Hercules. On our starboard lay the coasts of Spain and then Portugal, while North Africa lay to the south. After we passed through the Straits of Gibraltar, the African coast faded in the distance, but it was not until late in the evening when the tip of Portugal dipped below the horizon and we bid a fond farewell to Europe.

With all the experience I had gained over the years toiling in GI kitchens, I would have been very disappointed had they neglected to use my talents on our trip home. Sure enough, our squadron got the call on the third or fourth day out. Much to the gratification of us peons, even master sergeants were not exempt from doing their bit. We enjoyed watching them working in such an unfamiliar environment.

When we reported, I was dismayed to find out that pots and pans, my particular expertise, had been preempted by permanent scullery personnel. However, with the ingenuity possessed only by mess sergeants, they found a job which I could handle. Word must have spread about my tour of duty in Miami Beach where I had such great success in transporting cups from the dishwasher to the head of the chow line, because they assigned a dolly to me and asked me to take trays from the dishwasher to the front of the line.

Only four of us were toting trays, so I found out that speed was essential in order to keep the line moving smoothly. These trays were heavy devils so I gathered lots of momentum on my journey. I had no trouble until the ship made a sudden lurch to the starboard. A GI was talking to some of his pals and had strayed out of the chow line at this precise moment. I caught him perfectly as I careened along and carried him for about fifteen feet where he hopped off, none the worse for wear. I righted my course and continued on my way without breaking stride or looking back. I heard later that I might have saved him from a nasty fall. I was neither the first nor the last to hit somebody while toting trays. Those who stayed in line had nothing to fear, but anyone who strayed narrowed down our path considerably and was in imminent peril of taking an involuntary ride. When I finished my tour, I wept a gallon of crocodile tears. I realized that I had just finished my last day ever of KP. When I returned to our quarters, someone produced a bottle of smuggled whiskey and we toasted this freedom from the toils of KP with a nip or two.

Many of the areas where I had wandered freely on the *Mauritania* were restricted on the *Admiral Capps*. My favorite place at the bow was now off limits. This detracted from life on deck. Also, *The Capps* didn't have the open decks that passenger liners had. I spent some time topside, but the weather didn't cooperate. It got windy and cold, so I took advantage of a nice lounge to take a nap or do some reading.

Although it had windows, the view was not so hot, so I either read or played solitaire until we crossed the Gulf Stream. We had some sunny and warm days from then on, so I went back on deck. Since it was autumn, I also went up on deck for an hour or so each night in hopes of catching a glimpse of the Northern Lights but had no luck. I guess we were too far south.

The first evening on board, I stayed on deck till late and then went down to catch some sleep. Evidently I had missed the curfew since our room was pitch dark. I found my cot in the darkness and tried to get into my sleeping bag. For some reason, I was unable to do so. I fiddled around, muttering to myself and getting madder by the minute, until I heard a snicker in the background. This aroused my suspicion, and sure enough, somebody had put a belt around the middle of my sleeping bag which was about a close to a French sheet as they could come. If they hadn't given themselves away, I would have spent a cold night sleeping on top of bag, because I was completely baffled. As it was, I quickly straightened things out and hopped in my bag, chuckling at how many "innocents" I would question on the morrow.

We hit some rough water in mid-ocean, but nothing compared to the hurricane we faced going in the opposite direction. Our ship, as mentioned, was much slower than the *Mauritania*, and Marseilles was much farther away from the U.S. than Southhampton, so our trip took something like ten days instead of six. As we neared the U.S., we were disappointed to find that our port would be Portsmouth, Virginia instead of New York City. This meant no fireboats shooting water into the air, no big bands playing for our arrival, and no royal welcome. However, Portsmouth did its best; they had a brass band playing as we disembarked, but it was child's play compared to how GIs were welcomed in the Big Apple. However, it was still the States and it was still home.

We picked up our gear and hustled down the gangplank, home at last. We formed an amorphous group and strolled along, following the band toward our transportation. Here things happened with bewildering speed. First, trucks took us to a central point from which we got transportation to Fort George Meade, near Baltimore, Maryland. Next stop was a mustering-out station, which in my case was Fort Meade. However, most of my close friends were from Seattle, Texas, California, or the Midwest, so they proceeded on to mustering-out camps near their homes. Len Hitchman, for example, travelled to Fort Lewis, Washington, which took almost a week so he spent more time in the army than I did and he used to remind me of it. At Meade, we collected a few more addresses and then had our final farewells. By this time, it was late, well after dark, but the army still wanted to get rid of us in a hurry. We headed to the supply room to turn in our clothes. We thought that they would go through all our stuff with a fine tooth comb and deduct the cost of our missing clothes from our pay. When we got to the supply room, they indiscriminately grabbed our stuff, chucked the good stuff into bins, discarded the rags, and sent us on our way. One item I surrendered was the flight jacket that I had such a battle over in Belgium. This whole operation couldn't have taken more than ten minutes. Next door was a seamstress who sewed a funny little emblem, called a "ruptured duck" for some obscure reason, on our dress jackets as proof that we were discharged and not AWOL.

Next we reported to the paymaster and received our back pay which was a nice little nest egg, more money than I had ever held in my hands before in my life.

Next, I picked up my discharge papers and headed to the last door. Just before we got there, a recruiter gathered us together and asked us if any one wanted to re-up. If so, we could take a nice, long furlough and retain our present grade. I chuckled as I looked at my two tiny corporal stripes. I was tempted to come up with some smart remark such as, "Do you think you can afford it?" However, they had been very obliging to me at Fort Meade and were only doing their job, so I desisted. On the train to Philadelphia, I began to wonder why they would want us old vets. I had gotten into so many bad habits, militarily speaking, that I would have been more trouble than a dozen pliable recruits. I passed out the door, no longer a soldier but a veteran of World War II. I looked forward to civilian life with enthusiasm and hope.

Just outside the last portal was a sergeant who acted as a starter for the lineup of cabs which awaited us. He put four men in each cab and cautioned us to make sure that we split the fare, since the cabbies were not adverse to making each passenger pay the full fare. Three total strangers hopped in with me, and we took off to the railroad station in Baltimore. When we arrived there, rather than fuss about who paid what, we each paid the full fare.

I bought a ticket to Thirtieth Street Station in Philadelphia and called home. There was no answer. I arrived in Philly and caught a local to Germantown on the same line as I had taken when I learned about Pearl Harbor. Instead of heading straight home from there, I made a little detour and dropped in on my sister, brother-in-law, and a young niece whom I had never seen. Fortunately, they were still up and plied me with some super bourbon whiskey which they had saved for my return. I broke them in on what listening to combat veterans was all about with some super-duper, A-1 combat stories. Since this was still October and I was on the ground floor without any competition at this time, I poured it on thick. My audience was so interested that I wanted to stay all night. However, my brother-in-law had to work the next day, so I departed about two A.M. and walked home.

I knew that nobody would be home, but I also knew that in those innocent days, the front door of our house was seldom locked. Sure enough, when I arrived, I pushed the door open and walked in. I took a quick glance at the living room to see if any major changes had been made, and then out of force of habit, I looked into the refrigerator. When I saw that it contained nothing of interest, I went up to the third floor and my old room. I smiled wistfully as I looked at the decorations on the wall that I had suddenly outgrown. I glanced at some of my old books, reread my favorite chapter of *The Count of Monte Cristo* and decided to retire. My mattress was bare, so I grabbed a couple of blankets, put one underneath and the other on top, and lay down.

Gradually, all the immediate past faded away and a blank future took its place. This quickly changed. My first thought was how to con some unsuspecting college into ignoring my past record and letting me enroll. I saw no problem here, since I would be starting early enough to beat the rush. Next on my mind was the prospect of getting a job before classes began in January. Thirty some months of someone else doing my thinking faded away. I realized, suddenly, that for the first time in a long time, I was once again the master of my fate. A feeling of warmth and self-confidence enveloped me. I felt great, and with that, I fell asleep.

Chapter Twenty-six

Looking Back

Things look fairer when we look back at them
—James Russell Lowell

I was amazed at how writing these memoirs has refreshed my memory. On the few occasions over the years after I had read over my letters home, I could recall little except the incidents mentioned in them. However, when I started to write, I guess the tapping of my computer keys or the attempt to put things in proper prospective brushed the cobwebs from my memory, and I could recall events that had been long buried in my subconscious mind with amazing clarity. Instead of being a sterile narrative of long past and well-neigh forgotten events, these pieces of paper were suddenly transformed into a colorful and exciting history of a period of my life when the entire world was in turmoil. This demonstrated to me in a unique and wonderful way the vast difference between reading about past events and putting them on paper. Once again, I faced the miserable weather of St. Dizier, the *tête-à-tête* with our worthy supply sergeant, my many wrestling matches with pots and pans, and sitting in our tent with my five tentmates late at night, rehashing the events of a busy day on the line.

Digging up these old memories was as fascinating as it was useful. Many times when I had completed a chapter and started on the next, I'd recall an incident belonging to one I had just completed, so I would make a note of it and shoehorn it in at the proper place during a subsequent writing session. More than once, I had to remove a paragraph or two from one chapter and place it in another to make the narrative chronologically accurate. This took time, so my book was not written in a day.

For some strange reason, I had forgotten my one moment of glory, when I played the heavy at a USO show and got to kiss the girl. It was only when I had read Sam Weinberg's log that I remembered helping out in that show. However, it was only when I printed it out that all the exciting details came into focus. An opportunity like that comes once in a lifetime, and it would have been a sin not to have mentioned it.

Each draft brought out something new, and I am sure that this would have continued, although on a diminishing scale, as long as I continued to write. Going over my material and then putting it on paper has given me the opportunity to relive some of those momentous times of my years in the air forces. I recaptured the excitement, the boredom, the weather—both good and bad—the close relationships I had with many of my fellow soldiers, the adventures I experienced, and the sense of making history that were part and parcel of those times. Time has mellowed me so that the confrontations I had, which were of major importance then, have been reduced from torts to misdemeanors.

Unlike Shakespeare, I have discovered that in my case at least, "The good that men do lives after them, the evil is oft interred with their bones." I remember the fun and not the sorrow, my friends and not my adversaries. The army was an alien environment to all of us. Some adjusted easily; for others, it was more difficult, and for a small minority, it was impossible. We were either draftees or men who enlisted only for the "duration." Not one of our squadron was a professional soldier, except perhaps a pilot or two. The only career army men I met were Sergeant Spence in Walterboro and the West Point captain who socked me on the shoulder in Miami Beach. All our impressive accomplishments were made by a bunch of amateurs who had joined to fight the war.

As I study our squadron logs, I am amazed at what we accomplished. We were not a cohesive organization until just about Thanksgiving Day in 1943, two months after we had arrived at Walterboro. Here we switched from P-39's to the P-47's. Pilots had to start from scratch and learn to dive bomb and to shoot accurately. In less than seven months from that time, we were in England flying combat missions over an alien country. Our pilots were the main actors in this drama, but we ground crew members played an important part in their success. We rejoiced in their success and in the medals which they were awarded. We spared neither time nor effort to make certain that their planes were in excellent shape and that their guns were right on target.

Our squadron was just one of many who played a role in the historic and critical battles in Europe, and success against Germany would have been impossible without the use of air power. Heroism was not required of many of us, but on the few times it was, such as the times when Sergeant Feuer defused live bombs on our runways, we came through. What was required of us, we gave. Like Tennyson's Ulysses, "We were part of all that we have met."

When we arrived at New Cumberland Depot on that cold February day in 1943, I couldn't imagine that one year later, almost to the day, I would be part of a combat squadron overseas. At the time of my enlistment, I had no idea which branch of the army would be graced by my presence. I knew that the Allies had decided to defeat Germany first.

General George Marshall's decision to deal with Germany necessitated a rapid and exponential growth in the Air Force and I was drafted just as that buildup was underway. Thus my going into the air corps was not due to my test scores, as I had imagined, but to a decision that had reached as high as Churchill and Roosevelt. The branch of service in which each of us draftees served depended on the whim of a few leaders and the needs of the various branches at the time of induction. Had I been drafted at another time, I could easily have been in the tank corps or in the infantry. Timing was everything. However, no matter which branch selected me, I would have served with the same dedication and hard work as I did in the air corps.

Every action in life, voluntary or otherwise, influences all that follows. Army service did this for me. It is natural for anyone who served to wonder what his or her life would have been had they not been in the military or had they served elsewhere. Second guessing is one of the greatest sports there is.

I was at a crossroads in my life just prior to being drafted. I found out I didn't have the mathematical smarts to become an engineer and I realized that this was no hardship. I had entered engineering by default and not by actual desire, and this might well have accounted for some of my lack of success. I needed a respite from higher education and a good stretch in the army was probably just what the doctor ordered for me at that time.

Ads for the armed forces these days emphasize that they build character and prepare one for a productive future. This may be true now, but this was not so when I was drafted. The sole reason for our being drafted was to win a war, pure and simple. To accomplish that goal, the government of the United States was prepared to sacrifice the lives of thousands of its citizens and to interrupt the lives of countless others. We were all aware of this going in and accepted the risks and the inconveniences cheerfully. Shooting at people and having them shoot back may build character, but there was little future in it.

Discipline was a byword in the armed forces, and there were few of us at that age who didn't profit from that aspect of serving. Carrying out inane orders, an army specialty, was difficult at any age, but I think it was tougher for the young and inexperienced. Maintaining sanity under those conditions required a good sense of humor. We found humor in the "chicken-shit" OCS inspections in Miami, in KP assignments, and in many other ways in which we were losers to the vicissitudes of outrageous fortune. It soon became second nature with us to laugh at adversity. It was far better to laugh than to sulk, but learning this took time.

The discipline I learned in the military has stayed with me ever since and has been a great help in my subsequent careers as a student and as a businessman. While it is far easier to control one's life in the business world, there is still much that can't be changed and which makes no sense. However, at the time I was drafted, I was at loose ends and the army gave me almost three years to work things out. My service time couldn't have come at a more opportune time. I have often wondered how many others had the same problems at the same time as I did.

As the war progressed, I began reading books, which made me realize that I wanted to return to college when the war was over. Had I not had this time to think things out, I might have gotten so interested in making money that any thought of returning would have been smothered. The enormous size of the army made me realize that a small college would be more satisfactory than a large one like the University of Pennsylvania. In a small college, I would have the opportunity to exercise my limited talents as an athlete and take advantage of the intimacy of small classes to develop my scholastic aptitudes far better than I might in a large institutional factory.

Prior to my induction, I had traveled only as far west as South Bend, Indiana, as far south as Norfolk, Virginia, and as far north as Cobalt, Ontario. This made me one of the most traveled persons at New Cumberland! The army made a real nomad out of me. I took advantage of the opportunities to visit such towns as London, Paris, and Brussels which had been household words in our house for years. I visited art galleries, museums, palaces, and historic sights at every opportunity. This exposure to different countries created in me a desire to travel, to see different places, enjoy different cultures, and to try new things such as scuba diving and mountain climbing. I still have the desire to try new things and visit new and different cultures. My mild disappointment in not making sergeant was more than assuaged by my trips to Czechoslovakia, Heidelberg, and by my furloughs to Paris and Switzerland. Thus, my service time was a much greater plus than minus.

Life had some of the aspects of Edison's definition of genius. He claimed that genius is one percent inspiration and ninety-nine percent perspiration. Life is one percent luck and ninety-nine percent taking advantage of opportunities as they come along.

At the time of my being drafted, the war was still in a state of flux and the fighting was severe. I missed Guadalcanal, Kasserine Pass, and other great battles which had occurred just after the U.S. entered the war. I was fortunate enough to join at a time when I could still play a part in final victory but when most of the danger for us ground crews had passed. Most of my friends survived, but some made the supreme sacrifice. One in particular was inducted at the same time as I, went to ASTP, was yanked out at the time of the Bulge, assigned to the infantry, and was killed in action. Missing out on ASTP was a blessing in disguise.

Although we were not aware of it, the course of the war in Europe had been decided at the Falaise Pocket where most of the German reserves were destroyed in an ill-advised attack on the Allies. Fighter-bomber squadrons, including ours, played the vital role in the rout of the German counterattack. Our ruthless assault blunted and then routed the German forces and saved thousands of Allied lives. We left the German survivors with few vehicles and even less armor. Their retreating personnel were confused and disheartened. However, as decisive as was our success at Falaise, much remained to be done, and we had to absorb many casualties before the German Army was completely destroyed. Air power was vital to our invasion, the breakthrough at St. Lo, and the rout of the German attack at Falaise. After these great battles, it was no longer a matter of who would win but how quickly the Allies would achieve final victory.

Support by the Ninth Air Force was a vital ingredient of our ground successes. It was impossible for the Germans to move their troops without having them bombed and strafed by thousands of Allied aircraft. The Air Force not only destroyed German equipment at the front but also far behind their lines. Their communications were constantly being disrupted by our aircraft. Whenever our infantry were attacked, fighter-bombers came to their rescue, bombing and strafing the attacking enemy unmercifully. The German soldier, man for man, could easily have been the best fighting man in the world, but even he had no chance when we controlled the air. It is a tribute to their courage and devotion that they held out as long as they did.

My most important conclusion on war and this war in particular was the awesome power of the airplane and the moral questions raised by its use. Every major German city was destroyed by the heavy bombers of the RAF. They made no attempt to distinguish military from civilian targets. British night bombers dumped six-ton blockbuster bombs in the centers of German cities in a vain attempt to lower the morale of the German people. Thirty-two hundred Lancaster bombers were lost over the Reich, and in addition, many airmen were killed or wounded in the planes which were damaged but still able to return. The U.S. Eighth Air Force lost many B-17s despite the fact that our P-51 Mustangs were very effective escorts for them.

It was not until the U.S. Air Force under the direction of General Carl "Tooey" Spaats started the systematic bombing of German synthetic oil refineries that strategic bombing became effective. The German Luftwaffe was grounded for lack of aviation fuel, and gradually the entire German war machine ground to a halt for the same reason. This bombing occurred just as the German jet planes were coming on line. There was no telling what the result might have been had the Germans been able to use them in force. I have often wondered why we waited so long to attack such an obvious and such a vulnerable target. The RAF continued its ineffective attacks on cities, including an unnecessary and devastating raid on Dresden when the war was virtually over. Walking through the rubble of pulverized cities and observing the indifference of those who caused the damage has given me a horror of the insanity and bestial cruelty of war. William Tecumseh Sherman's observation that "war is hell", is an understatement. It doesn't convey the misery incurred by civilians who are theoretically not involved but who often suffer worse than the combatants. The damage we saw in towns like St. Lo and others strategically located has to be seen to be believed.

Both sides inflicted senseless damage on each other, and if innocents happened to be killed or maimed, it was chalked up to experience. Area bombing, carried out by both sides, effected the civilians, not the military, and served only to increase the resolve of the one who was bombed.

Twelve percent of the bombs dropped by the Allies were duds. Thus in a thousand plane raid, an average of one hundred and twenty bombers were subjected to attacks by enemy fighters and accurate antiaircraft might just dumped a bunch of duds on their target.

Several years after my discharge in October, 1945, I started to read some of the accounts of military writers such as Basil Liddell-Hart and the memoirs of Patton, Charles De Gaulle, and others. It appeared to me that they considered war just a game and in their books they discussed various tactics, and discussed battles as if they were discussing a chess game. Losses of troops, a fashionable word for soldiers, were equated to the loss of knights or pawns or a trick or two at bridge. Some of these generals made tactical mistakes which resulted in enormous casualties and never gave it a second thought. While these books make interesting reading because most of us have a fascination with military tactics and the likes of a General Rommel stir up the imagination, theirs is not the whole story. This reading should be supplemented by such books as *All Quiet on the Western Front* and by *Company Commander* and others which were written by those in the trenches who understood the danger and faced the cruelty of war. They cover such topics as gunning down unarmed German soldiers eating breakfast, setting barns on fire, and shooting paratroopers floating down, still in their chutes, and the endless lines of refugees plodding their way from nowhere to nowhere, carrying all their possessions in a small backpack. For every Rommel or Eisenhower, there are thousands of Paul Baumers and John Does who do the killing and are killed in turn. However, the history of war has always been written by historians, politicians, and the brass, and undoubtedly will always be. Few people are interested in the nitty-gritty of front line action.

Ten or so years ago, my wife and I took a trip to Egypt which included a trip to El Alemein where we saw and read a sampling of the headstones of those who had died there. A sizable part of the flower of the youth of Germany, Italy, and Great Britain were interred there, unsung and virtually unremembered. Now these tours there have been dropped for lack of interest.

We saw a similar sight in a beautiful park in Perth, Australia, where hundreds of trees had been planted by family members in memory of those killed in the "war to end all wars." Some of the inscriptions brought tears to our eyes—a tree planted by a young girl who had never seen her father or one planted by a couple who had lost their only son.

War involves too much destruction, death, and misery, and one great war breeds the next one. All in all, it reminds me of part of a quotation from Shakespeare's *Macbeth*:

> "It is a tale told by an idiot, full of sound and fury, signifying nothing."

Bibliography

Brewer, William B. *The Death of a Nazi Army*. Chelsea, MI: Scarborough House Publishers, 1985.

Frischauer, Willi, and Robert Jackson. *The Altmark Affair*. New York: Macmillan Co., 1955.

The Complete War Memoirs of Charles de Gaulle. New York: Simon and Schuster, 1964.

Hart, B.H. Liddell. *History of the Second World War*. 1st American ed. New York: G. P. Putman's Sons, 1971.

History of the U.S. Air Force. New York: Cresent Books.

MacDonald, Charles. *Company Commander*. New York: Bantam Books.

Patton, George S. *War As I Knew It*. Boston: Houghton Mifflin, 1947.

Unit History-511th Fighter Squadron, 405th Fighter Group, March, 1943 to August, 1945, Ninth Air Force. Declassified Official Microfilm records.